D1587830

Scottish Gothic

Edinburgh Companions to the Gothic

Series Editors
Andrew Smith, University of Sheffield
William Hughes, Bath Spa University

This series provides a comprehensive overview of the Gothic from the eighteenth century to the present day. Each volume takes either a period, place, or theme and explores their diverse attributes, contexts and texts via completely original essays. The volumes provide an authoritative critical tool for both scholars and students of the Gothic.

Volumes in the series are edited by leading scholars in their field and make a cutting-edge contribution to the field of Gothic studies.

Each volume:
- Presents an innovative and critically challenging exploration of the historical, thematic and theoretical understandings of the Gothic from the eighteenth century to the present day
- Provides a critical forum in which ideas about Gothic history and established Gothic themes are challenged
- Supports the teaching of the Gothic at an advanced undergraduate level and at masters level
- Helps readers to rethink ideas concerning periodisation and to question the critical approaches which have been taken to the Gothic

Published Titles
The Victorian Gothic: An Edinburgh Companion
    Andrew Smith and William Hughes
Romantic Gothic: An Edinburgh Companion
    Angela Wright and Dale Townshend
American Gothic Culture: An Edinburgh Companion
    Joel Faflak and Jason Haslam
Women and the Gothic: An Edinburgh Companion
    Avril Horner and Sue Zlosnik
Scottish Gothic: An Edinburgh Companion
    Carol Margaret Davison and Monica Germanà

Visit the Edinburgh Companions to the Gothic website at:
www.edinburghuniversitypress.com/series/EDCG

Scottish Gothic

An Edinburgh Companion

Edited by
Carol Margaret Davison and
Monica Germanà

EDINBURGH
University Press

Edinburgh University Press is one of the leading university presses in the UK. We publish academic books and journals in our selected subject areas across the humanities and social sciences, combining cutting-edge scholarship with high editorial and production values to produce academic works of lasting importance. For more information visit our website: edinburghuniversitypress.com

Edinburgh University Press Ltd
The Tun – Holyrood Road
12(2f) Jackson's Entry
Edinburgh EH8 8PJ

Typeset in 10.5/13 Sabon by
Servis Filmsetting Ltd, Stockport, Cheshire
printed and bound in Great Britain by
CPI Group (UK) Ltd, Croydon CR0 4YY

A CIP record for this book is available from the British Library

ISBN 978 1 4744 0819 6 (hardback)
ISBN 978 1 4744 0820 2 (webready PDF)
ISBN 978 1 4744 0821 9 (epub)

Contents

Acknowledgements

We would like to thank our series editors, Andy Smith (University of Sheffield) and Bill Hughes (Bath Spa University), for inviting us to collaborate on this research project, which, we hope, will pave the way for more work in the field of Scottish Gothic.

We also owe special thanks to Edinburgh University Press's Jackie Jones, Publisher, and Assistant Commissioning Editor, Adela Rauchova, for her ongoing support throughout the publishing process, and the Press for their financial support towards the illustrations in the volume.

We are also indebted to a number of agencies, scholars and colleagues who have helped us in various ways. Special thanks go to the Social Sciences and Humanities Research Council of Canada for a Standard Research Grant (2008–11) in support of research undertaken towards this volume, Alex Warwick (University of Westminster) for granting research time to support the development of this book, the University of Windsor for research support in the form of a Humanities and Social Sciences Research Grant (2015), Kate Turner (University of Westminster) for completing work on the collection's index, and Ashley Girty (McGill University) for editorial assistance on our joint Introduction.

Last but not least, we would like to thank the collection's authors for their tremendous patience and commitment to this project, and their insightful contributions that will offer innovative ways of thinking about Scottish Gothic for generations of future scholars.

Carol Margaret Davison
(University of Windsor)

Monica Germanà
(University of Westminster)

To my beloved parents,
Alexandra Mc Lean and William Davison,
whose intense relationship to their Scottishness
resonates at the heart of this book.

C. D.

To Elliott Patrick Germanà Murray (b. 14 January 2016),
for his spectacular entry into the world alongside this book.

M. G.

Chapter 1

Borderlands of Identity and the Aesthetics of Disjuncture: An Introduction to Scottish Gothic
Carol Margaret Davison and Monica Germanà

'How can a "Scottish Gothic" be conceived?' So asks Nick Groom in his provocative chapter in this collection, in the face of a historical, theoretical and political conundrum identified recently by other critics. In his article devoted to 'Shakespeare, Ossian and the Problem of "Scottish Gothic"', for example, Dale Townshend (2014) wrestles with the category of the Scottish Gothic given its union of seemingly irreconcilable terms whose yoking, he suggests, is counter-intuitive. According to Townshend, 'Scotland's political and historical relationship to things "Gothic" . . . [is] a vexed and complicated issue' that renders discussion of the anachronistic category of the 'Scottish Gothic' a fraught enterprise. One must adopt, he says, 'a greater sensitivity to [the] political history' of the eighteenth century (2014: 227), when the Goth and the Celt/Scot were generally positioned as discrete ethnographic categories.

The idea of a 'Gothic Scotland', however, did not prove difficult to conceptualise in the late eighteenth century and the early nineteenth when a Romanticised portrait of Scotland furnished the nation's most prevalent cultural image. As Ian Duncan astutely observes in regard to the politics of literary history, it was 'Scotland's fate to have become a Romantic object or commodity' rather than a site of Romantic production (Duncan et al. 2004: 2). Such an objectification was ironic given the existence of Scottish Enlightenment philosophy and its rationally fuelled preoccupations. That objectification was also, notably, expressed in two forms – in both the lighter and darker, more Gothic, shades of Romanticism. Despite the differences in these two manifestations, the Highlands served in both as a synecdoche for a Scotland that exemplified two primary attitudes towards 'British' history and rapid modernisation.

In the first, tourist literature of the era 'deprecate[d] Scotland's modern developments', imagining the Scottish nation as 'immune to the passage of time' (Grenier 2005: 136, 135). This immunity served an agenda grounded 'in specific cultural needs and anxieties which emerged in both England and Scotland in the beginning of the industrial era' (Grenier 2005: 11). In response to the advent of modernity and industrialisation, Scotland was nostalgically reconceptualised as a pre-modern domain of untouched, natural sublimity, a state from which Britain/England had, lamentably, fallen. In the second, the British Gothic's literary lens was diverted from Roman Catholic Europe and brought closer to home where it reconfigured the Highlands as a pre-modern site of Britain's most sublime scenery populated by foreign, Gaelic-speaking, Roman Catholic, tyrannical banditti. In dozens of Gothic works, many published by Minerva Press,[1] Scotland is repeatedly represented as a locale in thrall to mantology and marked by warfare and barbarism, a state out of which Britain/England had thankfully emerged.

Such split representations of the Scottish nation – and its culture – reflect not only the political bias of a dominant agenda outside Scotland, but also, and in a more complicated way, an inward-looking attitude towards national identity, whereby being Scottish becomes the equivalent, on occasion, of being foreign to oneself. That the word 'uncanny' originated in Scotland, that 'auld country' that has been so often, as Nicholas Royle adeptly describes it, 'represented as "beyond the borders", liminal, an English foreign body', is fitting, the Scots language itself being seen as uncanny, 'a language which is neither purely English . . . nor foreign' (2003: 12). The word 'uncanny' captures the in-between-ness that Scottish writers – especially those employing the Gothic – suggest is central to what might be called the 'Scottish condition' in the wake of the Act of Union. Informed by the concurrence of 'historical disjunctions', including, as noted by Ian Duncan, the 1707 Union of Parliaments – which resulted in the loss of Scotland's independence – and the nation's social and cultural fragmentation between primitive Highlands and modern Lowlands, a strong sense of divisive duality has always pervaded Scottish identity and culture (2004: 70). Indeed, the straitjacketing image of Scotland as a divided Jekyll-and-Hyde-monster of a nation rears its head in nearly every chapter in this volume, a spectre with which Scottish writers have had to wrestle since the Act of Union. In the twentieth century, intellectuals were significantly divided in their responses to cultural and political debates about Scottish independence. G. Gregory Smith coined the phrase 'Caledonian Antisyzygy' to define the contradictory core of Scottish culture, as characterised by an internal opposition between Highland/Lowland, primitive/enlightened and Roman Catholic/Protestant, among others (1919: 4). Hugh MacDiarmid, whose long poem *A Drunk Man Looks at the Thistle* (1926) exemplified his belief in the literary value of Scots, argued for the importance of Scotland's national language. Against MacDiarmid's attempt to breathe new life into Scotland's vernacular literature, in 1936 Edwin Muir famously blamed Scotland's lack of cultural unity on the fact that 'Scots feel in one language, and think in another' (1982: 8), promoting English, rather than Scots, as the literary language of Scotland. Significantly, such inner cultural division and, particularly, the emphasis on the Highlands' primitivism have continued to be pervasive motifs in literature and, as Duncan Petrie argues in his contribution to this collection, in the Scottish Gothic cinematic canon.

One might expect Scottish writers to reject the Gothic given Scotland's gothicisation in various British cultural productions since the eighteenth century. Indeed, as Colin Manlove problematically and provocatively stated in 1994, apart from some of Sir Walter Scott's short stories and James Hogg's works, Scotland was 'remarkable in having little or nothing to offer of the Gothic novels that flooded in such a stream from English presses from the 1760s through to the 1820s' (1994: 41). As Hamish Mathison demonstrates in his contribution to this collection, however, Scottish Gothic, in fact, represents an important cultural continuum that finds its roots in the oral literature of the ballad tradition and is carried into the works of Robert Burns and Allan Ramsay, before the rise of its golden age in nineteenth-century fiction. Disregarding such Scottish philosophers as Lord Kames, Dr Hugh Blair, Thomas Reid and Dugald Stewart, who 'saw tales of specters and superstition as an affront to reason and decency' (Lloyd-Smith 2012: 163), and drawing on the Border Ballads, Sir Walter Scott and James Hogg lay the foundation for a rich and diversified Scottish Gothic. Such tradition has, arguably, persisted into the twenty-first century and extends well beyond the mere gothicisation of Scotland as a 'Macbethian place of witches, ghosts, and regicide' (Townshend 2014: 240). Indeed, many Scottish writers, following Scott and Hogg, embraced that cultural mode as one with which they could engage and explore a broad spectrum of questions relating to issues of personal and socio-political identity. Why, one might ask, would Scottish writers consistently and repeatedly turn to the Gothic for their cultural expression? Adrienne Scullion has provided what is perhaps the most persuasive response to date, when she suggests that

> The role of mythology, legend and fable, the Gothic, the supernatural and the unconscious within the development of the Scottish imagination is not a symptom of psychosis but a sophisticated engagement with the fantastic that other cultures might celebrate as magic realism. (Scullion 1995: 201)

It is precisely this distinctive symbiosis of psychological introspection and supernatural subversion that, arguably, has consistently distinguished the Scottish Gothic, since its origins in the Ballad tradition, to the more recent works of such writers as Alan Warner, A. L. Kennedy and John Burnside.

Alongside explorations of the devastating psychological impact of social and religious repression, in the hands of Scottish writers the Gothic has been used to illuminate Scotland's own haunted history. While it is generally accepted that the past and the haunting secrets it holds is central to all Gothic narratives, it is also true that Scotland's relationship with its own complex history lends a distinctive quality to Scottish Gothic. As David Punter argues, 'Scottish Gothic will inevitably be different from – if never separate from – English Gothic because of the central importance of Gothic's dealing with history' (2012: 133). Scotland's ambivalent – at the best of times – relationship with its neighbour is behind the nation's problematic role within the history of the British Isles. Such ambiguities are rooted in Scottish Gothic; official versions of the historical past may still bear the marks of hegemonic subjectivity, but history is also read against the grain, to resist authoritative discourse and to promote an alternative notion of historical truth. Discussing the recurrent features of Irish and Scottish Gothic – the monument and the ruin – David Punter points to their significance as a reminder that Scottish history 'is constantly under the threat of erasure' (2002: 105). As several of the chapters in this *Companion* suggest, Scottish Gothic has helped bring to light the truth of Jonathan Oldbuck's declaration in Scott's *The Antiquary* (1816), that 'every mansion in this country of the slightest antiquity has its ghosts and its haunted chamber, and you must not suppose us worse off than our [English] neighbours' (2009: 89). Simultaneously, Scottish Gothic has not refrained from applying a critical eye to Scotland's own historical past sins, in particular, the complex role that the nation played within the development of the British Empire. The exploitation of colonial resources and involvement with the slave trade, for example, emerge as haunting secrets in such contemporary Gothic novels as Alice Thompson's *Pharos* (2002) and James Robertson's *Joseph Knight* (2003).

Such emphasis on critical revision, in turn, is reflected in the self-conscious textuality that has permeated the Scottish Gothic canon since the publication of James Macpherson's *Ossian's Fragments of Ancient Poetry* (1760). As Carol Margaret Davison's contribution to this volume proposes, the *Ossian* phenomenon turned Macpherson's literary artifice, which became an influential source of the Scottish Gothic, into the main target of Scotophobic criticism. Significantly, the work was presented – much like that of one of Macpherson's greatest critics, Horace Walpole – as a lost manuscript, a motif that would be embedded in much later Scottish Gothic fiction. The multiple narrative layers of texts such as

Hogg's *Private Confessions of a Justified Sinner* (1824) and Stevenson's *Strange Case of Dr Jekyll and Mr Hyde* (1886) are but two classic examples of a recurrent narrative strategy that exposes the contested nature of Scottish Gothic. As Angela Wright argues:

> Scottish Gothic is intimately concerned with distilling the right narrative from any story, with awarding equal attention to the stories of shepherds (as in Hogg) alongside self-appointed narrators of the nation, such as the 'editor' of Hogg's tale and the lairds and antiquarians of Scott's fiction. (Wright 2007: 76)

In constructing an apparently singular narrative, the Gothic, in fact, draws attention to the ways in which a story always emerges from a polyphony of clashing voices, throwing light on the fabricated nature of both story and history. As Wright claims, one of the distinctive qualities of Scottish Gothic is precisely that contested territory that the contradictory narratives of a Gothic text frequently uncover. The palimpsestic structure of much recent Scottish Gothic, from Alasdair Gray's *Lanark* (1981) to Janice Galloway's *The Trick Is to Keep Breathing* (1989) and James Robertson's *The Testament of Gideon Mack* (2006) – a rewriting of James Hogg's *Confessions* – demonstrates the multiplicity of forms this pervasive feature has manifested. Challenging the definition – and existence – of a singular truth, the coexistence of multiple voices and, frequently, multiple texts, erodes the foundations of hegemonic authority, allowing a plethora of 'other' voices to emerge.

Turning the tables on Scotland's earlier gothicisation, the Gothic has also been manipulated by Scottish writers, in both a direct and oblique manner, to shed light on the darker side of England's history, particularly with regard to its impact on Scotland. From Scott's *Waverley; or, 'Tis Sixty Years Since* (1814) and Stevenson's *Strange Case of Dr Jekyll and Mr Hyde*, to Iain Banks's *The Wasp Factory* (1984) and Alasdair Gray's *Poor Things* (1992), the Scottish Gothic has exposed such repressed, sometimes sinister realities, while lending expression, in some instances, to the terrifying prospect of the erasure of personal and national boundaries, a threat that reached its height, according to Cairns Craig,

> In the years of Thatcherism [when] there developed in Scotland what was known as the 'Doomsday Scenario' – a political and cultural obliteration of Scotland's differentiating features, its forcible incorporation into a Union which was no longer a partnership between nations but the Scottish nation's final submersion in English culture. With each victory of a Conservative government apparently oblivious to Scotland's separate history and identity, the apocalyptic expectations grew more intense. (Craig 2006: 138)

Following from the bitter disappointment of the failed Scottish Devolution Referendum of 1979, the rise of a second Scottish Renaissance in the last quarter of the twentieth century, signalled, as Douglas Gifford (1996) rightly notes, a significant 'return to magic' after the prevailing urban realism of post-war Scottish fiction. This meant, in turn, a noticeable re-engagement with the Gothic and myth that is visible across the literary spectrum in the works of Edwin Morgan, Iain Banks and Liz Lochhead, among others (Gifford 1996). Recent devolutionary years have significantly eased the threat but, as Scottish Gothic has reiterated since its inception, history has a peculiarly uncanny way – for better or for worse – of repeating itself.

Indeed when looking at Scottish literary productions since the late twentieth century, a strong sense of uncanny repetition emerges in the works of some authors who engage with the past with deliberate critical intentions. A regressive nostalgia to revisit the past does not lurk behind such works as Emma Tennant's *The Bad Sister* (1978), Alice Thompson's *Justine* (1996) and James Robertson's *The Fanatic* (2000); instead, they challenge linearity and monologism. The critical interrogation of binary essentialism, particularly with regard to gender and sexuality, remains an important drive in contemporary Scottish Gothic, as highlighted in Monica Germanà's and Kate Turner's chapters in this collection.

Considering the idea of 'Scottish Gothic' from a more contemporary, post-structuralist perspective that recognises the complexities in personal and national identity construction, volume contributor Timothy C. Baker has underscored the folly of attempting to arrive at a unified definition of 'Scottish Gothic'. In his recent book *Contemporary Scottish Gothic: Mourning, Authenticity, and Tradition* (2014), Baker points out the fitting union between Scotland and the Gothic given the Gothic's 'inherent instability and resistance to unified definitions'. As a mode that 'disrupts unified ideas of nation, community, or imagination', the Gothic is particularly well suited to accommodate Scotland's own cultural expression in what Baker provocatively describes as a 'national literary tradition' whose authors 'rarely attempt to define themselves in relation to a unified nation' (2014: 23). Indeed, Baker seems to revel in the multifarious manifestations of the 'Scottish Gothic' and sets, as the critical agenda of his own study, a reinvestigation of the ideas of 'Scotland' and 'the Gothic' (2014: 23). Each of the chapters in the present collection may be said to interrogate the 'Scottish Gothic' as a single and singular critical category, paying close attention to the sometimes disjunctive relationship between the two terms.

Recognising and expanding upon the Gothic's unique ability to challenge an often uncomfortable, uncanny, contentious and sometimes explosive terrain of issues relating to personal and national/religious identity and history, one might venture to say, as the chapters in this *Companion* suggest, that Scotland has put itself on the literary map by way of the Gothic, confronting in it a complicated understanding of its own cultural history and identity. Scottish Gothic, therefore, is defined as an aesthetics of disjuncture, looking both inward to the nation's own fragmented status as well as outward, offering a way of reflecting on identity that moves beyond essentialist binary forms of self-representation. Embracing this aesthetics, this collection aims to redefine the paradigms of Scottish Gothic by offering a comprehensive critical survey of Gothic cultural productions by Scottish novelists, poets, playwrights and film-makers, and to consider how and with which ramifications Scotland and its culture have been defined within the parameters of the Gothic as an aesthetic mode.

*

Opening the collection, Nick Groom's chapter, '"The Celtic Century" and the Genesis of Scottish Gothic' examines the Gothic in Scotland in the context of emerging Celtic identities, arguing that the Celtic was the product of a 'mutually antagonistic collaboration' with Whiggish Gothic ideology and politicised antiquarianism. Like the 'Gothic', Groom argues, the 'Celtic' had many different associations in the eighteenth century before it crystallised into a term that stood broadly in opposition to Anglocentric society and identity.

A different perspective on the role played by the Celticism of Macpherson's *Ossian*, and the contested position this text, as archetypal Gothic, occupies, is offered in Carol Margaret Davison's 'The Politics and Poetics of the "Scottish Gothic" from *Ossian* to *Otranto* and Beyond'. By way of key socio-historical and cultural phenomena and historiographical debates in the eighteenth century involving Scottish Enlightenment literati, Davison lays out the trajectory of the Scottish Gothic's inception while offering a bold reassessment of British literary history, particularly as regards the role played by *Ossian* in the rise of Gothic literature.

Continuing the investigation into eighteenth-century Scottish Gothic, Hamish Mathison's 'Robert Burns and the Scottish Bawdy Politic', argues that the preoccupations of Scotland's Gothic lie in a more deeply corporeal, more wholly libidinal manner of expression than those found in English writing of the same period. The analysis leads to an original redefinition of modern 'Scottish Gothic' literature as it emerges, in the eighteenth century, from deep, historical, libidinal tropes that combine concerns of social justice, faith and personal well-being.

Starting with the eighteenth century and reaching out to contemporary productions, Barbara A. E. Bell's 'Scottish Gothic Drama' locates the work of Scottish playwrights (1790–1820) amidst the welter of 'Gothic' performances set in Scotland. Looking back to earlier works such as John Home's *Douglas* (1756), the chapter assesses the influence of the London stage, state censorship, and the tension between the playwrights' breadth of invention and the physical delivery of theatrical effect, considering works by such authors as Joanna Baillie, Walter Scott, James Hogg and, more recently, Liz Lochhead and David Greig, to provide evidence of thematic through-lines.

Covering the much neglected field of Gothic poetry, Alan Riach's contribution to this collection explores Gothic aspects of the work of the 'Dark Poets' of the late nineteenth and early twentieth centuries – John Davidson, James ('B. V.') Thomson, James Young Geddes and Robert Buchanan. Scottish Gothic poetry may be described as engaging with the macabre, nightmare qualities of an unbearable or unresolvable vision, Riach suggests, yet its historical connection to medieval Gothic art – all the arts, from music to architecture – reminds us that this engagement has didactic purpose. Pointing to novel ways of looking at the concept of the Gothic, as well as reading Scottish Gothic poetry in a new light, Riach underscores medieval Gothic art's reminder that life is multifaceted and ultimately uncontrollable, often imposing itself inexplicably upon the best ideals of rational humanity.

With a specific focus on the nineteenth century, Alison Milbank's 'Calvinist and Covenanter Gothic' explores two contrasting literary responses to Calvin's doctrine of predestination: the literature of the second self and Covenanter Gothic. Tracing the Calvinist double from Hogg's *The Private Memoirs and Confessions of a Justified Sinner* through to Stevenson's *Strange Case of Dr Jekyll and Mr Hyde* and Robertson's *The Testament of Gideon Mack*, the chapter then considers Covenanter Gothic with particular attention given to John Galt's and Walter Scott's Gothicised histories. In both modes, the double functions to provide an alternative episteme that reconciles the notion of multiple identities at the individual and social levels.

Fiona Robertson's chapter addresses the key role of Sir Walter Scott in developing and popularising Scottish Gothic, while discussing his poems, plays, novels and analytical prose works as interventions in a complex, shifting, early nineteenth-century 'Gothic' field. A central focus of the chapter revolves around his fictions, in various genres, as Gothic narratives: detailed examples include *The Lay of the Last Minstrel* (1805), *The Tale of Old Mortality* (1816) and *The Bride of Lammermoor* (1819). The chapter also highlights Scott's role as an interpreter of Gothic narratives as evidenced by his 'Prefatory Memoirs' of Horace Walpole, Clara Reeve and Ann Radcliffe in *Ballantyne's Novelist's Library* (1821–4).

While continuing the critical survey of nineteenth-century Scottish Gothic, Scott Brewster's 'Gothic Hogg' rightly emphasises the influence of the vernacular storytelling tradition of Lowland Scotland on one of the key canonical figures of Scottish Gothic. The reanimation of folk culture challenged the discourse of improvement and cultural Anglicisation, counterposing the post-Enlightenment, secular rationalism of Edinburgh with the popular folk culture of the Borders. It is this disjunction between enlightenment and superstition, Brewster argues, that becomes a founding dynamic of early Gothic. In his uncertain relation to Edinburgh literary culture, and *Blackwood's* in particular, Hogg's Gothic inhabits both imaginative spaces.

Focusing more specifically on *Blackwood's*, Robert Morrison's '"The Singular Wrought Out into the Strange and Mystical": *Blackwood's Edinburgh Magazine* and the Transformation of Terror' argues that *Blackwood's* played a key role in the development of a new Gothic aesthetics. The magazine regularly published tales of terror that rejected the long and anxious narratives of late eighteenth-century Gothic novels and romances in favour of much shorter stories. This innovation, Morrison argues, set new standards of concentrated dread and precisely calculated alarm, signalling the emergence of a new Gothic aesthetics, which would prove to be influential beyond the Scottish literary scene.

The complex intricacies of the human condition form a core theme in Stevenson's oeuvre, the topic of Roderick Watson's 'Gothic Stevenson'. The chapter takes its cue from Stevenson's relationship to the familiarly 'Gothic' roots to be discerned in Scottish supernatural belief, oral folklore and Calvinism, and particularly visible in works such as 'Thrawn Janet' (1881) and 'The Merry Men' (1882). Watson moves on to explore a strain of existential anxiety in Stevenson's *Strange Case of Dr Jekyll and Mr Hyde*, read against Julia Kristeva's theory of abjection and alongside Stevenson's own essay 'Pulvis et Umbra' (1888). The chapter ends with an examination of 'Olalla' (1885), a short story not to be read just as a variation on the theme of vampirism, but more significantly in the context of Stevenson's work, as an exploration of the abjection of human desire.

Moving on to the twentieth century, Sarah Dunnigan's 'J. M. Barrie's Gothic: Ghosts, Fairy Tales and Lost Children' locates Gothicism at the heart of three works – *Peter Pan* (1904), *Mary Rose* (1920) and *Farewell Miss Julie Logan* (1931) – identifying not only the influence of nineteenth-century fairy-tale Gothic, but also demonstrating its reflection of the psychological complexities of contemporary Modernist supernatural fictions. In doing so, Dunnigan draws attention to Barrie's deployment of 'affective Gothic', visible, in particular, in his uncanny rendition of domestic settings, and the empathetic treatment of the haunter's figure.

A different kind of uncanny hauntedness pervades the fiction of Muriel Spark, whose work is given a comprehensively critical analysis in Gerard Carruthers's 'The "*nouveau frisson*": Muriel Spark's Gothic Fiction'. The chapter charts the development of Spark's fictive Gothic through her early novels, culminating in *The Prime of Miss Jean Brodie* (1961), alongside her mid-career period, most especially in *The Driver's Seat* (1970) and *Not to Disturb* (1971). While tracing the influence of the Scottish Ballads, as well as 'Scottish' antecedents, such as Hogg and Stevenson, Carruthers claims that throughout her career it is Spark's religious outlook that causes her to enlist the Gothic as part of a melo-dramatic fabric against which the lives of everyday 'fallen' human beings are in turn measured, satirised and sometimes even sympathised with.

Moving beyond textual fictions and engaging with Scotland's visual Gothic production, Duncan Petrie's 'Scottish Gothic and the Moving Image: A Tale of Two Traditions' examines two distinct manifestations of Scottish Gothic cinema. In one, Scotland is constructed by film-makers as the remote Celtic Other, explored and experienced from the perspective of the visitor from elsewhere. This is central to films like *The Brothers* (1947) and *The Wicker Man* (1973). In the other, more recent, tendency, the Gothic, however, seems to emanate from something more internal to the culture. Petrie argues that this invokes the legacy of Calvinism, in particular the dialectic of fearfulness/fear-inspiring as dis-cernible in such examples of the New Scottish Cinema as *Shallow Grave* (1994), *Orphans* (1998) and *16 Years of Alcohol* (2004).

Timothy C. Baker's 'New Frankensteins; or, the Body Politic' offers a critical survey of the literary production of the last thirty years, con-sidering key texts such as Alasdair Gray's *Poor Things* (1992) and Iain Banks's *The Wasp Factory* (1984), to examine the relationship between the individual and national body, and the complex overlaps of textuality and embodiment – the body as text – in works such as Elspeth Barker's *O Caledonia* (1991) and James Robertson's *The Fanatic* (2000). Far from suggesting that the discourse of textual embodiment is consistently rooted in all contemporary writing, Baker points to texts such as Alice Thompson's *The Falconer* (2008), which seemingly reject the linearity of textuality, and others that, like Val McDermid's *The Skeleton Road* (2014), point to the physical body as the holder of unutterable secrets.

Challenging the heteronormative aspects of traditional readings of Scottish identity and nationalism, Kate Turner's 'Queer Scottish Gothic' addresses the distance traditionally placed between 'Queer' and 'Scottish' and argues for the Gothic as a site through which 'Queer' and 'Scottish' can be reconciled. The analysis, which focuses on themes central to the Scottish Gothic tradition – such as hauntings, decaying castles and the supernatural – pays particular attention to Louise Welsh's *The Cutting Room* (2002), Zoë Strachan's *Ever Fallen in Love* (2011) and Luke Sutherland's *Venus as a Boy* (2004). Underpinning Turner's argument is an uncanny reading of both national identity and sexuality.

Closing the collection, Monica Germanà's 'Authorship, "Ghost-filled" Islands and the Haunting Feminine: Contemporary Scottish Female Gothic' investigates the question of authorship in contemporary women's Gothic, with specific references to the representative texts of Louise Welsh's *Naming the Bones* (2010), Alice Thompson's *Burnt Island* (2013) and Amy Sackville's *Orkney* (2013). While drawing attention to the persistent trope of the haunting feminine in Scottish Gothic, the chapter establishes a link between spectral femininity and these novels' interrogation of textual authenticity and authorial control. Such questions are grounded in the novels' strong engagement with the landscape, which, in the three works, is distinctly connected to the haunted geology and archaeology of Scottish islands.

*

Whilst attempting to provide a comprehensive account of Scottish Gothic cultural productions from the eighteenth century to the twenty-first century, we are conscious of the gaps the collection leaves open. With few exceptions – Andrew Smith and Jeff Wallace's *Gothic Modernisms* (2001) and, more recently, John Paul Riquelme's *Gothic and Modernism* (2008) – the relationship between the Gothic and literary Modernism still remains largely unexplored. With an eye to Riquelme's cogently argued claim that 'The transformations, adaptations, and other prominent traces of the Gothic in modern writing indicate the persistence of a cluster of cultural anxieties to which Gothic writing and literary modernism . . . continue to respond' (2000: 589), authors such as J. M. Barrie are given a fresh reassessment in Sarah Dunnigan's contribution to this collection. The influence of the Gothic on the Scottish Renaissance and the intermodernist decades (1930s–60s) also deserves more critical attention. While these decades were largely characterised by a distinctive preference for the aesthetics of realism, there may be further scope for Gothic exploration in the haunting landscapes of Lewis Grassic Gibbon's and Neil Gunn's narratives, the uncanny ambiguities of Naomi Mitchison's mythography and the darkness of Alexander McArthur's urban fiction. Similarly, we regret not being able to include an investigation of the important position of the Scottish ghost story in general, and the writing of Margaret Oliphant, in particular. Finally, while the collection attempts to assess the critical boundaries of Celticism in relation to Gothicism, we lament the fact that Gaelic Gothic has not been given more extensive attention. We hope that this collection has laid some fundamental groundwork about various manifestations of the Scottish Gothic generally, and provocatively engaged with the intricate ramifications of this complex classification. We are confident that other scholars will investigate areas overlooked by the present collection, and will branch out from the trajectories we have attempted to trace.

Note

1. According to Franco Moretti in his *Atlas of the European Novel, 1800– 1900*, 'Gothic stories were initially set in Italy and France, moved north to Germany, around 1800; and then north again, to Scotland after 1820' (1998: 16). Moretti's claim would support the case that Scotland became a popular Gothic locale only *after* the advent of Sir Walter Scott's Waverley series. While this claim may be true in the main, numerous Scottish-set Gothic narratives pre-date 1820, among them John Palmer's *The Haunted Cavern: A Caledonian Tale* (1796), F. H. P.'s *The Castle of Caithness: A Romance of the Thirteenth Century* (1802), Horsley Curties's *The Scottish Legend; or The Isle of St. Clothair* (1802), C. F. Barrett's *Douglas Castle; or, the Cell of Mystery, a Scottish Tale* (1803), Elizabeth Helme's *St. Clair of the Isles; or, the Outlaws of Barra* (1803), Mrs. Isaacs's *Glenmore Abbey; or, the Lady of the Rock* (1805) and Francis Lathom's *The Romance of the Hebrides; or, Wonders Never Cease!* (1809).

References

Baker, Timothy C. (2014), *Contemporary Scottish Gothic: Mourning, Authenticity, and Tradition*, Basingstoke: Palgrave Macmillan.

Craig, Cairns (2006), 'Devolving the Scottish Novel', in James F. English (ed.), *A Concise Companion to Contemporary British Fiction*, Oxford: Blackwell, pp. 121–40.

Duncan, Ian (2004), 'Walter Scott, James Hogg and Scottish Gothic', in David Punter (ed.), *A Companion to the Gothic*, Oxford: Blackwell, pp. 70–80.

Duncan, Ian with Leith Davis and Janet Sorenson (2004), 'Introduction', in Leith Davis, Ian Duncan and Janet Sorensen (eds), *Scotland and the Borders of Romanticism*, Cambridge: Cambridge University Press, pp. 1–19.

Gifford, Douglas (1996), 'Imagining Scotlands: The Return to Mythology in Modern Scottish Fiction', in Susanne Hagemann (ed.), *Studies in Scottish Fiction: 1945 to the Present*, Frankfurt am Main: Peter Lang, pp. 17–49.

Grenier, Katherine Haldane (2005), *Tourism and Identity in Scotland, 1770– 1914*, Aldershot: Ashgate.

Lloyd-Smith, Allan (2012), 'Nineteenth-Century American Gothic', in David Punter (ed.), *A New Companion to the Gothic*, Oxford: Wiley-Blackwell, pp. 163–75.

Manlove, Colin (1994), *Scottish Fantasy Literature: A Critical Survey*, Edinburgh: Polygon.

Moretti, Franco (1998), *Atlas of the European Novel, 1800–1900*, London: Verso.

Muir, Edwin [1936] (1982), *Scott and Scotland: The Predicament of the Scottish Writer*, Edinburgh: Polygon.

Punter, David (2002), 'Scottish and Irish Gothic', in Jerrold E. Hogle (ed.), *The Cambridge Companion to Gothic Fiction*, Cambridge: Cambridge University Press, pp. 105–23.

— (2012), 'Scottish Gothic', in Gerard Carruthers and Liam McIlvanney (eds), *The Cambridge Companion to Scottish Literature*, Cambridge: Cambridge University Press, pp. 132–44.

Riquelme, John Paul (2000), 'Toward a History of Gothic and Modernism: Dark Modernity from Bram Stoker to Samuel Beckett', *Modern Fiction Studies*, 46, 585–605.

Royle, Nicholas (2003), *The Uncanny*, Manchester: Manchester University Press.

Scott, Walter [1816] (2009), *The Antiquary*, Oxford: Oxford University Press.

Scullion, Adrienne (1995), 'Feminine Pleasures and Masculine Indignities: Gender and Community in Scottish Drama', in Christopher Whyte (ed.), *Gendering the Nation: Studies in Modern Scottish Literature*, Edinburgh: Edinburgh University Press, pp. 169–204.

Smith, G. Gregory (1919), *Scottish Literature: Character and Influence*, London: Macmillan.

Townshend, Dale (2014), 'Shakespeare, Ossian and the Problem of "Scottish Gothic"', in Elisabeth Bronfen and Beate Neumeier (eds), *Gothic Renaissance: A Reassessment*, Manchester: Manchester University Press, pp. 218–43.

Wright, Angela (2007), 'Scottish Gothic', in Catherine Spooner and Emma McEvoy (eds), *The Routledge Companion to Gothic*, London: Routledge, pp. 73–82.

Chapter 2

'The Celtic Century' and the Genesis of Scottish Gothic

Nick Groom

This may be called the Celtic century, for all Europe has been inundated with nonsense about the Celts. When we come to the truth about them, and time will always draw truth out of the well, the Celtic mist will vanish, or become a mere cloud. (Pinkerton 1814, vol. 2: 124)

The Celtic, insofar as it is applied to Scottish, Irish, Welsh and Cornish identity and culture, is, like traditional Scottish tartans, an invention. Barry Cunliffe describes the word in its current Anglophone usage as an 'ethnonym', and dates it to the eighteenth century (2003: 5). Seamus Deane (1997: 77) likewise places 'Celt' within scare quotes and suggests it is a late nineteenth- or early twentieth-century term carrying an anti-modernist agenda

transposed from its nationalist, antiquarian origins of the eighteenth century into a pan-European *combinatoire* of evolutionary destiny, the preservation of difference, even of anachronism, as a refusal of those adaptations needed to survive into the world of international capital and the nation-state. (Deane 1997: 88)

The 'Celt' and the 'Celtic' did not simply emerge in the mid-eighteenth century as an aspect of early Romanticism that reflected the growing literary taste for the ancient British past. Their genesis was instead in anti-quarianism, racial politics and national identity, and, as such, the terms are not dissimilar to 'Goths' and the 'Gothic'. The Gothic was politically Whiggish, describing a version of historical progress that was predicated on an irrepressible spirit of liberty that expressed itself through rebellion against tyranny and which was encoded in watershed events of English history: the Magna Carta, the Reformation, the Great Rebellion (the British Civil Wars), the Restoration and the Glorious Revolution. The consequence of all this historical turbulence had been to establish a form of government and civic representation that was liberal, Parliamentary and Protestant – and which underwrote eighteenth-century commercial society and the imperial economy. The ancient Goths themselves, a Germanic barbarian tribe, were the inspiration and the founding fathers of this ideology – in rebelling against Roman tyranny, sacking Rome itself and overrunning the Empire, the Goths had exhibited less a savage desire to lay waste to civilisation and rather an instinctive love of freedom, as well as values of honour, chivalry, monogamy and social equality – and an enviable energy and fertility – for which even Roman historians such as Tacitus held a grudging admiration when compared with the decadence, corruption and luxurious extravagances of Rome (Groom 2012: 2).

In the developing Whig theory of English history, the Goths were accordingly positioned as ancestors of the English (as 'Jutes', or as forebears of the Germanic Angles and Saxons), variously challenging Norman colonialism, Catholic repression and despotic sovereignty. The Goths had also, moreover, developed their own culture as an alternative to the austerity of classical art and architecture. The Gothic style was distinguished as being unrestrained by rule or order, restlessly decorative, vividly imaginative, intensely sublime – exemplified by the awe-inspiring cathedrals and abbeys of the Middle Ages and by medieval romance. The proximity of both ecclesiastical monuments and national folklore to the supernatural – whether in lurid depictions of Hell and the popular cult of the macabre in church art, or in the weird and perilous realm of folklore and Faërie – was also characteristic, and hinted at the darker side of the Gothic: namely, that if the political Gothic described the triumphal progress of the nation, then that progress had come at a great cost – the iconoclasm of the Reformation, the martyrdoms of the Counter-Reformation, the regicide of Charles I and the ensuing civil strife, and the brutal suppression of Jacobite resistance and rebellion in Ireland (the Williamite War, 1689–91) and Scotland (the '45). The Gothic aesthetic mixed northern anti-classical myths of purity with the nightmarish carnage of history and politics – it was uniquely suited to give voice to repressed fears of identity, to the unspeakable crimes of the past, to the anxieties of contemporary progress.

In literature, it is no accident that the Gothic came of age with *The Castle of Otranto* (1764), written by Horace Walpole: connoisseur, architect of the medievalist Strawberry Hill, Whig MP and son of the prime minister. Walpole's novel resolutely fixes the Gothic as an English form entangled in English Whig politics, from early antiquarianism to the current affairs of the court of George III, and consequently rooted in the nation's continuing and disputed history – all of which begs the question, 'how can a "Scottish Gothic" be conceived?' Is the Gothic exceptional to England, and are later iterations in Scotland and Ireland retrospective adoptions of the mere imagery of Gothickry rather than the deep-rooted political ideology of Whiggism (much as the category of the 'Gothic novel' itself is first employed as a critical category in 1889 to describe an idiosyncratic genre comprised of various stories of terror, horror, wonder and romance recognisable to writers and readers) (Gosse 1889: 301)?

Scottish Gothic sits uncomfortably with English Gothic, because Scottish history tells a different story: there is no celebrated advent of the Saxons, no ensuing Norman Conquest, no Magna Carta through which to develop the myths of national identity – but there is a Protestant Reformation, a mid-seventeenth century theocracy, the Act of Union with England and Jacobitism. To take the first of these as an example, the Roman Catholic priest Thomas Innes compared the Scottish Reformation to the Sack of Rome, complaining of John Knox, the founder of Presbyterianism, that he was the ringleader of the rioting iconoclasts:

> It is *Knox* himself who hounded out, or led on the furious mobb in this wretched expedition, that hath thought fit to record it, with many other such noble exploits, more becoming the *Goths* or *Vandals*, than an apostolical man, as he pretended to be. (Innes 1729: 569; see also 573)

So there is a thread of Scottish Whig history, which, Colin Kidd argues, is really the history of a single ecclesiastical party rather than of an ideology – of the Reformed tradition in general and of Covenanters in particular – that remained distinctive not only up to the end of the eighteenth century but throughout the nineteenth century (1997b: 98).

It is from out of these contexts that the Celtic also emerged, in a spirit of mutually antagonistic collaboration with Englishness, and as a constituent component of Britishness. Celticism is, perhaps, the earliest example of identity politics in Britain – a clear alternative to the Anglocentrism, urbanisation and commercial society beloved of the English Whigs. And because Celticism appears to give voice to the dispossessed and unenfranchised, it has been predictably adopted by academics through Michael Hechter's model of British 'internal colonialism', and is repeatedly used as a synonym for the ancient clans of the Highlands, Scottish identity in general, and Gaelic language and culture across Scotland, Ireland and Wales – what is now known, after Matthew Arnold, as the 'Celtic Fringe'.[1] But as Kidd again argues, 'The influential notion that Scotland belongs to a "Celtic fringe" reinforces a sense of Anglo-Scottish differentiation', and in particular, the use of the term 'Celtic' 'usually involves the projection of uninformed metropolitan attitudes towards a peripheral "other", and rarely pertains with any precision to the substance of Celtic-speaking cultures, however much intellectuals in the so-called "Celtic" countries have, in turn, appropriated the label for themselves' (2003: 874).

In other words, to use a term such as 'Celtic' is to initiate a hidden agenda that imposes an outdated sociological theory of internal colonialism on Britain and Ireland in order to distort the understanding of emerging British and Irish identities – especially, for the purposes of this chapter, in the eighteenth century. That distortion encourages the four nations to be perceived in a core–periphery relationship – of England and her satellites (that is, Anglocentric, or 'Anglo-British' Britain) – in which the peripheral nations, moreover, share a united experience and identity of disaffection, exclusion from power and oppression. But this is not borne out by the evidence of the time – a time dominated politically by the Irish statesman Edmund Burke, and a government that from 1762–3 was led by a Scotsman, the Earl of Bute; Scottish colonial ambitions also drove the imperial policy of the time (see MacKenzie and Devine 2011). Each nationality had, furthermore, its own learned societies – the Society of Cymmrodorion (1751), Society of Gwyneddigion (1771), Society of Antiquaries of Scotland (1780) and Royal Irish Academy (1785) – that respected and acknowledged English institutions as much as they did each other. More generally, the Welsh, for instance, felt no racial brotherhood with the Irish or the Scots – their ancestry lay with the ancient Britons and English Saxons, and as the author of *History of the Cymbri* (1746) argued, the Welsh and the Irish were separate: 'the Irish Celtae and the Cymbri were two different nations' (qtd in Kidd 1999: 198).

Despite these differences, there were plenty of connections within the archipelago due to geographical proximity, shared histories and migrations. These relationships ran deep. The Scots had a proud Saxon line of descent, particularly among Lowlanders, that united 'Gothic' and 'Celtic' pedigrees in a way comparable to the Union of the Crowns in 1603 and the Union of the Parliaments in 1707. The Gothic theorist Sir William Temple had suggested in the late seventeenth century that the Gaels (both Irish and Scottish) were northern Scythians, thereby sharing an eastern European genealogy with the Goths; likewise, later Scottish historians, including the novelist Tobias Smollett, combined the ancient Celtae, Cimbri and Teutons (Smollett 1757–8, vol. 1: 4–5). Saxonism, a general term for ancient northern Germanic peoples such as the Teutons, was as proud a cultural and racial identity as was Celticism. James Macpherson, the champion of *Ossian*, claimed Teutonic descent 'from the ancient Catti of Germany' and increasingly commended the

Saxon cultural influence on Lowland Scotland (Anon. 1796: 221). The polemical antiquarian John Pinkerton similarly argued that the Picts were of Gothic origin, alleging that the two races of Scotland were the Teutonic Lowlanders and the immigrant Celts. For Pinkerton, the unhappy marriage of these separate lineages had created a disastrously fractured identity that had sundered the Scottish people from the fortunes of Britain: 'two words, *Scots* and *Scotland*, have hitherto totally ruined our history' (1814, vol. 1: 324). Although undeniably contentious, Pinkerton's provocations nonetheless influenced later nineteenth-century historical researches, separating the Lowlanders from the Celts and acknowledging them as Saxons, Teutons and, for some at least, the true English (Kidd 2003: 886). It is no surprise then that Thomas Carlyle described the Lowland poet Robert Burns as 'a piece of the right Saxon stuff' (1993: 162).

Likewise, the political arena that defined the English Gothic enlisted the Scots as primordial Goths. William Camden was invoked for his claim that the 'Civiliz'd' Scots, 'who inhabit the East part of the Country, are not really Scots, but of the same German Original with us English' (1701, vol. 1: 42), while John Whitaker argued that the core settlement of Britain had been in the south from which the 'Scuites' ('Scots': literally wanderers or refugees) had successively settled Scotland and Ireland (1772: 184). The 1707 Act of Union could therefore be spun as a Gothic reunion. The anonymous author of *A Perswasive to the Union Now On Foot* (1706) mixes things nicely, asserting that the Goths were originally considered to be 'a *Celtick* Nation' (1706: 25), and goes on to argue that

> If the *Goths*, of whom, as it's said, the *English* are partly come, be *Scythians*, and that the *Scythians* are *Scots*, then in common consequence the *Scots* and *English* must have the same Original, and been at first one People; and if so, it is no wonder, that after they were severed they should be so desirous now to unite. (Anon. 1706: 26)

Scottish lawyers such as Andrew McDouall, author of *An Institute of the Laws of Scotland* (1751–3), likewise argued for the historical legitimacy of the Union and the Whig ascendancy, commenting in 1747 that 'It is to the *Gothick* Constitution that we owe our Parliaments, which are the Guardians of our Rights and Liberties' (McDouall 1747: 28). Perhaps most strikingly, the Scottish writer James Thomson, the best-selling poet of the age who was responsible for the imperial anthem 'Rule, Britannia', acclaimed English pan-Gothicism and a united British constitution in his political poem 'Liberty' (1735–6):

Of *Gothic* Nations this the final burst;
And, mix'd the genius of these people all,

Their Virtues mix'd in one exalted Stream,
Here the rich tide of *English* blood grew full.

(Thomson 1736: pt IV, ll. 742–5)

Consequently, as William Collins demonstrated in his 'Ode on the Popular Superstitions of the Highlands of Scotland' (1749, published 1788), the Scottish landscape could be figured as an outpost of the English Gothic imagination, rather than being a separatist Celtic terrain. For him, it was a realm of undead terror, one vast graveyard:

Yet frequent now, at midnight's solemn hour
The rifted mounds their yawning cells unfold,
And forth the monarchs stalk with sovereign power
In pageant robes, and wreathed with sheeny gold,
And on their twilight tombs aerial council hold.

(Collins, in Lonsdale 1969: ll. 150–4)

Ann Radcliffe too treated Scotland as such in her first novel, *The Castles of Athlin and Dunbayne* (1789), and Walter Scott went even further by dissecting English Saxonism in *Ivanhoe* (1820) and elsewhere interrogating historical Unionism to find a rightful place for Scotland within Great Britain. Scott was in any case heavily influenced by Thomas Percy's founding collection of Gothic balladry, *Reliques of Ancient English Poetry* (1765), to which Scott's first work *Minstrelsy of the Scottish Border* (1802–3, with James Hogg) was much indebted. Scott's *Minstrelsy* was also a response to Gottfried August Bürger's supernatural ballads and the German tradition, which also took inspiration from Percy's folkloric Gothicism.

So from certain perspectives, Goths and Celts were blood brothers, sharing common ancestry and attitudes, alike in their antipathy to Mediterranean classical civilisation, and almost synonymous. But Celticism was also figured as a strongly separatist identity, an alternative not only to Rome but to the Gothic. This has its origins in France. These 'Celts' were specifically 'born in *Gaul*, a part of *France*'; Julius Caesar had recorded that only the peoples of central France called themselves *Celtae*, and that they occupied the region between the rivers of the Marne, Seine, Rhine and Garonne (Blount 1656). They were noteworthy for their long moustaches and open homosexuality, and some claimed that the Galatians addressed by St Paul in the New Testament were also Celts, a claim for which there is now archaeological evidence (see Voigt 2003). But there is no evidence in antiquity that they ever visited or settled in Britain or Ireland. That claim did not arise until the late sixteenth century with the growing obsession with racial origins, ancient migrations and national character that was driving forward research into the Goths and the implications that their forms of governance had for the contemporary constitution and the monarchy.

Celtic separatism was properly inaugurated in 1703, when Paul Pezron published his *L'antiquité de la nation et de la langue des Celtes, autrement appellez Gaulois*, translated in 1706 by David Jones as *The Antiquities of Nations; more particularly of the Celtæ or Gauls, taken to be originally the Same People as our Ancient Britains*. That suggestive subtitle, 'the Celtæ or Gauls, taken to be originally the Same People as our Ancient Britains', on which the hopes of three nations would gradually be hung, was Jones's own contribution – and his own invention. Pezron's aim was to construct an Armorican national myth for France, replacing the Franks with the Bretons as the aboriginal French race and, in doing so, proposing the Celts as the forefathers of both the Gauls and Ancient Britons. The Keeper of the Ashmolean Museum in Oxford, Edward Lhuyd, who had encouraged Jones to translate Pezron, published his own *Archaeologia Britannica* in 1707 and took the cause of Celtic separatism further by linking the Cornish, Irish, Manx, Scots and Welsh languages to Breton: these languages, he decided, were 'Celtic/k' and the people who spoke them 'Celts'. Although Cunliffe suggests that Lhuyd only adopted such terms because 'Gaullish' sounded too French and implied Jacobite and Catholic sympathies, Lhuyd's work nevertheless gave momentum to the supposition that the Celts were a mysterious ancient race and a viable alternative to the Goths (Cunliffe 2003: 114, 48–9). Not unlike the English Gothic, the Celtic appeared to identify authenticity with ancestry, blending the fashionable cult of the sublime, as exemplified by wild and untamed landscapes, with the sentimentalisation of 'otherness' and alternative histories. Celtic culture, however, was oral rather than literate (unlike the Goths, who were the most literate of barbarians and had devised the Runic alphabet), and they identified themselves through a kinship with natural environments rather than via tribal history. Later commentators accordingly speculated that the Celts had built Stonehenge before sailing west to Ireland, and that the Celtic language was the universal language spoken before the scattering of tongues at the Tower of Babel – a theory espoused by such experts as John Cleland, better known for writing *Memoirs of a Woman of Pleasure* (or *Fanny Hill*) in 1748 (see Cleland 1766). But the Celt could also potentially be figured as the prototypical embodiment of an alternative to eighteenth-century Britishness focused on London: one that looked instead to the Scottish Enlightenment and its cultural pre-eminence, rising from the clash between Presbyterian and Jacobite politics and theology.

Such Celtic separatism forms the backstory to James Macpherson's hugely popular *Ossian* works (1760–5), which played on orality and voice, atmosphere and settings, as well as mixing Jacobite Romanticism with Scottish Enlightenment theories of social evolution. Macpherson's supporting essays on Celtic history and geography were deliberately anti-Anglocentric, aligning the Scottish literary heritage with that of Ireland – and in doing so infuriating Samuel Johnson, who responded to Macpherson's effectively archipelagic model of Scotto-Irish literary relations and alternative oral history by damning *Ossian* as a forgery because it sidestepped the Gothic authenticating devices of literate culture. But the case of *Ossian* is in fact far more complex than pitching the Celts against the Goths and demonstrates how rapidly Celtic separatism can collapse into English Gothicism. The strange and eerie lines of *Fragments* (1760), *Fingal* (1761) and *Temora* (1762) calculatingly evoked the sublime, weaving the fatalistic atmosphere of a lost and archaic age into daringly uncultivated scenes of rugged wilderness. Macpherson's repetitive, spectral style is exemplified by the 'Songs of Selma', which Wolfgang Goethe later transcribed at the end of *The Sorrows of Young Werther* (1774): 'It is night; – I am alone, forlorn on the hill of storms. The wind is heard in the mountain. The torrent shrieks down the rock. No hut receives me from the rain; forlorn on the hill of winds' (Macpherson 1996: 166).

As the Scottish Enlightenment professor Dr Hugh Blair argued:

> Accuracy and correctness; artfully connected narration; exact method and proportion of parts, we may look for in polished times. . . . But amidst the rude scenes of nature, amidst rocks and torrents and whirlwinds and battles, dwells the sublime. It is the thunder and the lightning of genius. It is the offspring of nature, not of art. (Blair 1763: 68)

Blair is suggesting that the *Ossianic* aesthetic is Celtic, as distinct from Gothic. And yet ironically, this literary style is really the offspring of the Whig cultural agenda forged by English writers earlier in the century, braiding political and cultural history, individualism and the passions into a new aesthetic vocabulary. Whig literary culture arose alongside post-Glorious Revolution commercial society to promote new artistic credos of originality and imagination, and as an alternative to neo-classicism: English literature was effectively developed as a cultural expression of a particular Whig identity (Williams 2005: 163–4). The philosophy of thinkers such as Anthony Ashley, Earl of Shaftesbury, and Edmund Burke (author of the highly influential *Philosophical Enquiry into the Origin of our Ideas of the Sublime and Beautiful*, 1757), and the 'Graveyard' fashion for vernacular superstition, haunted imaginings and mortal transience all influenced the deliberately self-absorbed work of Whig writers such as Mark Akenside and Edward Young, and in doing so contributed to a new and politically inflected literary scene.

Whig aesthetics is thus writ large throughout *Ossian*, and Macpherson's emphatic primitivism, so styled, did not challenge Whig notions of progress at all; rather, his account of ancient society – influenced as it was by Scottish Enlightenment thinking – confirmed the positive accounts of ancient Gothic society given in classical sources, and supported the prevailing attitude that the cultural remains of British antiquity could offer a credible political alternative to classical civilisation. And even the actual content of the *Ossianic* works – Macpherson's emphasis on bardism, dreams and ghosts, orality, the sublime and natural landscapes, as well as on memory, identity and the past – were consequently all very much within an emergent Whiggish tradition that was subsequently championed by later writers to become what was eventually known as Romanticism. Macpherson's writing is much more complex – or contradictory – than has often been recognised: for Kidd, Macpherson's politics are therefore a risky study in ambiguity, 'combining conventional Hanoverian Whiggism with sentimental Jacobitism, Scottish identity with a wider British patriotism, traditional conservative values with radical and liberal ideas' (1997a: 25). Likewise, Dafydd Moore comments that this 'fusion of Jacobite-cum-patriot Whig ideology with sociological Whiggism . . . proves itself unsustainable, as the contradiction between Macpherson's anathematization of property and praise of commerce or his ideas about the role of oral transmission suggest' (2006: 13). For John Kerrigan, this accounts for *Ossian*'s marginalisation and exclusion from the canon: 'The contradictions in Macpherson, Highland MP for a Cornish constituency, cultural-Jacobite unionist and "primitivist" favourite of Whig, commercial Edinburgh . . . help explain why Ossian has still not been assimilated by Eng Lit' (2008: 409).

Although the ambivalent influence of *Ossian* on later Gothic writing can consequently be seen as pervasive, it remains within a larger tradition of Whig aesthetics. *Ossian* was part of the cultural moment of the Whiggish English Gothic of the early 1760s, which takes its cue from Thomas Gray's poem 'The Bard' (1757), published in the same year as Burke's *Philosophical Enquiry into . . . the Sublime and Beautiful*, and as typical as Gray's own bardic invocations in, for instance, 'The Fatal Sisters' (1761), Horace Walpole's creative medievalism in *Anecdotes of Painting in England* (1762) and *The Castle of Otranto*, and Thomas Percy's revival of ancient Runic and ballad traditions in *Five Pieces of Runic Poetry* (1763) and *Reliques*. These works are filled with ghosts and dark landscapes, fragments and folklore; the past is heavy and inescapable, the only monuments megaliths and barrows. Indeed, in a rare moment of empathy with Macpherson, Johnson admitted that in the absence of written historical records, the testimony of ruins must suffice: 'Edifices, either standing or ruined, are the chief records of an illiterate society' (1984: 85).

But the prevalence, language and style of Whig culture is inescapable in *Ossian*, and perpetually stymies Macpherson's project: his attempts to develop an avowedly separatist Celticism remain entombed within the Gothic. Despite the heroic claims made for the Celtic in Macpherson's historicist essays, he is fatally aware of its own shortcomings and so mitigates it with Whig pragmatism in adapting the emerging tradition. At the moment of its defining literary achievement – *Ossian* – the Celtic is saturated in defeat and loss, indecisive and uncertain of its eventual fate, reliant on a half-century of Whig cultural formation, and always with a weather eye towards London. This cocktail of Scotticised English Gothic and self-repudiating Celticism was, however, itself enough, inspiring works that would brood on the contradictions of being, of a divided self.

James Hogg's gripping novel *The Private Memoirs and Confessions of a Justified Sinner* (1824), embodies these contradictions in the character of Robert Wringhim – a figure of questionable paternal legitimacy who, as an adherent of fundamentalist Calvinism, believes he is predestined. Through 'the rage of fanaticism', Wringhim therefore exposes the predicament of history, casting doubt on the validity of accounts of both origins and destiny (Hogg 1990: 93). The text itself is steeped in the rhetoric of antinomian election and reprobation as a perpetual reminder of how Wringhim as an individual (and Scotland as a country) is poised between past and future, a rhetoric of violent denunciation of sin that, as David Punter has pointed out, was commonplace in Scottish churches of the period (2002: 117). It is a narrative haunted by the preternatural apparition of the Brocken spectre, and is persistently on the verge of releasing a supernatural demonology into the plot, yet it is also doggedly mundane in its scenes and settings. The textual authority of Hogg's novel is also itself in question: it is a *manuscrit trouvé*, a mysterious document that has been entombed in a grave, disinterred and edited – it exists in different and competing identities, and through its recovery evokes the authenticity debates and antiquarian squabbles that plague Scottish culture.

Wringhim is a divisive sociopath whose 'presence acted as a mildew on all social intercourse or enjoyment'; he is bloody, abject and other (Hogg 1990: 33). He foments riot and internecine strife among the Whigs at the Black Bull inn: a reminder of civil war, the dangers of factionalism and the fragile peace of domestic politics. But in order to pervert social order, Wringhim adopts the guise of the dispossessed, of the separatist: he is a calculated anachronism. He is neither vampirically undead nor an evil genius, but is essentially a manifestation of the unspeakable Celt: diabolical, inscrutable, fanatical – thoroughly antithetical to English Whiggism.

The Gothic arose in Scotland in the context of emerging and complex Celtic identities, in what I have called a 'mutually antagonistic collaboration' with Whiggish Gothic ideology and politicised antiquarianism. Scottish Gothic consequently needs to be understood archipelagically and catachthonically. Archipelagic approaches move beyond 'four nations' and core–periphery models of British and Irish relations by challenging the assumption of English hegemony within the Isles and instead emphasising the range of cultural interactions at local, regional and national levels. Likewise, catachthonic thinking historicises this archipelagic understanding by analysing the historicity of historiographical theories of nationality and identity – effectively through a doubled, or subterranean history. Previous commentators have concurred that theories of racial origin were inextricable from cultural values, national identity and party politics, and that these were deeply structured by Whig thinking and its compelling influence on literature at the time. While it is difficult to disagree with Susan Manning's observation that, for the eighteenth century, we should 'regard the condition of Britishness as offering Scottish writers a range of rhetorical resources with which to explore the implications of "being modern" in the post-Union period' (2007: 47), what has been left out, however – at least in literary considerations – has been the problematic invention of the Celt and the Celtic, which adds a whole level of complexity to Scottish declarations of cultural self-determination.

And the Celtic does, uncannily, return. Celticism literally queers the pitch of Scottish Gothic, and indeed the topography of Scotland – the very notion of territory – became the ground on which the writing now categorised as 'Scottish Gothic' was tested. Land was debatable and unstable. From the misty panoramas of *Ossian* to the twisted cityscapes of Robert Louis Stevenson's *Strange Case of Dr Jekyll and Mr Hyde* (1886), the country and the city become phantasmal – spectral lairs of the other. *Jekyll and Hyde* is, like Hogg's *Confessions*, built of layered documents that draw attention to criminological detail in, for instance, styles of handwriting, although in this case the demon brother is unleashed through the agency of an impure drug: medicinal extremism rather than religious zealotry. While *Jekyll and Hyde* plainly gives voice to fears of corruption through the otherness of foreign drugs and the fear that Darwinian evolution may be a two-way affair in which the brutish can reassert itself, it is also a book about the character of the streets and locales of Edinburgh, split between the old and new parts of the city; as G. K. Chesterton pointed out as early as 1927, the story is 'very unmistakably happening in Edinburgh' (Chesterton 1991: 65). In this labyrinthine world, Hyde is the denizen of old Scotland, another dreadful Celt returned: primeval, bestial and elemental – the horrific Celtic alternative to British Unionism. This Celt lurks in the common places of Scotland. In literature, Deane argues that this sense of abiding menace amounts to 'an aesthetics of the actual . . . that remains immersed in the local, the folklorish, [and] refuses the theoretical' (Deane 1997: 17). This is how the Celtic does, catachthonically, subterraneously, enter into Scottish Gothic, as W. B. Yeats remarked of Ireland's cultural traditions (in a sentence that revives the shadow of the 'Celtic Fringe'):

> Folk-art is, indeed, the oldest of the aristocracies of thought, and because it refuses what is passing and trivial, the merely clever and pretty, as certainly as the vulgar and insincere, and because it has gathered into itself the simplest and most unforgettable thoughts of the generations, it is the soil where all great art is rooted. (Yeats 1959: 139)

The 'rootedness' in native soil here is highly suggestive. It is evident in Robert Burns's supernatural verse 'Tam o' Shanter' (1791), which, despite Burns's debts to *Ossian* elsewhere, presents itself as local tradition, peppered with notices of everyday reality – market days and ale drinking – before the warlocks frolic to the piping of the Devil in a spirited parody of the simple pleasures of country life: the communal dance. 'Tam o' Shanter' is extraordinarily vivid through a forensic level of minute detail and a resolutely vernacular diction – a style also adopted by Walter Scott for 'Wandering Willie's Tale', a ghost story extracted from *Redgauntlet* (1824).

Through such deviant familiarity, Celticism becomes not so much an archaic figure in the shade of the Goth, but a home-grown cultural practice: recovering and assimilating native traditions that can upset English Whig aesthetics. Legitimate Celtic history, then, is ardently parochial and, by being so can escape the bind of Whig history and its totalising narrative. As the nineteenth-century Scottish folklorist Andrew Lang wrote to his fellow writer the Englishman Edward Clodd, 'you believe in Progress, do you? I'd rather believe in wraiths' (qtd in Stocking 1996: 56).

Note

1. Matthew Arnold gave the O'Donnell lectures (1865–6) on the *Study of Celtic Literature* and was responsible for chairs of 'Celtic Studies'.

References

Anon. (1706), *A Perswasive to the Union Now On Foot, by Arguments from Nature, Reason, and Mutual Advantage*, London: The Booksellers.

— (1796), 'An Account of James Macpherson, Esq.', *The Scots Magazine*, 58 (April and June), 221–4, 365–7.

Blair, Hugh (1763), *A Critical Dissertation on the Poems of Ossian, the Son of Fingal*, London: T. Becket and P. A. De Hondt.

Blount, Thomas (1656), *Glossographia: or A Dictionary, interpreting all such Hard Words, whether Hebrew, Greek, Latin, Italian, Spanish, French, Teutonick, Belgick, British or Saxon; as are now used in our Refined English Tongue*, London: Thomas Newcomb.

Camden, William (1701), *Camden's Britannia Abridg'd; with Improvements, and Continuations, to this Present Time*, 2 vols, London: J. B. for Joseph Wild.

Carlyle, Thomas (1993), *On Heroes, Hero Worship, & the Heroic in History*, ed. Michael K. Goldberg, Joel J. Brattin and Mark Engel, Berkeley, Los Angeles and Oxford: University of California Press.

Chesterton, Gilbert Keith (1991), 'Robert Louis Stevenson', in *The Collected Works of G. K. Chesterton XVIII: Thomas Carlyle, Leo Tolstoy, Robert Louis Stevenson, Chaucer*, ed. George J. Marlin, Richard P. Rabatin, John L. Swan, Joseph Sobran, Patricia Azar, Joe Mysak and Rev. Randall Paine, San Francisco: Ignatius Press, pp. 39–147.

Cleland, John (1766), *The Way to Things by Words, and to Words by Things, being a Sketch of an Attempt at the Retrieval of the Antient Celtic, or, Primitive Language of Europe*, London: L. Davis and C. Reymers.

Cunliffe, Barry (2003), *The Celts: A Very Short Introduction*, Oxford: Oxford University Press.

Deane, Seamus (1997), *Strange Country: Modernity and Nationhood in Irish Writing Since 1790*, Oxford: Clarendon Press.

Gosse, Edmund (1889), *A History of Eighteenth Century Literature (1660–1780)*, London and New York: Macmillan.

Groom, Nick (2012), *The Gothic: A Very Short Introduction*, Oxford: Oxford University Press.

Hogg, James [1824] (1990), *The Private Memoirs and Confessions of a Justified Sinner*, ed. John Carey, Oxford: Oxford University Press.

Innes, Thomas (1729), *A Critical Essay on the Ancient Inhabitants of the Northern Parts of Britain, or Scotland*, 2 vols [continuously paginated], London: William Innys.

Johnson, Samuel (1984), *A Journey to the Western Islands of Scotland* and James Boswell, *The Journal of a Tour to the Hebrides*, ed. Peter Levi, London: Penguin.

Kerrigan, John (2008), *Archipelagic English: Literature, History, and Politics 1603–1707*, Oxford: Oxford University Press.

Kidd, Colin (1997a), 'Macpherson, Burns, and the Politics of Sentiment', *Scotlands*, 4, 25–43.

— (1997b), '*The Strange Death of Scottish History* Revisited: Constructions of the Past in Scotland, c. 1790–1914', *Scottish Historical Review*, 76: 201, 86–102.

— (1999), *British Identities Before Nationalism: Ethnicity and Nationhood in the Atlantic World, 1600–1800*, Cambridge: Cambridge University Press.

— (2003), 'Race, Empire, and the Limits of Nineteenth-Century Scottish Nationhood', *Historical Journal*, 46: 4, 873–92.

Lonsdale, Roger (ed.) (1969), *The Poems of Thomas Gray, William Collins, Oliver Goldsmith*, London and New York: Longman.

McDouall [MacDowall], Andrew, Lord Bankton (1747), *An Essay upon Feudal Holdings, Superiorities, and Hereditary Jurisdictions, in Scotland*, London: R. Lee.

MacKenzie, John M. and T. M. Devine (eds) (2011), *Scotland and the British Empire*, Oxford: Oxford University Press.

Macpherson, James (1996), *The Poems of Ossian and Related Works*, ed. Howard Gaskill, Edinburgh: Edinburgh University Press.

Manning, Susan (2007), 'Post-Union Scotland and the Scottish Idiom of Britishness', in Ian Brown (gen. ed.), *The Edinburgh History of Scottish Literature*, 3 vols, Edinburgh: Edinburgh University Press, vol. 2, pp. 45–56.

Moore, Dafydd (2006), 'James Macpherson and "Celtic Whiggism"', *Eighteenth-Century Life*, 30: 1, 1–24.

Pinkerton, John (1814), *An Enquiry into the History of Scotland*, 2 vols, Edinburgh: James Ballantyne.

Punter, David (2002), 'Scottish and Irish Gothic', in Jerrold E. Hogle (ed.), *Cambridge Companion to Gothic Fiction*, Cambridge: Cambridge University Press, pp. 105–23.

Smollett, Tobias (1757–8), *A Complete History of England, deduced from the Descent of Julius Cæsar, to the Treaty of Aix la Chapelle, 1748*, 4 vols, London: James Rivington and James Fletcher.

Stocking, Jr., George W. (1996), *After Tylor: British Social Anthropology, 1888–1951*, Madison: University of Wisconsin Press.

Thomson, James (1736), 'Liberty', in *The Works of Mr. Thomson*, 2 vols, London: A. Millar.

Voigt, Mary M. (2003), 'Celts at Gordion: The Late Hellenistic Settlement', *Expedition*, 45, 14–19.

Whitaker, John (1772), *The Genuine History of the Britons Asserted*, London: Dodsley [et al].

Williams, Abigail (2005), 'Patronage and Whig Literary Culture in the Early Eighteenth Century', in David Womersley (ed.), '*Cultures of Whiggism': New Essays on English Literature and Culture in the Long Eighteenth Century*, Newark: University of Delaware Press, pp. 149–72.

Yeats, W. B. (1959), 'By the Roadside', in *Mythologies*, London: Macmillan, pp. 138–40.

Chapter 3

The Politics and Poetics of the 'Scottish Gothic' from *Ossian* to *Otranto* and Beyond

Carol Margaret Davison

As Murray Pittock has cogently argued, the eighteenth century was 'the historic battleground of the formation of Great Britain' (1997: 1). In terms of Anglo-Scottish relations during this era, a shift occurred that saw the military battlefields of Culloden and Prestonpans give way to more intellectual battlefields and 'culture wars' (Moore 2003a: 46) where the question of national superiority rested upon the quality and innovation of cultural productions both ancient and modern, some of which, like James Macpherson's *Ossian*, notably chronicled martial struggles. Nationalist statements proliferated about literature, especially at mid-century, such as David Hume's comment in private correspondence in 1757 in the wake of the theatrical production of John Home's *Douglas* (1756), that Scots had become, despite the devastating losses of their 'Princes, ... Parliaments, ... Independent Government', in combination with the fact that they spoke 'a very corrupt Dialect of the [English] Tongue', 'the People most distinguish'd for Literature in Europe' (1932, vol. 1: 255). Lord Lyttelton echoed this viewpoint in his *Dialogues of the Dead* (1760), declaring that the Scots had 'discovered such Talents in all Branches of Literature as might render the English jealous of being excelled by their genius, if there could remain a Competition, when there remains no Destruction between the two Nations' (1970: 283). As various scholars have noted, national histories, which were published in unprecedented numbers over the course of the eighteenth century, were key battlegrounds that served either as unifying narratives in support of a sense of coherent Britishness post-Union, or divisive chronicles that underscored ethnic differences and consolidated national and cultural hierarchies. What appeared to be minor debates relating to ethnography, literature and history were pivotal in the development of the idea of Britishness and national identity, and reached an explosive height during the Scotophobic 1760s amidst 'the bitter factionalism of contemporary

English politics' (Hook 1986: 40). Of especial importance to cultural critics is the fact that literature played such a vital role in the development of new nationalist discourses (Groom 1996: 289) during a period that evidenced the efflorescence of Scottish Enlightenment thought and the seeds of Scottish Romanticism, an aesthetic that 'is still undergoing a process of conceptual recognition' (Pittock 2011: 6), alongside the development of various innovative novelistic forms, including the Gothic.

Looking back as a Gothicist across this era to consider *Ossian*'s role in the development of both Gothic literature and what Dale Townshend rightly refers to as the 'vexed and complicated', anachronistic category of 'Scottish Gothic' literature is a fraught enterprise requiring 'a greater sensitivity to political history of the period' (2014: 227). During the eighteenth century, 'Celts' and 'Goths' were generally positioned as discrete ethnographic categories, the Scots being associated – especially the Highlanders – with the Celts in opposition to the Goths. Significantly, the Celt–Goth distinction grew more pronounced in the wake of the publication of James Macpherson's first *Ossian Fragments* in 1760, a watershed event that inaugurated a new era in Scottish and British literary nationalism, igniting a battle for cultural dominance in the British Isles. What K. K. Ruthven calls the cornucopian 'mestizo corpus' of 'Macphossian' (2001: 7), now generally recognised as the product of 'an ideologically complex act of synthesis' (Duncan 2012: 125), served in part as a consolatory myth and 'a pro-militia statement' (Sher 1982: 60) for an embattled, defenceless Scotland after the definitive defeat of the Jacobites and Scotland's exclusion from the provisions of Pitt's Militia Bill (Sher 1982: 56). Macphossian's 'aesthetic call to arms' featured a warrior culture (Gibbons 2004: 21) and provoked a concerted response, as Nick Groom has noted, from a mixed set of people: 'Irish nationalists, Wilkesites, and textual pedants forged an unlikely alliance against the Scottish literati, poets, and antiquarian cranks' (1996: 287). *Ossian* inflamed various acrimonious nationalist debates that generated the publication in England of two landmark works of literary critical historiography – namely, Richard Hurd's *Letters on Chivalry and Romance* (1762) and Thomas Percy's *Reliques of Ancient English Poetry* (1765). These works strove, in direct response to Macpherson's *Ossian*, to 'reinvent the English poetic tradition' as 'Gothic' (Groom 1996: 294) – notably in the case of the *Reliques*, 'under the eye of [Samuel] Johnson' (1996: 294) – in conjunction with the myth of the valorous, liberty-promoting English 'Gothic' political tradition then being fostered. These works heralded 'Gothic' culture as superior to the 'Celtic' tradition represented by the *Ossian* poems, which were, virtually from the point of publication, denounced as a shamefully fraudulent fabrication by, as Horace Walpole vilified them, 'those Scotch impostors and their cabal' (1937–83, vol. 29: 240). This standpoint was retained into the nineteenth century by such writers as William Wordsworth, who deemed *Ossian*, in stark contrast to Percy's *Reliques*, utterly uninspiring and culturally without influence (1974: 207–8).

Walpole's condemnation of Macpherson bears closer scrutiny given its subsequent impact on literary critical assessments of *Ossian*'s role in British literary history, particularly in regard to the fields of Romanticism and 'Dark Romanticism', otherwise known as the Gothic. Despite Dr Hugh Blair's framing and discussion of the *Fragments* as epic, the form of choice for pre-literate societies (Moore 2003b: 36), romance operates in the poems, as Dafydd Moore has stated, as a barely repressed 'ghostly and at times threatening other . . . something that . . . [they] define themselves against and are constantly in danger of being subsumed within' (2003b: 22). While critics have considered *Otranto*'s role as a response to such Scottish works as David Hume's *The History of England* (1754–62) and recognised that Walpole, with an eye to expanding his readership, borrowed *Ossian*'s antiquarian framework, *Otranto* has not been considered within the context of the politically charged eighteenth-century ethnographic discourses and debates engendered by the *Ossian* poems in which Walpole was embroiled, as his correspondence attests, throughout the 1760s. There was a great deal at stake, nationally and aesthetically, in the fact that Walpole, in the wake of Hurd's and Percy's influential works that were written in direct response to *Ossian*, added the ethnographically loaded subtitle 'A *Gothic* Story' to *Otranto* in its second edition in April of 1765, the same year that saw the publication of the first popular Edition of *Ossian*'s collected works. In this instance, *Otranto* became the first prose work to be labelled 'Gothic', a weighty designation possessing aesthetic and political meaning, signifying things medieval during that period of Medieval Revival, while also signalling Walpole's explicit participation in the explosive contemporaneous debates fuelled in the wake of *Ossian* about England's mythic Gothic heritage.

Likewise overlooked by critics are the nationalist implications of *Otranto*'s second Preface where Walpole boldly and strategically attempts to distance his work from Ossian's given their status as forgeries, exposes *Otranto*'s fraudulent framing and celebrates what Walpole describes as his 'new species of romance' (Walpole 1982a: 12) combining ancient and modern forms (1982a: 7). He also identifies Shakespeare, 'the great master of nature', as his principal model (1982a: 8). Two years earlier, in his study delineating the 'pervasive influence of the apparently low literature of Gothic Romance (which he had not read)', according to Nick Groom, 'on the great English poets' (Groom 1996: 288), Hurd proclaimed Shakespeare the preeminent English author and the creator of Gothic terror, his best work including 'Gothic manners and machinery' (Hurd 1911: 117), the hallmarks of genius that rendered his work superior to the classical in its ability to produce sublime effects. Hurd's momentous conceptual and rhetorical yoking of the Gothic and the sublime – an association, notably, not forged by Burke in his famous essay from 1757 devoted to the sublime and the beautiful – must be underscored as must the fact that the sublime had been, repeatedly, critically identified as one of the key features of the *Ossian* poems. Hurd's Shakespeare–Gothic yoking is also significant for, as Robert Crawford notes, although Shakespeare was popularly conceived as England's national writer since the early eighteenth century, he was transformed into the national Bard in the 1760s concurrent with Ossian's canonisation as the Celtic Bard (2004: 127) amidst what I am describing as Anglo-Scottish culture wars.

As his correspondence attests, Walpole was extremely well acquainted with *Ossian*, being one of the few people in receipt, along with Thomas Gray and William Shenstone, of the first samples of Macpherson's *Fragments* (Groom 1996: 279; Moore 2003a: 42, n. 6). One of the foremost men of letters of his day and an authoritative and respected antiquarian, Walpole was an obvious choice for this assessment, his selection perhaps also being contingent on his bold declaration in *A Catalogue of the Royal and Noble Authors of England*, published in 1758, that Scotland was 'the most accomplished nation in Europe' (1759, vol. 2: 201). That grandiose statement earned him vicious rebukes from Wilkes's *North Briton* in 1762 where the 'mastery pen of Mr. Walpole' was condemned for national disloyalty (1762–3, no. 2: 11–12), the provocative Wilkes lamenting that the 'most rude of [Scottish] bards are [now] admired ... some choice wits ... [having] thrown aside *Shakespeare* and taken up *Fingal*, [being] charmed with [its] variety of character, and richness of imagery' (1762–3, no. 2: 11). Alongside Walpole's vilification of Scotland for, in his forceful words, 'debasing and disgracing [England] ... as a nation by losing America, destroying our Empire, and making us the scorn and prey of Europe' (1937–83, vol. 29: 105), his numerous, almost obsessive and consistently negative references to Macpherson that punctuate his voluminous correspondence attest to a radical sea-change in his attitude towards Scotland and *Ossian* in the early 1760s following George III's ascension to the British throne in 1760 and the promotion of the Earl of Bute to the position of Prime Minister.

Apart from his most explicit mockery of *Ossian* in the Preface to his *Hieroglyphic Tales* (Walpole 1982b, vol. 1: vi), Walpole's foremost critique of *Ossian* and Scottish literature more generally was its lack of originality, the highly prized hallmark of Romantic productions with which Walpole had stamped *Otranto* in his manifesto-like second Preface. Despite their striking differences, it is difficult not to see in the ostensibly antiquarian *Otranto* an innovative 'conflation of the ancient and the modern' (Moore 2003b: 34) that De Quincey deems 'a deliberate and audacious forgery' (1975: 125), with its outrageous giant helmet, walking portraits and buffoon-style servants, a comic and reductive riposte to *Ossian*'s sombre epic sublimity and powerful poetic treatment of the supernatural. Indeed, Walpole says as much in a letter to Hannah More where he relates that *Otranto* was written for sheer amusement in an age that was 'too somber', and where 'the flimsy giantry of Ossian . . . [had] introduced mountainous horrors' (1937–83, vol. 31: 221) – a 'flimsy giantry' *Otranto* seems to render literal as dismembered giant limbs and armour litter its landscape.

The fortunes of the Ossianic and the Gothic in the wake of the heated cultural debates of the 1760s offered up a mixed legacy for the Gothic generally and the Scottish Gothic more specifically. According to Fiona Stafford, Thomas Gray's enthusiastic response to the *Ossian* poems anticipated 'the rapid convergence of the Ossianic and the Gothic, and the way in which writers such as Ann Radcliffe . . . and Walter Scott would draw on Macpherson's image of Celtic Scotland to create their own romantic fictions' (1995: vi). Indeed, the dozens of early Gothic works set in Scotland that followed on the heels of the publication of Radcliffe's first novel *The Castles of Athlin and Dunbayne* (1789), most of them published by Minerva Press, furnish ample evidence in support of Stafford's claim. Drawing on what Murray Pittock identifies as the Whig historical narrative that alienised 'pre-Union Scotland as a dark age' resistant to progress (1997: 142), an image promoted in eighteenth-century Scottish tour narratives (Davison 2009: 193), the dominant Anglocentric line in British literary history rendered it Scotland's fate to become, in Ian Duncan's words, 'a Romantic object or commodity' rather than 'a site of Romantic production' (Duncan et al. 2004: 1), a strategic decision that denied Scottish writers their influential and rightful role in the development of Romanticism.

This problematic and pathological national image has been perpetuated by both Scottish and English critics alike, including Gothicists, into the twentieth century. In his theoretical overview of modern Scottish literature in 1983, for example, Alan Bold notes 'the abundance of grotesque characters and Gothic events' and declares that, in contrast to the

Great Tradition, 'the Scottish house of fiction is haunted' by the 'Grim Presence, the ghostly persistence of the frequently disastrous Scottish past' (1983: 164). Echoing Bold over a decade later, Cairns Craig claims that Scottish literature 'has a graveyard at its core' (C. Craig 1996: 132), a sentiment reiterated in David Punter's description of Scotland as 'a culture of lamentation, . . . a Gothicized culture in which images of past terrors, present malaise and future defeat loom large within a national iconography' (1999: 113). This semiotic and iconographic straitjacketing of Scotland constitutes a type of Frankenstein's monster from which scores of subsequent Scottish writers have since tried to liberate themselves. Indeed, if a pre-eminent spectre may be said to plague Scottish cultural history, it is this image of a melancholia-inducing, haunted graveyard of a nation that finds its provenance, ironically, in *Ossian*. As Andrew Hook states:

> Everything that is corrupt and debilitating, sham and distorting, in the Scottish cultural tradition – everything, that is, that is summed up by the Scottish Tourist Board's brand image of Scotland – may be traced back, it is implied, to James Macpherson and the kind of Scottish literary romanticism he did so much to create and diffuse. (Hook 1986: 39)

The problem of Scotland's gothicisation is compounded by a consistently inaccurate, selective assessment of the contributions to British literary history and the Gothic made by *Ossian*, the jewel in the crown of Scottish Romanticism. In the Anglo-Scottish culture wars that have persisted into the present day, *Ossian* continues to be denigrated and stripped of its powerful cultural influence in the annals of British literary history largely on the basis of its illegitimacy as an ancient text, its innovative aesthetic experimentation and influence being utterly disregarded in the process. Although some scholars have accepted American critic Jerome McGann's claim that *Ossian* was 'Enormously influential for European Romanticism . . . [as] it set the literature of sentiment and sensibility on a whole new footing' (1996: 33), the spectre of Walpole's indictment of *Ossian* as 'a heap of insignificant trash and lies' (1937–83, vol. 28: 192) has skewed and coloured subsequent assessments.

In his compelling essay 'Shakespeare, Ossian and the Problem of "Scottish Gothic"', Dale Townshend suggests that a less than friendly convergence of the Ossianic and the Gothic occurred in early Gothic fictions, an incessant conflict being registered 'between Ossian and Shakespeare, the Celtic and the Gothic . . . giving form at the level of fiction to a conflict that had played itself out within broader contemporary antiquarian and historiographical debates' (2014: 239–40). Townshend maintains that it was ultimately Shakespearean spectrality with its agenda of 'dramatic entertainment' and persistent and vengeful ghosts, 'ciphers of the unbearable persistence of the past' (2014: 237), that possessed staying power in the Gothic. In subsequent Gothic works that took Scotland as their backdrop, even Scotland was Othered as a site of 'witches, ghosts, and regicide' haunted by an aristocratic, Catholic past (2014: 240). In contrast, Townshend argues, the Ossianic supernatural was a 'matter of cultural anthropology' driven by an interest in exploring the nation's ghostly heritage (2014: 238), its spectres 'wholly unsuited to any extended uptake by the Gothic aesthetic, as preoccupied as it too might have been with the rendition of supernatural activity' (2014: 235).

Notably, much established *Ossian* criticism does not align with Townshend's view, characterising its spectral representations as evoking terror – *Ruath*, a word repeatedly used in the poems – due to their uncertain nature, thus exemplifying one of Edmund Burke's definitions of terror as advanced in his *Philosophical Enquiry into the Origin of our Ideas of the Sublime and Beautiful* (1757). In the words, most recently, of Wolf Gerhard Schmidt, 'the Ossianic spirits occasion terror just because they are nothing but cloudy forms, arbitrarily contoured by the imagination' (2004: 194). *Ossian*'s contributions to the Gothic have been obscured, therefore, by entrenched, long-standing Anglocentric biases. Various eighteenth-century and contemporary critical assessments of *Ossian* and *Otranto*, however, provide some direction in reconsidering this issue. Nathan Drake's popular and influential *Literary Hours, or Sketches Critical, Narrative, and Poetical* (1800) offers a mixed but telling examination of the *Ossian* poems. After lauding *Ossian*, the Bard, for 'the originality of his genius' (Drake 1970, vol. 1: VIII, 142), Drake denounces 'Mr. Macpherson', the translator, for his stiff, rigid style that undermines the ancient Bard's genius. While upholding the distinction between the Gothic and the Celtic, he positions the latter 'next to the Gothic in point of sublimity and imagination' with each form manifesting two distinct aspects – 'the terrible and the sportive' (1970, vol. 1: VIII, 141). He characterises *Ossian*, which he discusses repeatedly and at length, as lending expression to a sublime form of the terrible and advancing a new treatment of both the supernatural and the spectral, thus enhancing the 'Gothic':

> [*Ossian*] has opened a new field for invention, he has given fresh colouring to his supernatural agenda, he has given them employments new to gothic fiction: his ghosts are not the ghosts of Shakespeare, yet are they equally solemn and striking. (Drake 1970, vol. 1: VIII, 142)

It is significant that Drake nowhere considers *Otranto*. Anna Barbauld's subsequent classification of *Otranto* in Drake's 'sportive' category, calling *Otranto* 'the sportive effusion of a man of genius' (1987: 87), is likewise telling in terms of that work's impact and critical reception. Drake's assessment notably aligns with that of such critics as David Punter and James Watt who have been at pains to justify *Otranto*'s role as the Gothic's progenitor given its offhanded comic tone, that work being read 'spectacularly "after the fact" ... only once [readers] had encountered the extraordinary genius of Ann Radcliffe' who was popularly applauded for bringing the Gothic into being (Townshend and Wright 2014: 19). Punter draws a telling and useful distinction in this regard between mainstream 'chivalric Gothic' – as exemplified by Hurd and *Otranto* – with its 'bright daylight colours, the trysts and troubadours, [and] jousts and joyings of chivalric medievalism', and *Ossian*'s 'heroic Gothic' that privileges 'the Dark Ages, the forgotten corners of Britain, the shadows' (Punter 1995: 28). Ian Duncan extends this reading of *Ossian*, underscoring its invocation of Gaelic culture as 'a ghostly presence that always turns out ... to be facing away into some yet remoter anteriority', alongside Macpherson's employment of such Gothic tropes as the possession of the living by the dead (2012: 125).

By many critical accounts, therefore, *Ossian* features a more sublime spectrality than that featured in *Otranto*, a manifestation of the literature of the terrible known as the dark sublime, that was extremely suitable for Gothic uptake, as the works of Ann Radcliffe, the next major authorial link in the Gothic's historic trajectory, evidence. Unlike Walpole, Radcliffe did not traffic in what Blair described as the romantic taste of 'two ages ago ... [where] Giants, enchanted castles, dwarfs, palfreys, witches and magicians form the whole circle of the poet's invention' (qtd in Macpherson 1995: 217–18), and it was to her, significantly, not Walpole, that Michel Foucault ascribed the creation of the new discursive form known as the Gothic (1984: 114). Nathan Drake famously dubbed Ann Radcliffe 'the Shak[e]speare of Romance Writers' (1970: 359) and she identified Shakespeare as the source and inspiration for her posthumously published 1820 essay 'On the Supernatural in Poetry' (Radcliffe 2000) where she articulates her famous distinction between 'horror' and 'terror' Gothic. The strong and undeniable influence of *Ossian*, however, on Radcliffe's work, as opposed to Walpole, is in evidence from her very first publication, *The Castles of Athlin and Dunbayne*. In combination with its Romanticised/Gothic Scotland semiotics, the hero Osbert loves 'to wander among the romantic scenes of the Highlands, where the wild variety of nature inspired him with all the enthusiasm of his favourite art', the poetry of *Ossian* (1995: 5). One cannot imagine the creation of Radcliffe's works, especially the sublime, Romanticised landscapes in her masterpiece *The Mysteries of Udolpho*

(1794), without *Ossian*. In this regard, literary critics would do well to remember that the Gothic was a 'nascent' aesthetic, as Townshend has categorised it (2014: 234), in the late eighteenth century when it was being adapted, to quite diverse ends, by such innovative writers as Radcliffe, Godwin and Lewis, a process that continued well into the nineteenth century and beyond, exemplifying the Gothic's superiority in the generic survival of the fittest.

Despite long-established Anglocentric critical biases rooted in the culture wars of the 1760s that have often denied *Ossian* its due place in literary history, its legacy for the Gothic is indisputable given its serious introduction of the field of the ghostly, its elegiac tone and ventrilo-quising of the dead, its use of haunting, affective landscapes that lend expression to its protagonist's psyches, and its fixation on death and the memorialisation of the dead. Indeed, one could be forgiven for mistaking this list as constituting the key ingredients in Radcliffe's winning Gothic recipe, especially as they are manifested in *Udolpho*. Only by insert-ing *Ossian* back into literary history may we make sense of Radcliffe's works in a way that identifying *Otranto* as their primary precursor cannot. As Katie Trumpener's magisterial study *Bardic Nationalism: The Romantic Novel and the British Empire* (1997) has similarly illus-trated, marginalising or erasing *Ossian* from what Andrew Hook calls 'the grand parade of English literary historiography' (1986: 50) has had negative consequences, including the failure to recognise its impact on such novelistic sub-genres as the national tale and the Romantic regional novel (Moore 2003a: 38). Literary critics should likewise recog-nise *Ossian*'s and *Otranto*'s mutual roots in graveyard poetry, a poetic form whose progenitor Thomas Parnell and such followers as Robert Blair illustrate the noteworthy influence of the Celtic fringe during the eighteenth century, an era that saw a preponderance of 'cultural work devoted to death' (Walmsley 2009: 39) and mourning, an emotion that extended to rapidly changing/'dying' traditional societies and cultures.

Certain it is that James Macpherson's *Ossian* furnished a mixed legacy for the Scottish Gothic: while generating the image of Scotland as a site of sublime ruin, a fallen, melancholic nation haunted by a glorious past, a conception adopted by English authors to represent a dark, former age from which their nation had emerged, *Ossian* also advanced a novel treatment of the supernatural as a coexisting reality replete with intimate ghosts. This latter innovation opened the door to the titillating treatment of the psychological uncanny that was to become the engine of such great Gothic masterpieces of the nineteenth century as James Hogg's chilling *The Private Memoirs and Confessions of a Justified Sinner* (1824) and Robert Louis Stevenson's *Strange Case of Dr Jekyll and Mr Hyde* (1886). As one commentator has observed, *Ossian*'s 'dreary atmospherics' also carried forward into Romantic and Victorian literature, *Ossian* proving 'easy to recycle, consciously or unconsciously, when people like Byron, Emily Brontë or sundry Gothic novelists required darkly archaic effects' (D. Craig 1996).

Ian Duncan has noted how striking it is 'with what regularity the theory of modern Scottish culture condenses into a theory of Scott' (1995: 340). The same holds true for the Scottish Gothic as it is in the work of Scott, a dabbler in and aficionado of the Gothic, that the mixed Ossianic legacy is most compellingly in evidence, and it is out of his new historical novel that a low road to Scottish Gothic literature emerges. Following William Godwin, who employed the Gothic self-reflexively in relation to British national identity and politics, Scott both promoted and undermined the image of Gothic Scotland as an English bogey while laying the groundwork for the distinctive and strategic use of that literary aesthetic by Scottish writers for their own ends (Davison 2009: 191–200). Drawing in part on the Gothic, the first novelistic sub-genre to incorporate history as a theme, in combination with the supernaturally suffused Border Ballads, Scott's new historical novel self-consciously and strategically interrogated and exposed two interrelated issues: the blind spots of historiography and the terrors of history. The Scottish Gothic that developed therefrom represented '(with greater historical and anthropological specificity than in England) the uncanny recursion of an ancestral identity alienated from modern life' (Duncan 2012: 123), disrupting what Teresa Goddu nicely describes in relation to the American tradition as 'the dream world of national myth with the nightmares of history' (1997: 10). This involved meditating critically on what Nick Groom identifies as the dark side of the British nation and its proudly celebrated 'Gothic' constitution

> that had apparently progressed by resisting absolutism, by increasing liberties and rights, and by avoiding extremism, [but] had in fact within a few generations condoned regicide (the execution of Charles I), civil war, the invasion of William of Orange and the so-called 'Bloodless Revolution,' and the systematic repression and execution of Irish, Welsh, and Scottish rebels such as at Glencoe (1692) and the Battle of Culloden (1746), culminating in the mass extermination of Jacobite sympathizers by the notorious Duke of Cumberland – 'Butcher' Cumberland. (Groom 2012: 56)

The generally wavering narrator of Scott's *Waverley* (1814), a novel whose historical theme 'articulates a "Gothic" plot on the grand scale . . . [as] the 1745 Jacobite rebellion represents the disruptive resurgence of a pre-revolutionary past (Catholic, absolutist, feudal, tribal, pagan) into a still raw and uncertain modern dispensation' (Duncan 2012: 74), offers up such a meditation. After recounting the anti-Jacobite cruelties and execution of Fergus Mac-Ivor conducted by putatively 'brave and humane men', Scott expresses the aspiration at the novel's end that he 'shall never see the scenes, or hold the sentiments, that were general in Britain Sixty Years since' (1985: 464).

Piggybacking on Jonathan Oldbuck's provocative remarks in Scott's *The Antiquary* (1816), a novel that engages with the ethno-historiographic debates that proliferated in the wake of *Ossian* (2009: 64–6, 225), that 'every mansion in this country of the slightest antiquity has its ghosts and its haunted chamber, and you must not suppose us worse off than our neighbours' (2009: 89), Scottish writers subsequently brought the Gothic, self-reflexively, to bear on various politico-religious bogeys that ranged beyond Catholicism to include the Calvinist, the Covenanter, the Cameronian and the Jacobite. They extended its critique into the treacherous yet compelling terrain of the human psyche/ identity often plagued by mental disorders borne of such phenomena as religious fanaticism, misogyny and drug/alcohol addiction. The works of Scott, therefore, registered a significant transition from the idea of an objectified Gothic Scotland characterised by 'witches, ghosts, and regicide' (Townshend 2014: 240), to a self-reflexive 'Scottish Gothic' produced by Scottish writers for their own ends, both personal and political. In a passage rife with Gothic rhetoric that nowhere references the term 'Gothic', Cairns Craig unwittingly identifies the Gothic engine that drove the nineteenth-century Scottish novel inaugurated by Scott. That new 'tradition'

> confronted the historical in radical ways – by challenging it with what it had left out of its ideological conception of social life, by reminding it of what it had excluded but could not forget, by pointing forwards to the barbarity which would turn out to be waiting around every corner of the progress of civilization. (C. Craig 1996: 46)

Although Craig fails to mention the nationalist aspects of this critique, Scott often cunningly marshalled the English Gothic's interrogation of 'enlightened' modernity against England and its various certainties, including the Union. Subsequent Scottish writers, from James Hogg and Robert Louis Stevenson to Iain Banks, Liz Lochhead and James Robertson, have adapted the Gothic aesthetic to scrutinise the spectres of history and the treacherous domain of subjectivity and consciousness. In the process, they have produced works of penetrating psychological realism and socio-political critique that have established the tropic and thematic groundwork for Scottish Gothic literature while illuminating a myriad of synergies between the categories 'Scotland' and 'Gothic'.

References

Barbauld, Anna [1810] (1987), 'Introduction to *The Castle of Otranto*', in Peter Sabor (ed.), *Horace Walpole: The Critical Heritage*, London and New York: Routledge & Kegan Paul, pp. 86–8.

Bold, Alan (1983), *Modern Scottish Literature*, London: Longman.

Craig, Cairns (1996), *Out of History: Narrative Paradigms in Scottish and British Culture*, Edinburgh: Polygon.

Craig, David (1996), 'Letter' [in response to 'Post-Cullodenism', rev. by Robert Crawford of James Macpherson, *The Poems of Ossian and Related Works*, ed. Howard Gaskill, *London Review of Books*, 18: 19, 3 October 1996], *London Review of Books*, 18: 22, 14 November, <http://www.lrb.co.uk/v18/n19/robert-crawford/post-cullodenism> (last accessed 17 March 2015).

Crawford, Robert (2004), 'The Bard: Ossian, Burns, and the Shaping of Shakespeare', in Willy Maley and Andrew Murphy (eds), *Shakespeare and Scotland*, Manchester: Manchester University Press, pp. 124–40.

Davison, Carol Margaret (2009), *History of the Gothic: Gothic Literature 1764–1824*, Cardiff: University of Wales Press.

De Quincey, Thomas [1891/1893] (1975), 'Great Forgers: Chatterton and Walpole, and "Junius"', in Alex H. Japp (ed.), *Thomas De Quincey: The Posthumous Works*, New York: Georg Olms Verlag Hildesheim, pp. 125–31.

Drake, Nathan [1800] (1970), *Literary Hours, or Sketches Critical and Narrative*, 2 vols, New York: Garland Publishing.

Duncan, Ian (1995), 'North Britain, Inc.', *Victorian Literature and Culture*, 23, 339–50.

— (2012), 'Walter Scott, James Hogg and Scottish Gothic', in David Punter (ed.), *A New Companion to the Gothic*, Oxford: Wiley-Blackwell, pp. 123–34.

Duncan, Ian with Leith Davis and Janet Sorensen (2004), 'Introduction', in Leith Davis, Ian Duncan and Janet Sorensen (eds), *Scotland and the Borders of Romanticism*, Cambridge: Cambridge University Press, pp. 1–19.

Foucault, Michel [1969] (1984), 'What Is an Author?', in *The Foucault Reader*, ed. Paul Rabinow, New York: Pantheon Books, pp. 101–20.

Gibbons, Luke (2004), *Gaelic Gothic: Race, Colonization, and Irish Culture*, Galway: Arlen House.

Goddu, Teresa (1997), *Gothic America: Narrative, History, and Nation*, New York: Columbia University Press.

Groom, Nick (1996), 'Celts, Goths, and the Nature of the Literary Source', in Alvaro Ribeiro and James G. Basker (eds), *Tradition in Transition: Women, Writers, Marginal Texts, and the Eighteenth-Century Canon*, Oxford: Clarendon Press, pp. 274–96.

— (2012), *The Gothic: A Very Short Introduction*, Oxford: Oxford University Press.

Hook, Andrew (1986), '"Ossian" Macpherson as Image Maker', *The Scottish Review*, 36, 39–44.

Hume, David [1727–76] (1932), *The Letters of David Hume*, ed. J. Y. T. Grieg, 2 vols, Oxford: Clarendon Press.

Hurd, Richard [1762] (1911), *Letters on Chivalry and Romance* with the Third Elizabethan Dialogue, ed. Edith J. Morley, London: Henry Froude.

Lyttelton, George [1760] (1970), *Dialogues of the Dead*, New York: Garland Publishing.

McGann, Jerome (1996), *The Poetics of Sensibility*, Oxford: Clarendon Press.

Macpherson, James (1995), *The Poems of Ossian and Related Works*, ed. Howard Gaskill, Edinburgh: Edinburgh University Press.

Moore, Dafydd (2003a), 'The Critical Response to *Ossian*', in Gerard Carruthers and Alan Rawes (eds), *English Romanticism and the Celtic World*, Cambridge: Cambridge University Press, pp. 38–53.

— (2003b), *Enlightenment and Romance in James Macpherson's* The Poems of Ossian, Farnham: Ashgate.

Pittock, Murray J. (1997), *Inventing and Resisting Britain: Cultural Identities in Britain and Ireland, 1685–1789*, New York: St. Martin's Press.

— (2011), 'Introduction', in Murray J. Pittock (ed.), *Edinburgh Companion to Scottish Romanticism*, Edinburgh: Edinburgh University Press, pp. 1–9.

Punter, David (1995), 'Ossian, Blake and the Questionable Source', in Valeria Tinkler-Villani and Peter Davidson (eds) with Jane Stevenson, *Exhibited by Candlelight: Sources and Developments in the Gothic Tradition*, Amsterdam and Atlanta: Rodopi, pp. 25–41.

— (1999), 'Heart Lands: Contemporary Scottish Gothic', *Gothic Studies*, 1: 1, 101–18.

Radcliffe, Ann [1789] (1995), *The Castles of Athlin and Dunbayne*, Oxford: Oxford University Press.

— [1826] (2000), 'On the Supernatural in Poetry', in E. J. Clery and Robert Miles (eds), *Gothic Documents: A Sourcebook 1700–1820*, Manchester: Manchester University Press, pp. 163–72.

Ruthven, K. K. (2001), *Faking Literature*, Cambridge: Cambridge University Press.

Schmidt, Wolf G. (2004), '"Menschlichschön" and the Discursive Function of *Ossian* in Schiller's Work', in Howard Gaskill (ed.), *The Reception of Ossian in Europe*, London: Thoemmes Continuum, pp. 176–97.

Scott, Walter [1814] (1985), *Waverley; or, 'Tis Sixty Years Since*, Harmondsworth: Penguin.

— [1816] (2009), *The Antiquary*, Oxford: Oxford University Press.

Sher, Richard B. (1982), '"Those Scotch Impostors and Their Cabal": Ossian and the Scottish Enlightenment', in Roger L. Emerson, Gilles Girard and Roseann Runte (eds), *Man and Nature: Proceedings of the Canadian Society for Eighteenth-Century Studies*, London, ON: University of Western Ontario, vol. 1, pp. 55–63.

Stafford, Fiona (1995), 'Introduction', in James Macpherson, *The Poems of Ossian and Related Works*, ed. Howard Gaskill, Edinburgh: Edinburgh University Press, pp. v–xxi.

Townshend, Dale (2014), 'Shakespeare, Ossian and the Problem of "Scottish Gothic"', in Elisabeth Bronfen and Beate Neumeier (eds), *Gothic Renaissance: A Reassessment*, Manchester: Manchester University Press, pp. 218–43.

Townshend, Dale and Angela Wright (2014), *Ann Radcliffe, Romanticism, and the Gothic*, Cambridge: Cambridge University Press.

Trumpener, Katie (1997), *Bardic Nationalism: The Romantic Novel and the British Empire*, Princeton: Princeton University Press.

Walmsley, Peter (2009), 'The Melancholy Briton: Enlightenment Sources of the Gothic', in Miriam L. Wallace (ed.), *Enlightening Romanticism, Romancing the Enlightenment: British Novels from 1750 to 1832*, Aldershot: Ashgate, pp. 39–53.

Walpole, Horace [1758] (1759), *A Catalogue of the Royal and Noble Authors of England, with Lists of Their Works*, 2 vols, London: R. and J. Dodsley.

— [1733–97] (1937–83), *Correspondence*, ed. W. S. Lewis et al., 48 vols, New Haven: Yale University Press.

— [1764] (1982a), *The Castle of Otranto*, Oxford: Oxford University Press.

— [1785] (1982b), *Hieroglyphic Tales*, 8 vols, Los Angeles: University of California Press.

Wilkes, John (1762–3), *The North Briton*, 1–46.

Wordsworth, William [1815] (1974), 'Essay, Supplementary to the Preface', in W. J. B. Owen (ed.), *Wordsworth's Literary Criticism*, London and Boston: Routledge & Kegan Paul, pp. 192–218.

Chapter 4

Robert Burns and the Scottish Bawdy Politic

Hamish Mathison

Where are the *Jesters* now? the Men of Health
      Complexionally pleasant? (Blair 1743: 9; original emphasis)

Oft-times, Lowland Scots wrote of death in the eighteenth century without engaging in what we now call 'Scottish Gothic'. Witness Robert Blair, above, Edinburgh-born, as he brings the adverb 'complexionally' to an otherwise straightforward example of the ancient and melancholy *ubi sunt* trope.[1] Blair's melancholy is here expressed in a fantastically influential poem called *The Grave* (1743). Blair's fascinating poem, to which this chapter will return at its conclusion, is rightly held to be foundational for the study of what until recently was thought of as a pan-British 'Graveyard School' of poetry. That label describes an extremely loose collection of mid-eighteenth-century authors whose poems were written in a more or less 'standard' English, and often troped the graveyard. The category invokes such disparate poets as the English-born Thomas Gray and Edward Young or the Scottish-born James Thomson and James Beattie. There are many good poems on death, demise, and the supernatural realm written by Scottish and English authors during the eighteenth century. What actually differentiates a Lowland 'Scottish Gothic' poetry from not dissimilar poetry on death ('Gothic' or otherwise) in the eighteenth century is not only a turn to a Scots lexis but also a profound and foundational localism. The incorporation of local thought marks the difference between Scottish writing of the Gothic and all the other forms of expression that have come to take the adjective 'Gothic'. Since the eighteenth century, every attempt to ground a Gothic work in a particular time and place relies upon the temporal and spatial architecture laid down by early practitioners in the Scottish eighteenth century. What this chapter argues is that Scottish Gothic verse needs to be read carefully both in terms of its emergence in time as well as its geographical specificity. Consider the opening quotation from Robert Blair: his title offers the reader just 'the' grave. The definite article ('the . . .') is most indefinite: it is designed to indicate all of our graves; from that there follows the poem's ambitious scope. For the poem to succeed on its own terms, it cannot offer 'that spot just there' as we will find the Burnsian locale to be. The generic death of a 'complexionally pleasant' man in Blair's reference is very different, in that generality, from a discussion of John Wilson's death held just below the 'distant *Cumnock* hills out-owre' close by the road 'down on *Willie's mill*' (Burns 1968: 79, 80). The disjunction is between the grammatically general and the geographically specific. Cairns Craig makes the wider point well in *Out of History* (1996) when he argues that:

> The relationships of 'dependence' on outside forces through which peripheral cultures develop is, however, all too often seen as *only* a function of their relationship with the core, when, by virtue of the very fact that they feel themselves threatened and repressed by the core culture, their true relationships are not centripetal but centrifugal, not towards the core but towards the other marginal cultures who share a similar relation to the core. (Craig 1996: 28; original emphasis)

What the poetry that follows delivers is a realisation, in varying degrees of Scots, of a tension between an impossibly general 'core' and a deeply specific periphery. This chapter will argue that the Scottish Gothic articulates a profound resistance to centripetal ideas of order, and that in doing so it significantly facilitated the capacity of poetry in English to imagine the body as a site of resistance to hegemonic political, economic and cultural discourses of order and authority. The disordering of centre and periphery that this chapter examines is a complex one. On the one hand, we need to think of Scotland and Britain's geography: the relation, that is, between two disparate states that sought to become one in 1707. The Scottish, English and then British understanding of what was nationally central and nationally peripheral was uncertain throughout the seventeenth and eighteenth centuries. That spatial flux requires too that we bear in mind the internal geography of Scotland, a mindfulness that understands the poet of the '*Cumnock* hills' (Burns 1968: 79; original emphasis) of the south-west of the country to be peripheral to the nation's print capital: Edinburgh. That sense of disjunctive geography is paralleled in Scotland's early and fraught adoption of the Protestant Reformation. It is fraught not least because, whether it was Presbyterian Edinburgh speaking to the provinces or Episcopalian kingship in London or Oxford in the seventeenth century attempting to impose religious practice and texts on the wider Scottish nation, the spokes of religious control sought (and often failed) to run from contested centres of religious authority to a fractious backwoods.[2] If the literal and the spiritual geography of Scotland in the eighteenth century was, at best, contested and, at worst, hopelessly fractured, then that in turn impacted on how the nation's poets could represent it and themselves. The three poets examined in this chapter – William Lithgow, Allan Ramsay and, at greatest length, Robert Burns – all in their own way reject the idea that an imagined nation (Britain, let alone Scotland) is, on its own, a meaningful organising principle for verse. They turn instead to precise locales, to districts, to tiny instances of community in order from there to draw wider conclusions, or ask broader questions, about how we are to be governed – or are to govern and manage ourselves. The management of the self brings about the principal thrust of this chapter: if, as it will argue, a distinct localism with a keen sense of local being pervades Scottish poetry, then that is troped by the most 'local' site of all – the point of most minute spatial being, and location of a terrifyingly brief threescore years and ten – the human body. In fact, the calling into imagination of the narrator's threatened and vulnerable body in verse is the distinct marker of Scottish Gothic verse in the eighteenth century. That is where it, in a profound and personal localisation of anxiety, clearly differs from the work of Robert Blair, Edward Young, Thomas Gray and others. The body in the Gothic verse of the eighteenth-century Scottish Lowlands offers itself up as an exemplar of the local, specific, vulnerable and individuated.

The troping of the local, specific, vulnerable and individuated comes more deeply into focus in a process with two key moments. The first was 1603 when the Scottish James VI took to London and made a British throne in the Union of the Crowns. The second accelerated these tensions after 1707 when the Scottish political class moved to London to make a British Parliament in the Union of the Parliaments. Consequent on those two moments were the responses to Scottish self-determination that emerged in the fifty years following the Battle of Culloden in 1746. There, the forces of the 'Young Pretender' to the British throne, Charles Edward Stuart, were defeated by the forces of the Hanoverian incumbent, George II. To read Scottish culture in terms of these two moments and their aftermath is to begin to understand why so much verse of the eighteenth century, regardless of the author's provenance, so commonly grapples with problems of inclusion: how can this freshly minted state comprehend the inclusion of so many disparate parts? The answer, offered by both Scottish and English writers, was to theorise an invented state called 'Britain' with its 'British values'. Such material, penned by Scottish- or English-born authors, is seldom truly 'Gothic'.

Writing that insists on a synthetic whole cannot fully realise a realm outside established religion; a realm without tyranny beyond the parliamentary control of a king and citizenry; or there ever being a commerce that excludes barbarity. Where a discursive inclusivity is in place, where all are free under the Hanoverians, or Whiggish political liberty, or the established churches of the British Isles, then all that need be excluded is an imagined alterity: the Gothic. That alterity takes its being not from a discourse of inclusion, but from a discursive assimilation. Scottish Gothic is the expression of resistance to discursive assimilation, and it resists on the grounds of the local and the personal. It resists at the most basic level: by imagining, troping and insisting upon the moral consequence of each individual's biological, vulnerable, parlous human body. Take the late example of Walter Scott's 1805 *The Lay of the Last Minstrel*: had the Minstrel's belly been replete there would be no pathos or urgency to his song. Instead, for in need, 'He begged his bread from door to door' (1987: 256). Fiona Stafford is right to lock bardic voice into national anxieties of cultural loss in *The Last of the Race* (1994): in Scotland at least such wider implications of cultural loss tend to require the imaginative emplacement of a vulnerable and failing body which, in turn, ports a voice. This was true not just of poetry but also of Scottish prose fiction as it developed momentum in the early decades of the nineteenth century. Take, for example, the poet and novelist James Hogg's treatment of politics, mob, body and voice in *The Private Memoirs and Confessions of a Justified Sinner* (1824). In Edinburgh, the young George Colwan is part of a circle of Episcopal, Jacobitic, tennis-playing friends trapped by the Edinburgh mob in a tavern with a larger group, a 'Revolutionist faction' of Whigs (1969: 27). Hogg notes that the 'concourse of people that were assembled in Edinburgh at that time was prodigious; and as they were all actuated by political motives, they wanted only a ready-blown coal to set the mountain on fire' (1969: 26). Amidst this febrile atmosphere, both sets of young men become embroiled with the Edinburgh mob, and although the episode contains comedic effect (the Duke of Queensbury identifies, intra-diegetically, the event as a 'joke – an unlucky frolic, where no ill was meant on either side' (1969: 31)), it is set amongst a fractious and unstable populace who live in a city that 'swallowed up the multitude in a few seconds' and then 'vomited out its levies' (1969: 29). The mob would have 'swallowed them up', had both parties not retreated to the Black Bull, where the factions had originally met. Edinburgh itself, politicised and divided before the Act of Union, functions as a metaphorically sick body, swallowing and vomiting forth its own citizenry. The political bifurcation that leads to the metaphor is paralleled later in the text when Robert

Wringhim hears his servant Samuel Scrape, known as 'Penpunt', speak of Satan being 'the firmest believer in a' the truths o' Christianity':

> I confess, to my shame, that I was so overcome by this jumble of nonsense, that a chillness came over me, and in spite of all my efforts to shake off the impression it had made, I fell into a faint . . . 'Now, Penpunt, you may tell me all that passed between you and the wives of the Clachan. I am better of that stomach qualm, with which I am sometimes seized, and shall be much amused by hearing the sentiments of noted witches regarding myself and my connections.' (Hogg 1969: 197)

Hogg's novel is famously divided between the account of the editor and the account of Wringhim. Hogg allows both the editor, accounting for Edinburgh's public confusion, and Wringhim, explaining his own private loss of reason, to reach for the image of the sickened body in order to understand eighteenth-century Scotland's depth of political and religious turmoil. In concluding his tale, Hogg makes literal the 'jumble of nonsense' using the figure of the suicide's grave and the decomposing body we are led to believe is Wringhim's:

> A number of the bones came up separately; for with the constant flow of liquid stuff into the deep grave, we could not see to preserve them in their places. At length great loads of coarse clothes, blanketing, plaiding, &c. appeared; we tried to lift these regularly up, and on doing so, part of a skeleton came up, but no flesh, save a little that was hanging in dark flitters about the spine, but which had no consistence; it was merely the appearance of flesh without the substance. (Hogg 1969: 249)

What Hogg's text delivers both narratologically and in its thematic and metaphoric content is the absence of authority: the 'jumble of nonsense' that maddens the seeker after political, religious or textual certainty. The order of death, of the grave, is interrupted by the seeker after truth: without irony, 'we could not see to preserve them [the bones of the skeleton] in their places'. In celebrating 'the appearance of flesh without substance', the text recalls Scotland's eighteenth-century political disorder and its loss of cultural authority: whether understood through the lens of the 'Revolutionist faction' and the dissolution of Parliament leading to Union in 1707, or the 'Jacobite order' and the key military and cultural losses of 1715 and 1746. Read thus, Robert Wringhim's disordered religious fundamentalism is a consequence of Scotland's maddening political and religious state, not its cause.

Scottish Gothic in the eighteenth century, having lost its king-in-history, its Parliament-in-history and, most recently in 1745–6, any disruptive military agency, leaps beyond English elegy and the 'Graveyard

School' to propose that, long before the death of the author, poetry can and must imagine the absence of the authoritative (Punter 2012: 133). The most important part of the Scottish Gothic's proposition is that the individual flesh always and already bears the anticipation of its own demise, and certainly Hogg's work is centred on this proposition. This is diametrically, pointedly and knowingly opposed to how the British state was imagined: an eternal, synthetic and providential settlement underpins (the Scottish) James Thomson's 'Rule Britannia'. Prayers to a providential God which hymn a Kingdom do, after all, tend to disregard the bodily frailties of named individuals. In one way, Scottish Gothic writing offers a beguilingly simple disruption of the smooth aesthetic of national aspiration offered by a song such as 'Rule Britannia': the mind in melancholia knows always the demise of its carriage, the body.[3] Within that body, nothing is more vulnerable than the belly, and it is our belly's vulnerability that draws the Scottish Gothic.

There are at least two ways of reading the belly: one more clearly subject to patriarchal control than the other. It is the space that digests food, according to Samuel Johnson: 'That part of man which requires food'. It can also be 'The womb'. It is, said Johnson, hedging his bets, 'That part of the human body which reaches from the breast to the thighs' (1755). The belly exists between ingestion and excretion, a liminal space. It is also the site of procreation, generation and nurture; it is subject to patriarchal authority, not to mention the laws of state and faith. Johnson's definitions of this contested space offer the generative vector first, the digestive second. The belly is, I would suggest, a Gothic space: an in-between of both pregnancy and digestion. Simultaneously real and imagined, fruitful and vulnerable, the belly is policed for its outward expression of individual excess or conjugal transgression. In identifying the belly's two functions, Johnson was following a Scotsman: James VI. The Jacobean Bible offers the belly as a bifurcated space in need of some restraint. In 1 Corinthians 6: 13 Paul offers the following:

> meats for the belly, and the belly for meats: but God shall destroy both it and them. Now the body is not for fornication, but for the Lord; and the Lord for the body. (Anon. 1769)

Paul's association of fornication and meat is a close one, and the Pauline belly is a site of explicit danger, as seen in Philippians 3: 18–19:

> For many walk, of whom I have told you often, and now tell you even weeping, that they are the enemies of the cross of Christ: Whose end is destruction, whose God is their belly, and whose glory is in their shame, who mind earthly things. (Anon. 1769)

It is not that Paul's epistles are the only way of reading the Gothic belly in late early modern and eighteenth-century Scotland, but there is a clear and unambiguous troping of the belly as a site of shame and physical, carnal frailty. What we find in eighteenth-century Scottish poetry is a trace of that Jacobean position. The belly is, after all, only as significant as that which it holds. Its contents justify its being – but to see the belly's contents outwardly marks either violent death or successful birth: terminal evisceration or instigative evacuation. Between these extremes, there exists only a holding area ripe for inscription and wonder: a skin, a skein, a truly Gothic occlusion of essence. What the belly contains, in eighteenth-century Scottish poetry, is poetry itself. For eighteenth-century poetry it is a site both of digestion and of generation, a filthy site and a site of weakness, and yet a powerful image of satiety, fulfilment and creativity. The eighteenth-century Scottish belly is haunted by memories of political disempowerment: pursued by Pauline disgust, it comes to be marked by Johnsonian imprecision.

In 1633, William Lithgow published a substantial poem entitled *Scotlands welcome to her native sonne, and soveraigne lord, King Charles*. In it, Scotland welcomes the accession of Charles I yet deplores the loss of the Scottish court and courtiers to London:

> And thus they take my money all away
> To spend abroad; whilst it should rather stay,
> For to enrich my *Bowels*; and to barter,
> For Cornes and Merchandise in evry quarter.
> [...]
> In comes *Thom Tumbler* with his bags and bellie,
> To alter *Tackes* and *Rentals*; I must tell *Thee*,
> I pitty my poore *Commouns*, and their toile,
> Made to new Upstarts and their greed a spoile.
>   How can my *Tennants* live? How can they thrive?
> How can they growing stand? When dead alive,
> Slane by oppression, extortion, debate,
> From Laird to Laird, in their *Camelion* State ...
> (Lithgow 1633: B3; original emphasis)

The 'dead alive' are in Lithgow's '*Camelion* State': this is a fruitful image for it suggests in this extended passage not just the Lairds, who are as Chameleons between Scotland and England following the Union of the Crowns, but also the ambiguity of the full belly. Scotland must be fed, her 'bowels' must be enriched. Yet at the same time, the Laird's man, Thom Tumbler, is marked by his 'bellie', his 'greed'. His fat condition starves the poor: corpulence means that the tenants are as 'dead alive', the bowels of the living dead are empty. Fat is a marker of 'oppression, extortion, debate', and yet the bowels of the living dead still demand their food. Lithgow's text very nicely highlights the early modern belly as a site of contest – national, ethical and moral. Nevertheless, death follows – as Lithgow picks up the Pauline fear of the immoral belly: 'Then in a word, its gluttonie and lust, / That brings so many headlong to the dust' (1633: B3). That 'gluttonie and lust' should be run together is maybe no surprise: the link between sex and food is an association carried over from the seventeenth into the eighteenth century in Scottish poetry. What Lithgow achieves is the marriage of post-1603 anxiety about Throne and State with a simple and effective libidinal trope. Allan Ramsay, writing a few generations after Lithgow, takes this forward with a sophisticated elegy that places ideas of satiety and fertility to the fore in a contemplation of the post-1707 political settlement.

Allan Ramsay wrote his 'Elegy on Lucky Wood in the Canongate' in 1717 and published it in 1718. Lucky Wood was the female proprietor of an alehouse who was celebrated by Ramsay for her liberality. As Lithgow used the belly in the previous century to reflect on the loss of the Scottish court to London in 1603, so Ramsay begins his poem with a reflection on the loss of the Scottish Parliament in 1707. In both cases, reflection upon plenitude is a reflection upon loss. 'Loss', it should be added, is an odd word to use as Scotland did not 'lose' a king or misplace a parliament; the Scots knew precisely to where and to whom they had fled: to '*London* and Death' (Ramsay 1944: 18). Ramsay begins by personifying a few hundred yards of Edinburgh, an awkward space on the Royal Mile between Holyrood Palace and the Cathedral of St Giles/ Parliament Square known now as the 'Canongate':

> O *Cannigate!* poor elritch Hole,
> What Loss, what Crosses does thou thole!
> *London* and Death gars thee look drole,
>   And hing thy Head;
> Wow, but thou has e'en a cauld Coal
>   To blaw indeed.
>
>   (Ramsay 1944: 18; original emphasis)

From the local to '*London* and Death', the association is pointed and is foundational for the study of the emergence of Scottish Gothic. The bathos too is pointed: the poem is set between Holyrood's (absent) throne and St Giles's (reformed) Kirk and Parliament Square's (lost) chamber. All that remains in this in-between space is 'cauld Coal': yet the geography in turn is only as significant (and no more so) as the death of the noted and named landlady, Lucky Wood. Scotland has been emptied of its contents, both personally and politically; now Ramsay and his peers in a drinking club called the 'Facers' are to be starved, literally:

> It did ane good to see her Stools,
> Her Boord, Fire-side, and facing Tools;
> Rax, Chandlers, Tangs, and Fire-Shools,
>   Basket wi' Bread.
> Poor Facers now may chew Pea-hoofs,
>   Since Lucky's dead.
>
> (Ramsay 1944: 19)

'Since Lucky's dead' the bread basket is as empty as Holyrood House, or the Scottish Parliament, and the representative wealth of Scotland lost, along with the 'Rax, Chandlers, Tangs, and Fire-Shools' of Lucky's tavern. The grand and political sits alongside the absolute minutiae of sociability and of the comestible. She was honest too, her accounting was fair, there was no 'Lawin fause' and her unadulterated beer turned no stomach:

> SHE ne'er gae in a Lawin fause,
> Nor Stoups a Froath aboon the Hause,
> Nor kept dow'd Tip within her Waw's,
>   But reaming Swats;
> She never ran sour Jute, because
>   It gee's the Batts.
>
> (Ramsay 1944: 19)

The poem suddenly and explosively dives inside the reader's belly. Lucky's clientele is guaranteed a solid bowel action for 'She never ran sour Jute, because / It gee's the Batts'. As the reader is asked to consider their own experience of diarrhoea, they simultaneously must deal with this stanza's four negatives and weigh those voids against the satiety she supplied '*gratis*'; such food as one could ever need:

> SHE had the Gate sae well to please,
> With *gratis* Beef, dry Fish, or Cheese;
> Which kept our Purses ay at Ease,
>   And Health in Tift,
> And lent her fresh Nine Gallon Trees
>   A hearty Lift.
>
> SHE ga'e us aft hail Legs o' Lamb,
> And did nae hain her Mutton Ham;
> Then ay at *Yule*, when e'er we came,
>   A bra' Goose Pye,
> And was na that good Belly Baum?
>   Nane dare deny.
>
> (Ramsay 1944: 20; original emphasis)

Her food was 'good Belly Baum', soothing and filling, and 'Nane dare deny' it. Her food, then, brought a community together; marked by the plural acknowledgement that no one could deny the poet's claims. Together, then, the writers and drinkers of a post-Parliamentary Scotland had their needs assuaged by Lucky Wood. But now and in the future the belly will be empty, the stomach without its balm. That is where the Gothic inserts itself: well-being slips into memory, and all that the belly's plenitude once was becomes narrative, subject to memory, decay and revision. There is a disjunction between the satiated past and the unfulfilled present, and Ramsay associates this quite explicitly with political absence, political loss. Where the poem begins with and sustains a political gesture, so it ends with an even more sophisticated, and nascently Gothic, one.

> O LUCKY *Wood*, 'tis hard to bear
> The Loss; but Oh! we maun forbear:
> Yet sall thy Memory be dear
>   While blooms a Tree,
> And after Ages Bairns will spear
>   'Bout Thee and Me.
>
>   (Ramsay 1944: 21; original emphasis)

To risk two rhetorical questions: why will the children of the future, as long as there is springtime, talk about Lucky Wood and Allan Ramsay? Why will they be yoked together so? On the one hand, the elegiac strain offers us an answer: there is a conventional yoking of narrator, or speaker, with subject or addressee at work here. But the poem remembers the connection between feeder and fed, supplicant and succour. The narrator himself suggests that his association with Lucky Wood may have been more than that of landlady and drinker. The hope that this was the case, thus guaranteeing the poem's authority, is matched and set against the early eighteenth-century Presbyterian dislike of any suggestion that as Lucky Wood filled Allan Ramsay's belly, so Allan Ramsay filled Lucky Wood's wame. The 'Epitaph' tightens fulfilment's gap:

> *Beneath this Sod*
> *Lies Lucky* Wood,
> *Whom a' Men might put Faith in;*
>   *Wha was na sweer,*
>   *While she winn'd here,*
> *To cramm our Wames for naithing.*
>
>   (Ramsay 1944: 21; original emphasis)

How reassuring that all men could put their faith in Lucky Wood. The double meaning only exists because of what we now recognise as a well-established doubled treatment of, or turn to, the word 'wame' as synonym for 'belly'. Ramsay is perfectly capable of using the word 'belly' ('good Belly Baum' (1944: 20)) but then chooses 'wame' in the epitaph. The belly here is both and neither stomach and womb: it is both the lost political past and the lived personal present. The fullest realisation of these tensions, wherein the past is always-already present in the vulnerable human body and thus the vulnerable human belly, is in work by the poet most influenced by Allan Ramsay: Robert Burns.

Allan Ramsay died in 1758. Robert Burns was born in 1759, and his poem 'Death and Doctor Hornbook. A True Story' was composed around 1785. It was first printed in 1787 as part of the second edition of Burns's poetry. A discussion maintained with a figure who announces that his 'name is *Death*', the 'queerest shape that e'er *I* saw' (1968: 80; my emphasis), it neatly combines the profound geographic localism and bodily trope that we find in Ramsay with references to wider eighteenth-century discourses on and of superstition, as well as the management of the self both immediately and politically. The narrator finds himself on the road home having paid for drink ('I was na fou, but just had plenty', he reassures us (1968: 79)) and still paying attention to the undead (he 'took tent' to scan 'hillocks, stanes, an' bushes' for 'ghaists and' witches' (1968: 79)). He meets a '*Something*' bearing an 'awfu' scythe, out-owre ae shouther' (1968: 80) and casting care aside has a familiar chat:

> Its stature seem'd lang Scotch ells twa,
> The queerest shape that e'er I saw,
> For fient a wame it had ava,
>   And then its shanks,
> They were as thin, as sharp and sma'
>   As cheks o' branks.
>
> 'Guid-een,' quo' I; 'Friend! Hae ye been mawin,
> 'When ither folk are busy sawin?
> [...]
> It spak right howe – 'My name is *Death*,
> 'But be na' fley'd.'
>
> (Burns 1968: 80; original emphasis)

The line break in 'My name is *Death*, / 'But be na' fley'd' (roughly: 'but don't go worrying') is one of the better line breaks in eighteenth-century verse. It is certainly one of the funniest: poor Death, it transpires, has been hard at it for nearly six thousand years because 'Folk maun do something for their bread' (1968: 81); yet Hornbook deprives him of a living despite what Burns records in his own footnote to the poem as 'An epidemical fever [that] was then raging in that country' (1968:

81). What binds the narrator to the reader, and the reader in turn to the poem's figure, are the shared vagaries of life.

'Doctor Hornbook' (no doctor at all, but in fact a local quack called John Wilson) is proving more efficient at dispatch than Death. Death gives the narrator a couple of examples of Wilson's fine work, cast in the 'Standard Habbie' stanza form seen in Ramsay's poetry but which Burns was making his own. Hornbook has recently killed a country laird and a pretty girl:

> 'A countra Laird had ta'en the batts,
> 'Or some curmurring in his guts,
> 'His only son for Hornbook sets,
> > 'And pays him well,
> 'The lad, for twa guid gimmer-pets,
> > 'Was laird himsel.
>
> 'A bonie lass, ye kend her name,
> 'Some ill-brewn drink had hov'd her wame,
> 'She trusts hersel, to hide the shame,
> > 'In Hornbook's care;
> 'Horn sent her aff to her lang hame,
> > 'To hide it there.[']

(Burns 1968: 83–4)

Both stanzas foreground transformational qualities, inversions, achieved not so much by death itself as by the ingestion – the taking into the belly – of what promised to settle it: quack medicine. The reader should note how the ailments in both are of the midriff in the first place: some 'curmurring in his guts', a rumbling stomach, leads the laird to Hornbook's cure and to his death. In the second stanza, Burns puns on 'wame' much as Ramsay did: the pretty girl has taken an 'ill-brewn drink [that] had hov'd her wame', her swollen belly the figure of extramarital pregnancy. Those who benefit from Hornbook's intercession are figures of disjunction: the laird's son becomes 'laird himsel' in return for a couple of 'guid gimmer-pets', healthy sheep. The poem asks: did the boy know what he was doing? Was his trust misplaced, or is this patricide by physician? The poem allows both readings. These are real questions, fired by a male narrator we are invited to trust: as Fred Botting puts it of reason's dismissal of the supernatural: 'it is no more than an effect of a silly . . . imagination associated with women' (2014: 63). There is a little reference possibly in the second stanza to Burns's own sexual behaviour: 22 May 1785 saw the birth of his illegitimate daughter Elizabeth. Thus are licit and illicit sex and its consequences foregrounded therein. But this young girl is managing herself and her standing, managing the consequences of the communal judgement upon her of a pregnancy outside marriage; the bungling Hornbook kills two birds with one stone – mother and unborn child dead, sent not afar but to the 'lang hame'. That first stanza is comic for at stake is rural capital and primogeniture; the second stanza is tragic as everybody dies. It is wholly right of Botting to state that 'the gothic figures that appeared in so many novels, as well as critical, aesthetic and political discussions, became signs of a pervasive cultural anxiety concerning the relation of present and past, and the relationship between classes, sexes and individuals' (2014: 81), and one may add poetry to the long list of forms which expressed such anxieties.

To paraphrase Thomas Gray's *Elegy*, the paths of contentment and social conformity lead but to the grave. Well-being, normalcy, fitting in, convention: these are the characteristics of society that Hornbook challenges and erodes. We might detest, but the poem needs, Hornbook. Care from a local physician – that which should be comforting and familiar, that which should be easeful and morally commonplace – is what leads to death. This is Scottish Gothic: truly *unheimlich* poetry beginning to explore the lyrical and narrative pathways that lead beyond Burns's grave to the disgraced, dislocated, disempowered and disjunctive voices of William Wordsworth and Samuel Taylor Coleridge's *Lyrical Ballads* (1798), Walter Scott's *Chronicles of the Canongate* (1827), Robert Browning's *Dramatis Personae* (1864) and beyond. What a disruptive figure such as Hornbook allows is an astonishingly horrible and local levelling of class (the laird), sex (the pretty girl) and the individual (the narrator faced with death).

There is a social necessity to the Gothic: it reinforces and oils the expression of our mental unease whilst imagining change. In this poem the social order is maintained: the lairdship is passed to the younger and presumably less bilious son; the social obloquy of extramarital sex is stopped in its parturition. Social order is maintained in both instances: the genius of the Gothic is surely how it manages to imagine conformity efficiently even as it holds that social order under critique. Here, as elsewhere in Scottish Gothic, that conjunction of the desperately voiced knowledge of conformity's triumph is voiced at the intersection of satire, the supernatural and narratological self-denial. When Cairns Craig suggests, paraphrasing David Hume, that history 'can only be written when there *is* a composed order in the world, and it is only the composed order of the world that can be written by the historian' (1996: 68) then it is truly worth bearing in mind, *contra* Hume, exemplary counter-examples of Scottish narrative verse such as this, moments of decomposition. Here, in verse, closely held memories lie in wait to challenge narrative explication and to add an irresolvable supernatural disorder which only local lore (designedly untestable by outsiders) allows as even faintly reasonable.

Let us not forget that the narrator is drunk: the shrewd expression of communal values, nascent capitalism and moral transgression is brought about by one who admits that 'I was na fou, but just had plenty'. What facilitates this tightly packed erasure of narratological authority, social hierarchy and generative well-being is, very precisely, the belly: the wame. Sore guts or a child inside are 'cured' by the ingestion of quack medicines justified by Hornbook's progressive learning:

'Calces o' fossils, earths, and trees;
'True Sal-marinum o' the seas;
'The Farina of beans and pease,
    'He has't in plenty;
'Aqua-fontis, what you please,
    'He can content ye.

'Forbye some new, uncommon weapons,
'Urinus Spiritus of capons;
'Or Mite-horn shavings, filings, scrapings,
    'Distill'd *per se*;
'Sal-alkali o' Midge-tail clippings,
    'And mony mae.'

(Burns 1968: 82–3)

This stuff is what we need to rid ourselves of painful digestive conditions and illegitimate children (Hornbook descries no difference). There's a litanic quality to the first stanza's use of the short-line: as we receive unto ourselves the spurious nouns indicative of Hornbook's learning – and of his quackery – so we receive the responses with capitalised pronouns: '"He has't in plenty;"' '"He can content ye."' There is thus an almost sacramental quality to the ingestion of Hornbook's 'Urinus Spiritus' and other transformational matter. The poem decants into the (mis)management of the individual belly the incanted rhythm of the nation's religious history, drawn from pulpit, private study and psalm. The intangible Presbyterian communion, the rejection of the Book of Common Prayer, the adoption of the Westminster Directory, and the direction of worship in Scotland following the Reformation, are present in rhythm and voice, alongside the tangibly deceased laird and that bonnie lass with her unborn child. This is, as Cairns Craig would have it, no 'fragmentary failure . . . of the failed nature of Scotland's past' (1996: 110) but an angry and locally coherent assertion of legitimate, regional self-imagination.

The joy, and the horror, of the poem is that Death is most probably correct in his assessment of Hornbook. According to Death, Hornbook's ignorance of Hippocratic practice, derived principally from William Buchan's *Domestic Medicine* (1769), is doing the Grim Reaper out of business. In part, this is perhaps an acknowledgement of what Kenneth Simpson calls the Scottish 'instant and instinctive suspicion of what appeared to be the Romantic emphasis on the individual' in the face of a 'Scottish tradition of community' (1988: 247). To laugh with this poem is to laugh outwardly at the world's quackery and yet – in the same instant – to sigh inwardly for fear of one's better medical attention.

For most of the poor, or even most of the provincial middling sort in eighteenth-century Scotland, the likes of Hornbook/Wilson (a reasonably well-educated fellow who was literate and keen to see where autodidacticism took him) represented the acme of bodily care. The satire, as Malcolm Nicholson quite reasonably suggests, is not just on Hornbook himself: it is also satire upon the state of affairs where he is the best that a body can expect (2010: 25). As the Scottish universities, turning themselves into the finest sites of medical learning in Europe as the eighteenth century transitioned into the nineteenth, sent their finest graduates abroad, or to the armed forces, what the Scots are left with are the tender mercies of a well-read Hornbook: schoolmaster, apothecary and latterly, session clerk in the Gorbals. As Robert Blair describes men like Hornbook:

> Here! the great Masters of the *healing Art*,
> These mighty Mock-Defrauders of the *Tomb*!
> Spite of their *Juleps* and *Catholicons*,
> Resign to Fate. Proud *Æsculapius'* Son!
> Where are thy boasted Implements of Art,
> And all thy well-cramm'd Magazines of Health?
>
> (Blair 1743: 18; original emphasis)

Blair does not answer his own rhetorical questions. Burns did not need to pose them: the sophistication of both the metrical and propositional content of his poem, especially when contrasted to Blair's work on a similar topic, means they need not be made explicit. 'Proud *Æsculapius'* Son' is a rhythmically challenged figure in a metrically awkward line: the characters of Hornbook, Death and Narrator in Burns do not require, with their deep and immediate localisation, much in the way of generalist flourish. Burns draws upon, and his poem remembers, a tradition of writing about the endangered body and a version of Scottish history that hungers for what it has lost. In doing so, he brings to the fore deeply troubled and uneasy literary tropes of geography, faith, politics, the individuated self and its body that cumulatively ground the emergence of Scottish Gothic verse.

Together, these poems represent the emergence into the late eighteenth century of Scottish Gothic poetry's most distinctive feature, a localism centred on the vulnerable individual body. In the centuries that followed Burns's 'Hornbook', a tormented and contested body remained a key marker in poetry and prose of Scottish Gothic practice: whether in Scott's *Marmion* (1808), Stevenson's *Jekyll and Hyde* (1886) or James Kelman's *How Late It Was, How Late* (1994). The belly, hungry and medicalised, was rarely to be a marker of physical contentment. The belly and its well-being, a marker of our frailty and disempowerment in the teeth of forces beyond our control, still serves as a staple metaphor for the Gothic vulnerability of the Scottish voice.

Notes

1. *Ubi sunt* is a Latin phrase that means 'Where are[?]'. This rhetorical device has a deep literary history from Latin and, in English, the earliest Old English works. Blair is therefore displaying his classical learning and knowledge of literary history whilst also indicating the universality of his observations.
2. This was especially the case in the Highlands, which retained a substantial Catholic and Gaelic-speaking population all through this period, and the south-west of Scotland, a hotbed of Covenanting dissent in the late seventeenth century.
3. Thomson's work is, of course, far more subtle and far more anxious about the well-being of Britain and British poetry than the contexts in which this particular song is now typically rendered can or would allow. An argument may well be made that this is a consequence of Scotland's early and full engagement with the Protestant Reformation. Predestination's ethic of the select meant that how one lived in life no longer pointed to where one's soul reposed after death. The birth of a distinctive Scottish Gothic poetry is commensurate with the emergence of a post-Reformation national identity.

References

Anon. (1769), *The holy Bible, containing the Old and New Testaments: Translated out of The Original Tongues: And with the Former Translations Diligently Compared and Revised, By His Majesty's Special Command. Appointed to be read in Churches*, Oxford: T. Wright and W. Gill.

Blair, Robert (1743), *The Grave*, London: M. Cooper.

Botting, Fred (2014), *Gothic*, Abingdon: Routledge.

Burns, Robert [1787] (1968), 'Death and Doctor Hornbook. A True Story', in Robert Burns, *The Poems and Songs of Robert Burns*, ed. James Kinsley, 3 vols, Oxford: Clarendon Press, vol. 1, pp. 79–84.

Craig, Cairns (1996), *Out of History: Narrative Paradigms in Scottish and British Culture*, Edinburgh: Polygon.

Hogg, James [1824] (1969), *The Private Memoirs and Confessions of a Justified Sinner*, ed. John Carey, Oxford: Oxford University Press.

Johnson, Samuel (1755), *A Dictionary of the English Language*, London: J. and P. Knaptor, T. and T. Longman, C. Hitch and L. Hawes, A. Millar and R. and J. Dodsley, K18.

Lithgow, William (1633), *Scotlands welcome to her native sonne, and soveraigne lord, King Charles wherein is also contained, the maner of his coronation, and convocation of Parliament; the whole grievances, and abuses of the common-wealth of this kingdome*, Edinburgh: Iohn Wreittoun, B3.

Nicholson, Malcolm (2010), '"Death and Doctor Hornbook" by Robert Burns: A View from Medical History', *Medical Humanities*, 36: 1, 23–6.

Punter, David (2012), 'Scottish Gothic', in Gerard Carruthers and Liam McIlvanney (eds), *The Cambridge Companion to Scottish Literature*, Cambridge: Cambridge University Press, pp. 132–44.

Ramsay, Allan [1718] (1944), 'Elegy on Lucky Wood in the Canongate', in Allan Ramsay, *The Works of Allan Ramsay*, ed. Burns Martin and John W. Oliver, 6 vols, Edinburgh: Scottish Text Society, vol. 1, pp. 18–21.

Scott, Walter [1805] (1987), *The Lay of the Last Minstrel*, in Thomas Crawford, David Hewitt and Alexander Law (eds), *Longer Scottish Poems*, 2 vols, Edinburgh: Scottish Academic Press, vol. 2, p. 256.

Simpson, Kenneth (1988), *The Protean Scot: The Crisis of Identity in Eighteenth Century Scottish Literature*, Aberdeen: Aberdeen University Press.

Stafford, Fiona (1994), *The Last of the Race*, Oxford: Clarendon Press.

Chapter 5

Scottish Gothic Drama
Barbara A. E. Bell

Scottish theatre, from the mid-eighteenth century onwards, has been characterised by a distinctive performance culture that values anti-illusionist techniques, breaking the fourth wall, music and song, strongly physical acting styles and striking visual effects. These were accepted traits of the Georgian theatre as a whole; however, they endured in Scotland through the music hall and pantomime traditions, when late nineteenth-century Western theatre was focused on realism/naturalism. Their importance to the search for a distinctive Scottish Gothic Drama lies in the way that the conditions of the Scottish theatre during the Gothic Revival valued these skills and effects. That theatre was heavily constricted in what it could play by censorship from London and writers were cautious in their approach to 'national' topics. At the same time a good deal of work portraying Scotland as an inherently Gothic setting was imported onto Scottish stages. The result, for much of the period, was a fractured 'Scottish Gothic' stage presence, with imported works easily outnumbering native pieces, whilst Scottish writers experimented with Gothic tropes and the 'industry' playwrights, actors and managers, some of them Scots, trod a fine pragmatic line between audience approval and the law. This chapter seeks to separate the multiple strands of Scottish Gothic Drama and uncover the enduring legacy of the Gothic Revival theatre in Scotland. It also explains how contemporary Scottish playwrights and theatre-makers have embraced that 'Gothic' heritage in ways best explained through theories of site-specific performance.

In his pioneering work *English Melodrama*, Michael Booth claimed that 'Scottish Gothic, created mainly by Scott, simply transplanted the usual characters and situations of melodrama ... [adding] a dash of nationalism, to vaguely historical and strongly romantic Scottish settings' (1965: 77–8). His later *Prefaces to English Nineteenth-Century Theatre* emphasised the importance of the 'particular relationship between a play and the theatre that first performed it' (1980: viii). This point, if pursued, would have revealed that what had appeared a homogenous group of 'Scottish Gothic' included many works from the 'Covent Garden Caledonian' (CGC) style of theatre, and others from the Scottish National Drama. Covent Garden Caledonian gave a fashionable tartan dressing to pieces originating outside Scotland, such as Charles Farley's 1803 ballet *Red Roy; or Oswyn and Helen* (Bell 1998). By contrast, the National Drama was a nineteenth-century dramatic genre emerging around 1815 and unique to Scotland, that dealt largely with Scottish historical subjects, treating them seriously and with some scenic realism. The core of the National Drama comprised adaptations of Scott's *Waverley* novels. Recent studies in theatre history have begun to deal with Scottish theatrical representation in more depth. Michael Ragussis argues persuasively for the need to view the repertoire, changing nightly, in its totality, given that the Georgian theatre 'mirrored and reproduced the nation as a contested space' (2010: 13).

The case of Scottish Gothic Drama is additionally complicated by the eighteenth-century intellectual scrimmaging around *Macbeth*, *Ossian* and the way that 'Gothic' was to be understood as supporting differing sides in the struggle to define Scotland's place in Britain. Dale Townshend, citing Robert Crawford, reminds us that Shakespeare was designated a 'national' poet during the 1760s in response to the Scots' focus on Ossian. Townsend concludes that *Macbeth* 'is appropriated in Gothic writing as a means of asserting Scotland's otherness . . . Scotland becomes as Gothic as Radcliffe's Italy . . . literally "another country" of darkness and distance' (2014: 239–40).

As a general definition, Ian Duncan refers 'schematically' to Scottish Gothic representing '(with greater historical and anthropological specificity than in England) the uncanny recursion of an ancestral identity alienated from modern life' (2000: 70). Evaluating the differing characters and fortunes of closet pieces, mainstream theatre and popular performance against this definition entails mapping the relationships between the Gothic Drama in general, Scottish Drama, the National Drama and the CGC pieces (Figure 5.1).

Within the proto-Gothic Drama category of early plays that contain 'Gothic' tropes and devices sit John Home's 1756 *Douglas* (1756) and Shakespeare's *Macbeth* (1606). *Macbeth* is not a Scottish Gothic play. Written by Shakespeare, the subject matter treated more with a view to Stuart England's future than Scotland's past or future, its popularity on English stages as an example of 'Scottish Gothic' is a result of celebrated productions by W. C. Macready and Charles Kean, among others. Analysis of what was seen on Scottish stages reveals that over

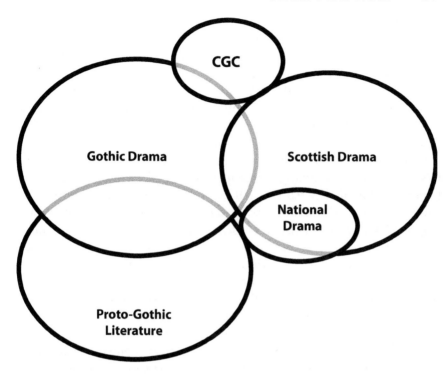

Figure 5.1 A model of the interplay of Scottish and Gothic Drama.
(© Barbara A. E. Bell, 2015. Reproduced with permission.)

150 years, *Macbeth* was most often a gesture to Scottish audiences by visiting guest artists. Many works sit on the borders between genres and styles, demonstrating the fluid utility of the Gothic to playwrights and theatre-makers alike. *Douglas* encompasses the intersection of the proto-Gothic, National Drama and Scottish Gothic Drama categories, a hugely successful blank verse tragedy by a Scottish playwright, regularly revived on the Scottish stage for the next 100 years, with a lost heir, feuding clans, a hidden marriage, numerous violent deaths and rugged castle settings.

The distinctive Gothic imagery of ruined chapels and haunted glens crosses the competing categories. Gothic Revival drama is a strongly visual form and the impact of scenes of Scottish views on the Gothic stage cannot be overstated; the major artists who painted for Scottish theatres, notably Alexander Nasmyth, David Roberts and Clarkson Stanfield, played a significant role in its development. James C. Dibdin reports that painter, architect, designer and civil engineer, Alexander Nasmyth, not only created scenery for *The Castle Spectre* – which was adjudged 'sublime and beautiful' (1888: 233) – in 1798, but also designed the interior of the New Theatre Royal, Edinburgh (1809), for Henry Siddons, who was himself introducing a technical innovation, a darkened auditorium, to intensify the audience experience. These changes were not universally welcomed and Dibdin quotes the critic of the *Courant* complaining that 'the Gothic effect of the ornaments excites rather a sombre than a cheerful impression, and . . . this effect was aided last night by a deficiency of light, everywhere except on the stage' (1888: 259).

CGC pieces relied strongly on their visual impact. In 1805, the Olympic Circus, Edinburgh, presented a 'Grand, Serious, Tragic and Heroic Pantomime, called OSCAR & MALVINA . . . as performed at Covent Garden'. The scenery, 'painted expressly for the occasion by Mr. Wilson', later a Scottish marine artist, included 'The Inside of a Romantic Cavern, Secret Passages, &c' and 'The Grand Armory of Fingal, representing implements of War, arranged in a fanciful manner, and in an ancient style' (*Caledonian Mercury* 1805). *The Lady's Magazine* (1791) reviewed Byrn(e)'s original 1791 production, declaring it 'one of the most superb and interesting entertainments of its species, and . . . [exhibiting] the united powers of painting, music, and dancing' (1791: 597–8). This description was significant. Much 'Scottish' content on Scottish stages during this period was in dumb-show, the native voice muted by statute. Genre restrictions that applied generally to minor theatres were overlaid with censorship by the Lord Chamberlain's Office, to ensure that nothing of an inflammatory, 'national', nature could be seen. *The Lady's Magazine* outlines the scenario, including 'A trial of strength and skill, after the manner of the Highland peasantry' (1791: 597). The physicality of romantic acting and dance was emphasised in numerous 'serious' pantomimes and Scotch ballets, such as *The Scotch Ghost; or, Little Fanny's Love* (Capelletti 1800).

Within the model it seems clear, for example, that *The Scotch Ghost* sits within the CGC/Gothic grouping; however, the many adaptations of genuinely Scottish materials by non-Scots, such as *Gordon the Gypsey* (Peake 1822) from Hogg, are more difficult to place. Other plays not written by Scots, like J. W. Calcraft's adaptation, *The Bride of Lammermuir* (1822), which became stalwarts of the National Drama, hover at the edges of the Scottish Gothic proper. Another key CGC text is J. R. Planché's *The Vampyre; or, the Bride of the Isles* (1820). At one level, it is a straightforward reworking by an English playwright of a French adaptation (by Charles Nodier in 1820) relocated in Scotland, of a tale by John Polidori. However, Polidori had based his tale, *The Vampyre* (1819), in part on earlier works by Byron, *The Giaour* (1813) and 'Augustus Darvell' (1819), and on Caroline Lamb's portrait of

Byron in her novel, *Glenarvon* (1816) to the extent of borrowing Lord Ruthven's name and something of his appearance. Polidori's was the tale which turned the vampire from a blood-spattered night-stalker to a decadent aristocrat, able to pass as a normal, albeit charismatic and aloof, figure. Planché, in emphasising Ruthven's Scottish roots and his mesmeric effect on his victims, male and female, fixed in audiences' minds his association with the 'dangerous' Lord Byron and the Gothic character of northern Scotland. Frederick Burwick (2009: 257) sees Ruthven serving as an 'apt post-Revolutionary commentary on an aristocracy feeding upon the lower classes' whilst Mair Rigby warns that 'whether gothic texts such as *The Vampyre* uphold or subvert dominant sexual ideology is never clear cut' (2004–5: 14). In production, the celebrated vampire trap that allowed Ruthven to disappear before the audience's eyes is equalled in its impact and legacy by the iconic 'attitude' that T. P. Cooke as Ruthven took in the opening Vision, lowering over Helen, asleep in Fingal's Cave (Figure 5.2). The printed text advises a 'grey cloak, to form the attitude as he ascends from the tomb' (Planché 1820: ix).

Eighteenth-century commentators disputed the nature of Gothic effects, a major issue being the difference between the 'avowed supernatural' of earlier works such as *The Vampyre* and the 'explained supernatural' in which the thrills were available for immediate enjoyment, but eventually explained (Cooke 2004). The inherently uncanny stage space became additionally fascinating and John Aikin (1794) and Joanna Baillie (2001: 69–70) explored how known fictions could generate real emotion in observers. Both emphasised the power of the collective spectator experience and Marjean Purinton (1998), after Burroughs, calls women Romantic playwrights 'the foremothers of contemporary performance theory'.

Within the overlap between Scottish Drama and Gothic Drama, that includes Gothic works by Scots – not necessarily focusing on Scotland – and Scottish Gothic Dramas – written by Scots about Scotland – should sit pieces as varied as Joanna Baillie's *Witchcraft* (1836), Scott's *Doom of Devorgoil* (1818) and Byron's *The Deformed Transformed* (1824). By a Scottish writer, but set outside Scotland and arguably outside Duncan's definition of the Scottish Gothic, *The Deformed Transformed* is an unfinished play about a Faustian pact exchanging deformity for conventional beauty, in which Sharon Snyder sees Byron 'recognizing that a performance-based art can effectively transform "the deformed" by positing disability as a flexible narrative entity' (2005: 272).

Whilst Scott's novels generally confined the supernatural elements to an individual character seen as having uncanny powers or a superstition

Figure 5.2 'Scene in The Vampire', Lyceum Theatre, London, 1820, by J. Findlay. (© V&A Images/Victoria and Albert Museum, by permission.)

long held, within his few plays he was bolder in his use of Gothic elements. In *The Doom of Devorgoil*, Scott tried to splice the avowed supernatural and explained supernatural together, but admitted that *Devorgoil* had failed in part because 'mimic goblins . . . are intermixed with the supernatural machinery' that was thought 'objectionable' (1838). The leading playwright of her day, committed to exploring the limitations of theatrical effect, Joanna Baillie wrote plays that are generally Gothic in tone.

Her exposure to the published medical work of relatives gives her depictions of madness, in particular, some weight. Her Scottish Gothic plays, *The Family Legend* (1810), *The Phantom* (1836) and *Witchcraft* (1836) (see Baillie 2007), reflect Duncan's notion of the relationship of 'ancestral identity' to modern life. All three feature Scottish characters entangled in situations brought about by prejudices presented as outmoded, although they vary in terms of the Gothic elements used to drive forward the action. In *The Family Legend*, the legendary gift of precognition is presented as inherently false and suggestible, used to sway the weak and superstitious, and the warring clansmen as too prejudiced to embrace the desired peace. Twenty years later in *The Phantom*, Baillie employs the 'avowed supernatural' in the appearance of a ghost, neither illusion nor trickery, instead, according to Purinton (2004: 230–1), requiring the audience to 'reconceptualis[e] phantasmagoria' between earlier Gothic tropes and contemporary scientific knowledge. In *The Phantom*, Baillie employs a chorus of townspeople, commenting on a passing funeral, to voice the entrenched prejudices that have brought about the tragedy and raised the ghost of Emma Graham; the same effect occurs in *Witchcraft*, when the townspeople crowd about the stake ahead of the anticipated witch-burning. Here Baillie returns to the explained supernatural, but builds tension through the agency of characters who genuinely believe themselves to have supernatural powers. All three works share a focus on the role of women as powerless within ancestral formations.

Whilst the Covent Garden Caledonian continued to depict Scotland as 'other', and Baillie and writers such as Scott, Galt and Hogg wrote works rarely if ever performed, the National Drama provided what was clearly Scottish audiences' preferred style of Scottish Gothic. Scotland's history is recognisable and the limited supernatural elements sit within a realistic setting. The most regularly performed nineteenth-century Scottish 'Gothic' character was the gipsy queen, Meg Merrilies from Scott's *Guy Mannering* (1815). Described in the novel as a 'sybil' [sic] (1815: 63) and in Daniel Terry's adaptation as 'a witch' (1816: II, ii), Meg's heightened, prophetic, language is contrasted by the naturalistic prose of the other characters. Whilst Baillie's *The Family Legend* might be the most 'complete' Scottish Gothic Drama in terms of its array of Gothic devices, it was an expensive undertaking, with a large cast and complex machinery and merited occasional revivals for a single performance. By contrast, Meg Merrilies, unknowable, uncanny but essentially benevolent, strode across Scottish stages large and small, decade after decade. As the century progressed, Gothic work survived on popular stages but declined at major theatres in favour of sensation drama. Changes to theatrical copyright also had an impact on the adaptation of popular narratives and *fin-de-siècle* concerns with, notably, medicine and masculinity, combined in a fascination with and horror of the monstrous. The two issues collided in intense press speculation about the authorised adaptation of Robert Louis Stevenson's *Strange Case of Dr Jekyll and Mr Hyde* (1886). Where once many theatres would have reworked the material for their particular audiences, now the story's reach was restricted by an effective copyright. This focused attention on the minutiae of the production arriving from America and particularly on how the 'transformation' was to be effected (Anon. 1887). Significantly, the story owed much to Stevenson's earlier play with W. E. Henley, *Deacon Brodie; or The Double Life* (1882). This piece, based on the true life, double life, of a respectable Edinburgh craftsman by day and master criminal by night, provided Stevenson with the initial impetus for the more famous work.

The Victorian–Edwardian period produced a clutch of characters from Scottish writers who transcend ready categorisation as Scottish or Gothic. Stevenson and Conan Doyle were writing forms of Scottish-inflected urban and imperial Gothic in the case of Doyle's adaptation of a Sherlock Holmes story, *The Speckled Band* (1910). Ian Brown examines the case of characters such as Jekyll and Hyde, Sherlock Holmes and J. M. Barrie's uncanny man-child, Peter Pan (1904), seeing them as 'manifestations of fundamental human types or psychological states . . . entities in the global imaginative mindscape and . . . evacuated of their Scottish genesis' (Brown 2012: 1). Their legendary status is thus added as another layer to the Scottish mythology of faithful soldiers, groundbreaking scientists, clever doctors and innovative engineers. Both *Jekyll and Hyde* and *The Speckled Band* featured doctors whose greed, intellectual in one case and monetary in the other, was driving them to ever more extreme actions and it is another doctor, Dr Knox, in James Bridie's 1931 play *The Anatomist* (2007) who brings onstage two notorious figures from Edinburgh's past, in the bodysnatchers, Burke and Hare.

By mid-century commentators were openly voicing their dissatisfaction with Scotland's theatrical image. *The Scotsman* (Anon. 1949) lamented the strange misconceptions abroad and wryly exhorted Scots to see *Brigadoon* for instruction in how to be Scottish. In fact, as shown by Bridie's 1943 *Mr Bolfry* (2007), in which he demonstrated a playful ability to utilise and undermine Gothic elements at will by raising a most unconventional Devil, change was afoot. Twentieth-century Scottish theatre-makers found a new flexibility in their engagement with the Gothic, unfettered by the political censorship of the Gothic Revival period, at ease with anti-illusionist performance styles, and with an ability to take ownership of whatever elements of the Scottish Gothic persona best fitted their stage-world view. Several of Liz Lochhead's works exemplify this freedom. *Mary Queen of Scots got her Head Chopped Off* (1989), for instance, explores moments in history that resonate up to the present, examining the origins of myths about women in history, whilst presenting audiences with thematic and visual parallels and/or doubles. In *Mary Queen of Scots*, the actresses playing Mary and Elizabeth become each other's servants and ultimately contemporary children, still playing out old enmities in chilling playground rhymes. Lochhead's early career as an art teacher would suggest a skilled eye for stage picturisation and the opening scene, with its ragged ringmaster, La Corbie, speaking Lochhead's thrilling call to audience engagement, is a masterly theatrical image. Lochhead indicated that her 1985 adaptation of *Dracula* (2009) was influenced by theories of the unconscious; however, Benjamin Poore suggests that the work is more inflected with the 'uncanny' (2013). As he argues, Lochhead's rearrangement of character creates a series of uncanny doubles, dead and undead. Perhaps most importantly, Poore quotes Frances Babbage who, writing in 2009 on the challenge of creating stage presence in adaptations, considering a production of *Dracula*, noted that the novel's 'unstageable' elements are now more readily accessed by audiences who are familiar '"with anti-illusionist stage conventions" and the use of physical theatre' (qtd in Poore 2013: 90).

Alongside the vitality in its playwriting, the contemporary Scottish theatre has seen the emergence of performance-based companies whose work challenges genre boundaries and production practices, using found spaces, digital media, mashing-up art forms and stretching the audience's sensation of time, place and action. Studies of site-specific performance by Clifford McLucas (2000) and Cathy Turner (2004) have articulated the relationship between the found spaces and the events held within them as being that between a 'host' and a 'ghost'. Pearson (2010: 35–6) explains that the prompt towards conceptualising this relationship was a show by the Welsh company *Brith Gof* (PAX 1991) in which part of a Gothic cathedral was built out of scaffolding within an existing space. According to Pearson, the 'site itself became an active component in the creation of performative meaning, rather than a neutral space of exposition' (2010: 36); it is in seeing Scotland's Gothic persona as the 'host', providing echoes of its history to be over-layered, added to and revealed by the event in a live, real-time palimpsest, that the contemporary playful engagement with the Gothic is explained.

The work of two Scottish companies, Grid Iron and Fire Exit, embodies the creative interplay of Scotland's 'Gothic' persona with contemporary performance. Trish Reid's (2013) study of Grid Iron begins by considering *The Bloody Chamber* (1997). This adaptation of Angela Carter's retelling of the Bluebeard myth was both theatrically exhilarating and culturally significant, inhabiting Mary King's Close, an underground labyrinth of streets reputedly haunted by the spirits of plague victims. Discussing his early site-specific shows in Edinburgh, *Burke and Hare* (1994) (Edwards 1993), *The Bloody Chamber* and *Gargantua* (1998), director Ben Harrison noted that these all occupied a 'kind of Gothic imaginary space' (qtd in Reid 2013: 185). For *The Bloody Chamber*, the main character, the Bride, had been divided into two figures, one meeting her fate in the present, the other conjuring her story up from her past. In Mary King's Close, he felt that Carter's story 'found a suitable space for an exploration of the darker reaches of female desire' (Harrison n.d.a). Reid notes that the production had been revived in other locations but 'never recaptured the atmosphere supplied by Edinburgh's gothic past' (2013: 180). Describing the interplay of 'host' and 'ghost', Turner comments that 'Whether the site haunts the work or vice versa often seems intriguingly unclear' (2004: 374). *Sub Rosa* (Leddy 2008) is a promenade piece anchored in Scottish theatre history that originally inhabited the backstage spaces of the Glasgow Citizen's Theatre in a co-production, before being revived in a Masonic Temple for the 2010 Edinburgh Festival, by the Glasgow-based artist/director/writer David Leddy and his company, Fire Exit. Once transferred to a different environment, the audience underwent an orientation before entering the building, lectured on the connections between the Masonic movement and the nineteenth-century theatre. The principal protagonist is Flora McIvor, twelve years old and sharing a name with the Jacobite heroine of *Waverley*, who joins the company at a variety theatre to discover that the Manager is, literally, getting away with murder. As small groups were led through the Citizen's warren of technical areas, characters recounted their involvement in the power struggle between Flora, supported by her only ally, the strong-man, and the Manager's accomplices who, living and dead, ultimately make the audience complicit in their plotting. Louise Welsh's Preface to the printed text, calls Flora 'a classic gothic female' but shifts *Sub Rosa* from terror into horror as a 'Grand Guignol world with its casual deaths, infanticides, under age sex and intimations of incest' (2008: 1). As in *The Bloody Chamber* the extensive physical and sexual violence is never displayed but is described in awful detail, an example of Scots storytelling, powerfully underplayed by the characters.

Alongside the space, the audience are actively engaged in creating meaning in site-specific performance. As Ben Harrison suggests, 'because it is an imaginative act created between strangers, [promenade performance] has a dangerous, flirtatious and erotic charge' (n.d.b). This seductive energy can be seen at work in David Greig's *The Strange Undoing of Prudencia Hart* (2011), which straddles the space between site-specific promenade and building-based work as a 'theatre ballad' developed to be performed in pubs or anywhere, to paraphrase the stage directions, that is warm and where drink is flowing. The playful exuberance of the dialogue, in ballad form and boldly rhyming couplets and a chilling encounter with the Devil after a night of revelry, might echo 'Tam o' Shanter', but Greig has targets beyond a raucous folk night in a pub for his linguistic darts, beginning with postmodern academia. His heroine is an earnest young woman, a folklore specialist, who makes her Gothic journey of discovery heading south in a snowstorm. The conference at which she speaks is conjured up with painful accuracy; however, it is once the plenary is over and she finds herself in the pub with her fellow panellists, a raucous chorus of karaoke 'corbies' and a lock-in pending, that Prudencia's world begins to spiral away into a very personal hell.

> Landlord: Call it what you like – it's that moment when
>   We look back at the past and then forward again
>   And then leap – jump over time's crack
>   Between looking forward and looking back,
>   A fractional second of universal still
>   When what 'was' is, and what is – is 'will'
>   And all time and everything stops
>   Even the ticking of the clocks
>   A midnight moment, when past and future kiss.
>   (Greig 2011: I, vi)

Despite warnings that tonight is the Devil's Ceilidh, Prudencia plunges out into a snowy Kelso and finds herself beguiled by Nick from the B&B into entering his bungalow with its acre-long library 'Paradise' of all the volumes that she could desire. The second part of *Prudencia Hart* becomes a haunting exercise in power play and a journey towards self-knowledge as Prudencia learns how to defeat Nick during the endless night that she spends in the B&B. Finally, she is not only reconciled with her erstwhile enemy, Colin Syme, but also, as she tempts the Devil, saying, 'But what if love's not impossible in poetry?' (2011: II, xi), she discovers that her beloved Border Ballads can become lived-in spaces with their own signposts to freedom.

A CGC-type of cultural referencing has not entirely disappeared, its survival evidenced, for example, in Matthew Bourne's *Highland Fling* (1994), a reworking of the prototypical Romantic ballet, *La Sylphide* (1836). Bourne relocates the story of young James, lured away from his bride by a sylph whom he pursues and ultimately kills, from a romantic Highland glen to contemporary Glasgow. His research embraced Highland folklore, *Peter Pan*, *Trainspotting* and 'the cliché of the Scottish character: hot-tempered, violent, abusive with drugs and drink' (Macaulay and Bourne 2011: 158).

A major stage production embodying the contemporary Scottish Gothic play, combining multidisciplinary production values with a Gothic-inflected text, is Peter Arnott's *The Breathing House* (2003). It could be considered 'urban Gothic'; however, set in Victorian Edinburgh, the 'host' location offers myriad accompanying stories that murmur alongside the dialogue. Arnott calls the city 'Robert Louis Stevenson's Edinburgh of the Mind' (2007: 1). The description is apt as *The Breathing House* pits surface respectabilities in the New Town against corruption bubbling up from the Old Town cesspools that the play's central male characters, John Cloon and Gilbert Chanterelle, are documenting. The scale of emotional and physical contagion is revealed in the array of interlocking tales, told in twenty-three scenes that flow one into another: widower Cloon is captivated by his redoubtable servant Hannah but struggles to accept her as an independent woman; her sister, gripped by religious mania, conceives of an apocalyptic redemption; and the abandoned maidservant, Agnes, ends on the gallows. The play repeatedly foregrounds the slippery nature of surface appearances, despite the efforts of Cloon with his careful photography and Agnes with her hurried charcoal sketches that attempt to capture and hold onto them. The rhythm of the piece is punctuated by long, still, photographic exposures and driven forward by an unsettling sound-scape as walls breathe and choirs sing sweetly amidst the squalor.

The Production Notes to the printed text explain that it was only through the use of technology, in light, sound, stage revolves, video and back-projected photography, that the required pacing is achieved, adding that 'whatever the chosen style of production, a degree of abstraction in the settings is probably necessary' (Arnott 2007: 5). With this intent, director Kenny Ireland approached Scottish artist Calum Colvin to design the show, after seeing his exhibition, *Ossian: Fragments of Ancient Poetry*, at the Scottish National Portrait Gallery in 2002 (Figure 5.3). Tom Normand's Commentary in the exhibition catalogue notes the 'dark core to Colvin's photography' that has 'described landscapes in decay, a world littered with ambiguity, and a humanity sated by doubt and uncertainty' (2002: 20). In private correspondence (23 January 2015), Colvin identifies Scotland's storytelling tradition as a major influence on his work. The designs for *The Breathing House* that compress and expand street scenes and interiors have hung amidst their creep-

Figure 5.3 'The Breathing House', I, i, Royal Lyceum Theatre, Edinburgh, 2003. (© Calum Colvin. Reproduced with permission.)

ing walls portraits of Scottish writers, embodying 'the Scottish mix of success, private disaster and scandal reverberating through the narrative elements', notably Byron in an opium den, and Walter Scott in Gilbert's study (Colvin n.d.).

Conclusion

Looking back across the period under investigation, it is not immediately obvious that there is an unbroken strand of Scottish Gothic in the drama; however, an unravelling of specifically Scottish work from other species of 'Scottish' and Gothic Drama has revealed something potentially more enduring at work.

Scottish culture, with its heritage of narrative forms, oral and written, in one language or several, its traditions of intellectual enquiry, practical ingenuity and physical prowess saw nineteenth-century Scottish writers and theatre-makers ride the wave of 'Scottish' Gothic despite official constraints, to create what suited their audiences/readers. Today, Scottish writers and artists are engaging readily with the Gothic and also with Scotland's Gothic persona; the 'host' and the 'ghost' convey the symbiotic relationship between an external imposed/internally tolerated historical context and present creative realities so that Duncan's 'ancestral identity' is no longer 'alienated from modern life'.

References

Aikin, John [n.d.] (1794), 'On the Impression of Reality Attending Dramatic Representations', *The Scots Magazine*, 56 (January), 19–21, reprint from *The Memoirs of the Literary and Philosophical Society of Manchester*, 4: 1.

Anon. (1887), 'Music and the Drama', *The Glasgow Herald*, 6 June.

— (1949), 'A Scotsman's Log: Through the Looking Glass', *The Scotsman (1921–1950)*, 19 May, <http://connect.nls.uk/docview/482101616?accoun tid=12801> (last accessed 2 July 2015).

Arnott, Peter (2007), *The Breathing House*, Edinburgh: Fairplay Press.

Baillie, Joanna [1798] (2001), 'Introductory Discourse', in *Plays on the Passions*, ed. Peter Duthie, Peterborough, ON: Broadview Press, pp. 67–113.

— (2007), *Six Gothic Dramas*, intro. Christine A. Colón, Chicago: Valancourt Books.

Bell, Barbara (1998), 'The Nineteenth Century', in B. Findlay (ed.), *A History of Scottish Theatre*, Edinburgh: Edinburgh University Press, pp. 137–206.

Booth, Michael (1965), *English Melodrama*, London: Jenkins.

— (1980), *Prefaces to English Nineteenth-Century Theatre*, Manchester: Manchester University Press.

Bridie, James (2007), *The Devil to Stage: Five Plays by James Bridie*, ed. Gerard Carruthers, Glasgow: ASLS.

Brown, Ian (2012), *Our Multiform, Our Infinite Scotland: Scottish Literature as 'Scottish', 'English' and 'World' Literature*, Glasgow: ASLS.

Burwick, Frederick (2009), *Romantic Drama: Acting and Reacting*, Cambridge: Cambridge University Press.

Byrn(e), James (1791), *Oscar and Malvina*, ballet, Covent Garden, London, 20 October.

Byron, George Gordon (1824), *The Deformed Transformed: A Drama*, <http://www.lib.ru/POEZIQ/BAJRON/byron_deformed.txt> (last accessed 15 January 2015).

Calcraft, J. W. (1822), *The Bride of Lammermuir*, Theatre Royal, Edinburgh, 1 May.

Caledonian Mercury (1805), 'Olympic Circus, College Street', advertisement, 18 February, 13019, 1.

Capelletti, Giuseppe (1800), *The Scotch Ghost; or, Little Fanny's Love*, ballet, Drury Lane, London, 8 February.

Colvin, Calum (n.d.), 'The Breathing House', <http://calumcolvin.com/the-breathing-house> (last accessed 26 January 2015).

Cooke, Arthur L. [1951] (2004), 'Some Side Lights on the Theory of the

Gothic Romance', in Fred Botting and Dale Townsend (eds), *Gothic: Critical Concepts in Literary and Cultural Studies*, London: Taylor & Francis, pp. 19–26.

Dibdin, James C. (1888), *The Annals of the Edinburgh Stage*, Edinburgh: Cameron.

Duncan, Ian (2000), 'Walter Scott, James Hogg and Scottish Gothic', in David Punter (ed.), *A Companion to the Gothic*, Oxford: Blackwell, pp. 70–80.

Edwards, Owen Dudley (1993), *Burke and Hare*, Edinburgh: Mercat Press.

Farley, Charles (1803), *Red Roy; or Oswyn and Helen*, ballet, Haymarket Theatre, London, 10 August.

Greig, David (2011), *The Strange Undoing of Prudencia Hart*, London: Faber and Faber.

Harrison, Ben (n.d.a), 'The Bloody Chamber', <http://www.benharrison.info/productions/the-bloody-chamber/> (last accessed 13 February 2015).

— (n.d.b), 'Why I Do Site Specific Work', <http://www.benharrison.info/articles/site-specific-work/> (last accessed 13 February 2015).

Harrison, Ben and *Grid Iron* Theatre (1997), *The Bloody Chamber*, unpublished performance text.

— (1998), *Gargantua*, unpublished performance text.

Home, John [1756] (2010), *Douglas: A Tragedy*, ed. and intro. Ralph McLean, London: Humming Earth.

The Lady's Magazine; or, Entertaining Companion for the Fair Sex (1791), 'Account of the New Pantomime called Oscar and Malvina', 22, 597–8.

Leddy, David (2008), *Sub Rosa*, Edinburgh: Fairplay Press.

Lochhead, Liz (1989), *Mary Queen of Scots Got Her Head Chopped Off*, London: Penguin.

— [1985] (2009), *Dracula*, London: NHB Modern Plays.

Macaulay, Alastair and Matthew Bourne (2011), *Matthew Bourne and His Adventures in Dance*, London: Faber and Faber.

McLucas, Clifford (2000), 'Ten Feet and Three Quarters of an Inch of Theatre', in N. Kaye (ed.), *Site-Specific Art: Performance, Place and Documentation*, London: Routledge, pp. 125–38.

Normand, Tom and the Trustees of the National Galleries of Scotland (2002), 'Calum Colvin's Ossian', in *Calum Colvin – Ossian: Fragments of Ancient Poetry*, Edinburgh: National Galleries of Scotland, pp. 11–56.

Peake, Richard Brinsley (1822), *Gordon the Gypsey*, play, English Opera House, London, 5 August.

Pearson, Mike (2010), *Site-Specific Performance*, Basingstoke: Palgrave Macmillan.

Planché, James Robinson (1820), *The Vampyre; or, the Bride of the Isles*, play, English Opera House, London, 9 August, London: Cumberland, vol. 27.

Poore, Benjamin (2013), 'Liz Lochhead and the Gothic', in Anne Varty (ed.), *The Edinburgh Companion to Liz Lochhead*, Edinburgh: Edinburgh University Press, pp. 86–104.

Purinton, Marjean D. (1998), 'Revising Romanticism by Inscripting Women Playwrights', *Romanticism on the Net*, 12 (November), <http://www.erudit.org/revue/ron/1998/v/n12/005822ar.html#re1no3> (last accessed 2 February 2015).

— (2004), 'Pedagogy and Passions: Teaching Joanna Baillie's Dramas', in

Thomas C. Crochunis (ed.), *Joanna Baillie, Romantic Dramatist: Critical Essays*, London: Routledge, pp. 221–40.

Ragussis, Michael (2010), *Theatrical Nation: Jews and Other Outlandish Englishmen in Georgian Britain*, Philadelphia: University of Pennsylvania Press.

Reid, Trish (2013), '"Angels and Modern Myth": Grid Iron and the New Scottish Theatre', in Patrick Duggan and Victor Ukaegbu (eds), *Reverberations Across Small-Scale British Theatre*, Chicago: Intellect/University of Chicago Press pp. 175–94.

Rigby, Mair (2004–5), '"Prey to some cureless disquiet": Polidori's Queer Vampyre at the Margins of Romanticism', *Romanticism on the Net*, 36–7 (November 2004, February 2005), <http://id.erudit.org/iderudit/011135ar> (last accessed 20 January 2015).

Scott, Walter (1815), *Guy Mannering, or The Astrologer*, Edinburgh: James Ballantyne, vol. 1.

— [1830] (1838), 'Preface', *The Doom of Devorgoil*, in *The Poetical Works of Sir Walter Scott, first series, containing Minstrelsy of the Scottish Border, Sir Tristrem, and Dramatic Pieces*, Paris: Baudry's European Library, p. 426.

Shakespeare, William [1606] (1992), *The Tragedy of Macbeth*, London: Wordsworth Editions.

Snyder, Sharon L. (2005), 'Unfixing Disability in Lord Byron's *The Deformed Transformed*', in Carrie Sandahl and Philip Auslander (eds), *Bodies in Commotion: Disability and Performance*, Detroit: University of Michigan Press, pp. 271–83.

Terry, Daniel (1816), *Guy Mannering; or, The Gipsey's Prophecy: A Musical Drama*, London: John Miller.

Townshend, Dale (2014), 'Shakespeare, Ossian and the Problem of "Scottish Gothic"', in Elisabeth Bronfen and Beate Neumeier (eds), *Gothic Renaissance: A Reassessment*, Manchester: Manchester University Press, pp. 218–43.

Turner, Cathy (2004), 'Palimpsest or Potential Space? Finding a Vocabulary for Site-Specific Performance', *New Theatre Quarterly*, 20: 4, 373–90, <http://dx.doi.org.connect.nls.uk/10.1017/S0266464X04000259> (last accessed 14 November 2014).

Welsh, Louise (2008), 'Preface', in David Leddy, *Sub Rosa*, Edinburgh: Fairplay Press, pp. 1–2.

Chapter 6

Scottish Gothic Poetry
Alan Riach

The first sentence of the Preface to Émile Mâle's magisterial study of religious art in thirteenth-century France, *The Gothic Image*, reads: 'To the Middle Ages, art was didactic' (1972: vii). Gothic Scottish poetry may be described as engaging with the macabre, nightmare qualities of an unbearable or unresolvable vision, yet its historical connection to medieval Gothic art – all the arts, from music to architecture – reminds us that this engagement has didactic purpose. It teaches us how life is multifaceted and ultimately uncontrollable, how the irrational imposes itself inexplicably upon the best ideals of rational humanity. This is one reason why the term 'Gothic' was originally pejorative and opposed to the ethos of certainty and assurance promulgated by *Classicism*.

In architectural terms, the most conventional meaning of 'Gothic' is that of a style of accretion, a design that might elaborate upon itself, irregularly prompted by what came before, rather than a design that was pre-planned, symmetrical and balanced. Again, this is why it was originally a scornful term used by purists. These two principles of the 'Gothic' – of didactic purpose and irregular structural design – both apply to poetry as much as to architecture, and are evident as a major strand in Scottish poetry. In this designation, Scottish Gothic poetry is didactic, opposed to unquestioning faith, and takes shape according to its own dynamics, not according to preordained designs.

Furthermore, Mâle's identification of the relation between the sacred and the profane in medieval Gothic architecture anticipates and helps explain the relation between pre-Enlightenment Gothic art, both pagan and Christian, and the post-Enlightenment trust in rational belief systems. In Scottish poetry, this relation can be understood in the ways that medieval and Renaissance poets brought energy in language and vision into formal structure. Edwin Morgan put this clearly in an essay on William Dunbar: 'we are dealing with ordered energy, not with energetic orderliness' (1990: 38). In many examples of Gothic literature, forces or figures from history or society arise in defiance of priorities of public order, not to be suppressed. This is most evident in supernatural tales and has been examined closely by Colin Manlove in his book on Scottish fantasy (1994) but the same principle applies generally to sexual energies, the urgencies of forbidden languages, the silenced understanding of chaos whose eruption is a perpetual threat to any ordered world.

Thus, the didactic quality of Gothic art is not confined to any single orthodoxy prescribed by any conventional authority. It is not the property of any church or state, and cannot be learned as dogma, posing as perpetual truth. It is rather something that takes different forms in different genres or ages, and demands recognition whatever its context. For Robert Henryson (c. 1460–c. 1500), William Dunbar (c. 1460–c. 1513) and Gavin Douglas (1476–1522), the whole world was Gothic: medieval and early Renaissance sensibilities were entwined. Precise dates for many of the poems are not available but the ethos pertains to them all. Henryson's 'Testament of Cresseid' (c. 1490) might endorse religious orthodoxy at one level but there is a proto-humanist compassion in his presentation of Cresseid's victimisation by the gods who parade before her in an arrogant display of authority. Dunbar's 'Dance of the Seven Deadly Sins' (c. 1504–7) is one of the most vivid presentations of allegorical grotesquerie in poetry – childishly eager humour comes into a horrific, macabre dance, a brazen exhibition of ferociously adult lusts and desires. In Gavin Douglas's translation of Virgil, *The Eneados* (1513), wild and human nature are in fearful balance, particularly in his representation of the northern seasons and seas. These poets are intrinsically Gothic in Mâle's sense: they are practitioners of a didactic art, deadly serious in moral implication. Their religious commitment is not mere piety but social priority. The energy of their language is continuously critical, allowing for no mere idolatry. They know full well to what temptation can lead.

The Ballads: Gothic Conflict

The Border Ballads are stories in song, great poems by virtue of succinct expression, cutting poignancy, razor-like humour and depth of pathos. In their didactic purpose, they teach us about human relations, weaknesses and strengths, and every one of them involves cross-purposes between people, of one kind or another. They are the equivalent in Scottish poetry of Jacobean drama in English literature. Their form arises from oral delivery, extemporisation and extension of story through the immediate engagement of an individual performer, in song or recitation. Once captured in print, variant texts may be read, but in performance a flexibility is understood to be required. Ballad metre is regular but ballad length can vary according to the event and its moment. All ballads are about conflict. None are tranquil, festive or easily conducive to serenity and joy. Some of the most lively enact a dance of defiance and self-realisation in the face of insuperable odds. When the king and his men surround the outlaw leader, Johnny Armstrong, he sees that he is outnumbered and asks for mercy, but the king sentences him to be hanged. Johnny recognises his position and maintains his dignity:

'To seik het water beneth cauld yce,
　　Surely it is a great folie;
I haif asked grace at a graceless face,
　　But there is nane for my men and me.'

(Child 1965, vol. 3: 371)

The truths the ballads embody are lasting, in human terms, and vividly realised. Descendants of 'The Twa Corbies' still sit on fences or branches of trees by motorways waiting for roadkill. In the ballad, they are waiting to get at a slaughtered knight, talking to each other about how, fortunately for them, not only has his hawk gone to the hunting and his hound left to fetch the wild fowl, but even his lady has taken another husband, so fickle love and love's betrayal are not all bad: the corbies can look forward to an enjoyably uninterrupted meal:

'Mony a one for him makes mane,
　　But nane sall ken where he is gane;
Oer his white banes, when they are bare,
　　The wind sall blaw for evermair.'

(Child 1965, vol. 1: 253)

'The Battle of Harlaw' exists in numerous versions from different periods, and while it ostensibly refers to a battle that set limits to the power of the Lordship of the Isles, it leaves us in some doubt about whether any side could claim it as a victory (Rideout and Purser 2011). 'True Thomas' refers to the historical Thomas of Ercildoune, but there are other ballads, traditional and more recent, that involve journeys to another world. In James Hogg's 'Kilmeny' (1813), this sense of mystery is paramount. Writing at a time when Walter Scott and not long before him, Burns, were transcribing songs from the oral tradition and publishing them with their music for performance in polite society in the drawing rooms of cities and big country houses, Hogg was part of a much wider literary, musical and storytelling ethos, both folk and genteel. This overlap between oral and literary worlds extends beyond Scott, especially in 'Proud Maisie' (1818), to Robert Louis Stevenson, in his poems depicting the imagined worlds of children, the land of counterpane, or the Galloway ballad-legend of 'Heather Ale' (1890), and is essential to their representations of religion and psychology in the ways history, memory and language are depicted and used in their poetry as much as their fiction.

Mysterious travels, mythical locations, grim portents, potent images and narrative tension that keeps resolution suspenseful – all these animate the ballads. Inexplicable things have a direct effect upon us. The three sons of 'The Wife of Usher's Well' leave their mother and she gets word of their deaths, but then they reappear, returned from the Gates of Paradise to visit her, before even more poignantly bidding farewell for a second time. The grief of this loss is piercing. In 'The Demon Lover', the pain and consequence of too ready trust and absolute betrayal cut deep. The story is interpreted in a classical music idiom in the orchestral tone poem of the same name by John Blackwood McEwen (1868–1948) (McEwen 1993). A similarly terrifying and haunting presentation of human fallibility and vulnerability is in 'The Cruel Mither', where a young unmarried mother kills her two babies at birth, then is tortured to damnation by her own guilt. Looking out at young children playing with a ball, she sees them turn to her with reproach, saying, 'But now we're in the heavens hie, / And ye've the pains o hell to drie' (Child 1965, vol. 1: 221). The implication of a social context of hierarchy and subjection, physical desire and need, the pain of childbirth, the speed of the killing, the long agony of guilt, all are evoked in tiny phrases and, when heard in performance, chilling, unelaborated, utterly unsentimental musical construction. It might be performed as a song, in a folk idiom, but in the arrangement for voice and string quartet by Edward McGuire (1995), it crosses into the world of concert performance.

The world of the ballads is social, material, palpable, and even when haunted, earthly. As Nick Groom says of them, 'Death is not presented as an escape or state of grace, it is not a form of sacrifice – it is merely a crushing reassertion of the material nature of reality' (2012: 36). Since ghosts have no place in the Protestant world, anything haunting has an evident material consequence, if not always a verifiable material source. In this respect the ballads are distinct from tales of the supernatural or unearthly intervention whose primary purpose is entertainment through frissons of fear and horror. And they possess an unmistakeable sense of humour, what Norman MacCaig, in the poem 'Space Travel', called 'the homicidal hilarity / of a laugh in a ballad' (2005: 196–7). The lasting influence of the ballads on modern Scottish poetry is evident, and it is also there in plays such as David Greig's *The Strange Undoing of Prudencia Hart* (2011) and in fiction such as Andrew Greig's novel *Fair Helen* (2013).

The ballads give Scottish poetry a key coordinate point of Gothic authority, both in didactic purpose and freedom of development, which evades the extremes of, on the one hand, orthodoxies in religious solemnity and piety, and on the other, the ephemerality of frivolous entertainment. What they have to teach does not come in the form of repeatable dogmatic formulae but arises from the experiences they depict through characters in contexts of uncertainty. Thus their didacticism is experiential, rather than preordained, and therefore distinct from the certainties of an absolute ruling dogmatism. As literary art, they have permanent value and their significance extends into the eras of Enlightenment and Romanticism. As works which arise and circulate among different readerships, the polite and the coarse, they embody the worlds of both literate and illiterate people, each group, potentially, in different ways, highly educated. Ballads, oral Gaelic songs and stories of Celtic myth and legend, the printed texts by James Macpherson, all had currency among different people. In the transition in the works of Scottish poets from the eighteenth and nineteenth centuries, the Gothic is a continuity. From Dunbar to MacDiarmid, the appropriateness of the gargoyle grinning by a saint can be seen in the juxtaposition of decorum and vulgarity.

The Dark Poets: Gothic Realism

Industrialising Scotland changed the nation (see Leonard 1990, *passim*). Thomas Campbell, in 'Lines on Revisiting a Scottish River' (1828), laments so-called progress as industrial effluvia have turned the rippling beauty of the Clyde into a seething, polluted mess: 'And call they this Improvement?' Campbell's Clyde is now a place where 'brick-lanes smoke, and clanking engines gleam' in the effort 'To gorge a few with Trade's precarious prize' (Gifford and Riach 2004: 104–5). In 'Glasgow' (1857), by Alexander Smith, the city is depicted in vivid images of haunting ferocity and spectacle. There is a feeling of dark belonging in this poem which takes pride in the scale of industrialisation and identification of the poet with a world of 'Black Labour' and 'secret-moaning caves': 'City! I am true son of thine' (Whyte 1983: 7).

The poetry of the neglected James Young Geddes (1850–1913) also presents the sense that industry might have a strange, terrible beauty but it is charged with moral force at the civic hypocrisies evident in industrial Dundee. 'Glendale & Co. (After Walt Whitman)' begins with the great American poet's sense of social justice and employs Whitman's long line and free verse, chanting a litany of bitter indignation as the firm of Glendale & Co. is described, 'grown great from small beginnings' to something now hellish that 'dominates the Town' (Geddes 1879: 122). This is Gothic vision at its most vivid, yet it seems scarcely exaggerated but rather a factual description of what can be seen. The reductive factuality enhances the political outrage at the misuse and exploitation of humanity by the impersonal firm, the company that employs human beings to keep the economy running: 'Lit up at night, the discs flare like angry eyes in watchful supervision, impressing on the minds of the workers the necessity of improving the hours and minutes purchased by Glendale & Co.' (1879: 122). The bitterness and irony of the poem escalates in Blakean indignation. Other important works include 'The New Jerusalem': 'Machineries / Are there whose vast pulsations tear and thrash / The groaning air' (1879: 26), 'The New Inferno', full of 'harsh dissonance' (1879: 39), and 'The Spectre Clock of Alyth' (1886). Geddes is Scotland's most radical social poet between Burns and MacDiarmid.

Both John Davidson (1857–1909) and James ('B. V.') Thomson (1834–82) were significant influences on T. S. Eliot and Hugh MacDiarmid. Thomson's visionary poem, *The City of Dreadful Night* (1880) is a phantasmagorical nocturnal journey through a nightmare city of sleep-walking, enervated, alienated individuals. It begins: 'The City is of Night; perchance of Death, / But certainly of Night' (Thomson 1993: 29). As we enter the city, we meet its inhabitants: 'step for step with lonely sounding feet / We travelled many a long dim silent street' (1993: 32). Deeply read in Dante and Leopardi (whom he translated), Thomson's vision belongs in their company as well as that of early modern Scottish poetry. It is not, like that of Geddes, one of an actual industrialised city, nor, like Davidson's, one of moral turpitude firmly based in historic fact. It is rather a metaphoric, illuminated nocturnal metropolis, like Dante's subterranean Inferno, whose people are doomed by something more inescapably human than alterable social conditions. The implication is that all cities bleed into one emblematic 'dreadful' city in a vision where industrialism has brought about a dark spiritual uniformity.

In Thomson's vision, the city is imbued with something more than realism. Darkness also characterises many of the poems of Robert Buchanan (1841–1901), who could write Robert Browning-like dramatic monologues such as 'Fra Giacomo' (1866), in which an Italian Renaissance aristocrat addresses a priest and gives him a glass of wine, while his wife lies dead in the bedroom upstairs, only to reveal in the course of the poem that he has discovered the priest was his wife's

secret lover. The orchestral setting by Cecil Coles (2002) is a miniature masterpiece of operatic grand guignol. He then reveals that the
wine is poisoned, and just in case, he stabs the priest repeatedly and
has his corpse thrown into the canal below (Buchanan 1884: 8–9).
This grotesque poem skilfully and with absolute assurance indicts all
its characters. Ostensibly a self-revealing monologue similar to Robert
Browning's 'My Last Duchess' (1842), 'Fra Giacomo' verges on the neo-
or pseudo-Gothic of exaggerated effect, the Gothic as sensationalised
display, that takes its most extreme forms in cinema of the 1960s and
1970s, with horror films whose priorities are commercial rather than
didactic. Generally, however, Buchanan is far removed from this. His
city-poems 'London' (1860–2) and 'Vanity Fair' (1872) and his portrait-
poem, 'The Ballad of Judas Iscariot' (1872), teem with people and make
an immediate formal appeal to a popular readership, but their subject
is alienation. Desolation, loneliness and elemental, inhuman nature are
most powerful in 'Sonnets written by Loch Coruisk, Isle of Skye' (1870).
'We Are Fatherless' (1870) ends with Nietzschean finality: 'There is no
God – in vain we plead and call, / In vain with weary eyes we search and
guess – / Like children in an empty house . . .'. And the location of the
poem 'Desolate!' (1870) delivers an unforgettable sense of the Godless
universe characteristic of the era:

> Deepening silence. Hush! the dark profound
>   Groans, as some gray crag loosens and falls sheer
> To the abyss. Wildly I look around,
>   O Spirit of the Human, are Thou *here?*
>
> (Buchanan 1884: 249)

There is no answer. Perhaps the solitude is registered so forcefully
because of the formal English of the poem's language and syntax. Yet
this is a Gothic realisation of a Nietzschean world, theatrical in one
sense, but materialistic in terms of geology or scientific analysis, which
aligns him with John Davidson.

For Davidson, the Nietzschean character rises most strongly in the
pessimistic *Testaments*. 'The Testament of a Vivisector' (1901) (1973,
vol. 2: 324–9) is perhaps the most repulsive poem ever written, a coldly
objective description of the flaying of a horse: 'I study pain, measure it'
(1973, vol. 2: 327, l. 168) and the proof is in the surgery:

>   I fixed
> The creature, impotent and moribund,
> With gag and fetter; sheared its filthy mane;
> Cut a foot's length, tissue and tendon [...]

And made this faithful, dying, loathsome drudge,
One diapason of intensest pain [...]

(Davidson 1973, vol. 2: 327, ll. 155–66)

The conclusion is the discovery that 'Matter in itself is pain . . . being evermore / Self-knowledge' (1973, vol. 2: 328–9, ll. 223–9). This line, linking the material universe, human self-knowledge and pain, is a key to understanding the Scottish Gothic mode in modern poetry. The emphatic importance it gives to critical comprehension of humanity, and the materialist conviction from which this arises, are crucial. The atheism of Davidson and his contemporaries is a new departure, of course, from the Gothic world of the earlier medieval and Renaissance poets, but it is in tune with the black ironies of the ballads and, as we shall see, the questioning loneliness of MacDiarmid, looking into the space where God was.

It was too much for Davidson, who killed himself in 1909, but it is an enduring strength in his poetry. Scientific chill runs all through 'Snow' (1909) (1973, vol. 1: 185–6). Davidson turns the objective gaze upon himself in 'The Testament of a Man Forbid' (1901), which begins, 'Mankind has cast me out' (1973, vol. 2: 329). Formally, many poems connect with the ballads, especially 'Thomas the Rhymer' (1891) (1973, vol. 1: 37–9) and 'A Runnable Stag' (1905) (1973, vol. 1: 159–61), and other works designated 'ballads', yet Davidson is also a culmination of the tradition of Romantic sinners, from Milton's Satan to Melville's Ahab and others. Even when Davidson writes in the working-class voice of the wage-slave in 'Thirty Bob a Week' (1894), sympathetic compassion and class solidarity fail to alleviate the human waste enacted by the industrial world: 'a naked child against a hungry wolf'; in the end, 'we fall, face forward, fighting, on the deck' (1973, vol. 1: 63–4). If this is Gothic realism, its product is despair, and leads to suicide.

MacDiarmid: Return of the Gothic

Any number of Hugh MacDiarmid's early lyrics might be considered with reference to the Gothic imagination, pre-eminently 'The Innumerable Christ' and 'The Diseased Salmon' from *Sangschaw* (1925), and 'The Dead Liebknecht' from *Penny Wheep* (1926) but it culminates in *A Drunk Man Looks at the Thistle* (1926). Here, the perception of the appropriateness of the proximity of gargoyle and saint, carved out in the sculptured stone of the Gothic cathedral, restores to modernity a medieval sense of humanity, similar to the work of James Joyce. This is a resumption of relational, as opposed to polarised, reality. Declan Kiberd, in his book, *Ulysses and Us*, says that Joyce worked towards 'a return to a vibrant medieval world in which sacred and obscene stood side by side' (2009: 33). MacDiarmid was endorsing exactly this in the 1920s in his appraisal of G. Gregory Smith's idea that in the best of Scottish literature there was an implicit understanding of the rightness of this Gothic world:

> Grinnin' gargoyle by a saint,
> Mephistopheles in Heaven,
> Skeleton at a tea-meetin'
> Missin' link – or creakin'
> Hinge atween the deid and livin'
>
> (MacDiarmid 1987: 36, ll. 426–30)

The original passage from Gregory Smith reminds us that the medieval aspect of this is crucial:

> Scottish literature is more medieval in habit than criticism has suspected, and owes some part of its picturesque strength to this freedom in passing from one mood to another. It takes some people more time than they can spare to see the absolute propriety of a gargoyle's grinning at the elbow of a praying saint. (Smith 1919: 35)

Memorably, Smith called this appropriate juxtaposition of the sacred and profane, the 'Caledonian Antisyzygy' (1919: 4) and MacDiarmid took what he did from that. This was not an isolated phenomenon. As Kiberd says, it is an understanding equally characteristic of Joyce. Joyce maintained that the medieval was the essential spirit of Europe and that Ireland at its best was in touch and in tune with that. *Ulysses* reconnects with the Ireland before colonial occupation. And that is exactly what the Scottish Literary Renaissance of the 1920s attempted to do in Scotland: to reconnect with, through, beyond and before, the centuries of being caught up in Britishness and Empire, to connect back to an ethos before the unions of parliaments and crowns, to a Gothic world of didactic art taking form in irregular, unpredicted, limber structural design.

A Drunk Man Looks at the Thistle may be described in external, theatrical terms, as if the reader were watching a play of the story enacted on a screen: a man, after drinking in a village pub, is walking home to his wife, falls in a ditch and looks up at the stars in the night sky; the poem is comprised of his rambling thoughts. His physical condition interrupts him as he has a bout of hiccups (MacDiarmid 1987: 22, ll. 233–7), vomits (1987: 118, l. 1571) and finally resolves to head for home. So far, this is no more than a frame resembling Burns's 'Tam o' Shanter', but it is banal. The imagery provides a set of cross-references and a kind of coherence; Roderick Watson discusses recurring paired images: thistle/ rose, whisky/moonlight, sea serpent/woman (1972: 94–116). This is accurate, but much of the poem is speculative, philosophically dark, tonally wry and not hinged to prevailing symbols.

A different way of accepting and accommodating the poem's formal waywardness would acknowledge its drive and purpose, without need of classical coherence. This connects the principles of Scottish Gothic I have been discussing with MacDiarmid's embrace of Nietzschean, Dionysiac abandon, the purpose of intoxication, to lose inhibitions and let loose possibilities. This confirms the poem's structure: it is an enquiry rather than a conclusion. There is didactic intention, but it is only found in sympathetic understanding of the forensic self-anatomising of its exposed humanity; it is as if a mask had been stripped off, and everything beneath was made visible to the surgeon's eye and scalpel:

> My face has flown open like a lid
> – And gibberin' on the hillside there
> Is a' humanity sae lang has hid! ...
>
> (MacDiarmid 1987: 32, ll. 374–6)

That which humanity has hidden for so long, through the Victorian rectitudes of polite society and imperial exploitation, MacDiarmid now promises he will expose to the scrutiny of modern readers. He will do this through an exploration of five main themes: Scotland, Sexuality, Identity, Purpose and Potential. Beyond the simple narrative frame and the twinned recurring sets of images, these themes give a kind of coherence, forming coordinate points from which explorations might arise and lead off in almost any direction. This is the meaning of the title: the thistle is a symbol for Scotland, and the vision of a 'drunk man' may be limited by its mid-1920s context, but it is uncontrolled by reason or objectivity. Even the opening line tells us the poem is unreliable: 'I amna fou' sae muckle as tired – deid dune.' The man is not drunk but exhausted, a state in which rambling, dreaming, nightmare visions might take him along the nerves of his own perception without prediction. Sustained in the idiom of Scots, the poem refers to the General Strike; it evokes small-town or village morality, social hypocrisy, the usurping centrality of the Burns cult to literary culture, to mention only obvious aspects particular to Scotland contemporary with its composition. The Burns cult especially warrants scorn and contempt since the idolatry at its centre is as corrupting as Mariology was before the Reformation. Idolising Burns is a symptom of guilt, born of inept post-Protestantism, misplaced Roman Catholic reverence. MacDiarmid's attack is Gothic in its extremism, severity, black humour and linguistic verve. Beyond specific reference, though, the thistle is a thorny weed that stings, a perpetual mystery in itself. It may be a strong symbol but it is not to be defined. It cannot generate security, let alone complacency, any more than Scotland can.

Just as the title announces the masculinity of the poem's speaker, sexuality is a main theme in its exploration. In 1926, when ideals of purity, virginity, fidelity and sexual rectitude were so much more important than they are in the West in the twenty-first century, it may be difficult to comprehend the shock the poem delivered: 'It's queer the thochts a kittled cull / Can lowse or splairgin' glit annul' (1987: 48, ll. 583–4). The Freudian comprehension of psychological and physical realities combines with MacDiarmid's sensitivity to the conventional repressions of his upbringing, so that degradation and idealism (gargoyle and saint) are seen in human terms as essentially linked, not to be severed from each other. Identity is at the core of the poem's central command:

And let the lesson be – to be yersel's,
Ye needna fash gin it's to be ocht else.
To be yersel's – and to mak' that worth bein'.
Nae harder job tae mortals has been gi'en.

(MacDiarmid 1987: ll. 743–6)

But to be or become yourself, and make yourself valid and worthwhile, identity must be enacted, and when action takes place, it is always in relation to other identities. One's identity is always realised in relation to other people and things. This in turn involves relations of power between different positions, different identities. Apply this to the Gothic image with which we began: the gargoyle and the saint. The question becomes central to Scottish Gothic poetry generally: which possesses more power? What is the relation of power between them? Is this juxtaposition of these two figures itself an empowerment? Any single form of identity – political, national, linguistic, gendered, religious, cultural, familial, tribal – is similarly relational. Identity is a function of position, and position is a function of power. So, to fulfil the injunction, 'To be yersel's – and to mak' that worth bein'', relations of position and power have to change, and for that we have to be convinced in a purpose.

What purpose? Scottish independence perhaps, as in lines 751–70, the section entitled 'My Quarrel with the Rose', or in lines 2371–94, 'My Quarrel with England'; socialist egalitarianism might be another one, as in the section on the General Strike of May 1926, lines 1119–218, 'Ballad of the Crucified Rose'. There are others. Whatever purpose you set yourself upon brings with it an implicit sense of drive towards the fulfilment of a destiny. We might take this drive further through fanatic devotion, another kind of intoxication, going beyond alcohol, risking annihilation, failure or simply exhaustion such as that noted at the poem's opening. This is the tragic ambiguity in the line, '*The thistle rises and forever will!*' (1987: l. 2231; original emphasis). It rises in defiant resistance and perpetual opposition to everything that oppresses it, but it also rises over the graves of generations gone.

MacDiarmid drew much of this dynamic from Nietzsche and his early champion A. R. Orage, editor of *The New Age* to which MacDiarmid contributed regularly in the 1920s. He knew Orage's 1906 book about Nietzschean ideas, and recognised the conflict described there between Apollo and Dionysos, standing respectively for law and liberty, or form and life, or, we might suggest, the Classical and the Gothic: 'Each is necessary to the other, but in active opposition ... Apollo must build continually more beautiful, more enduring forms, which Dionysos, in turn, must continually surmount and transcend' (1906: 34–6).

This delivers the final theme of MacDiarmid's poem: human potential, recognising the aptitude for waste as well as fulfilment, seeing more of the former than the latter, yet both present in the aftermath of the First World War, the Easter Rising in Ireland, the Communist Revolution in Russia, and Scotland in the cradle of a Europe coming to self-consciousness in this historical epoch, in the returning comprehension of the appropriateness of the Gothic idea. Or as Nietzsche puts it: 'Only where there are graves are there resurrections' (qtd in Orage 1906: 10).

From Modern to Contemporary: Gothic Challenge

After the Second World War, the great poets Sorley MacLean (1911–96), Norman MacCaig (1910–96), Iain Crichton Smith (1928–98), George Mackay Brown (1921–96), Robert Garioch (1909–81), Sydney Goodsir Smith (1915–75) and Edwin Morgan (1920–2010) were less given to the wildness of imagination in which MacDiarmid exulted. One might acknowledge Gothic aspects in MacLean's nightmare vision poem, 'Dogs and Wolves' (1939), or Morgan's science-fiction poems, 'The Gourds' (1973) or 'In Sobieski's Shield' (1968), but the predominant urge was towards a re-establishment of the foundations of Scottish nationality from the specific local attachments of their favoured places: Orkney, the Hebrides, Lochinver, Edinburgh or Glasgow. Yet in the poets arising through and after the 1970s, pre-eminently women, led by Liz Lochhead (b. 1947), the Gothic idea in poetry emphatically returns. It was appropriate for a period the American poet Edward Dorn (1929–99) termed 'The Rawhide Era' of Thatcher's Britain and Reagan's America. One might examine Gothic aspects in the poetry of D. M. Black (b. 1941), Frank Kuppner (b. 1951), John Burnside (b. 1955) and Peter McCarey (b. 1956), whose *The Devil in the Driving Mirror* (1994) and *Tantris* (1997) are especially apt for such analysis.

For Lochhead, though, even in apparently domestic locations, the Gothic is present, particularly in *The Grimm Sisters* (1981) and 'Mirror's Song' from *Dreaming Frankenstein and Collected Poems 1962–1984* (1984), in which the Nietszchean idea of destruction leading to regeneration is enacted in feminist terms to shattering effect:

> Smash me looking-glass glass
> coffin, the one
> that keeps your best black self on ice.
> Smash me, she'll smash back –
>
> (Lochhead 2011: 70)

The poem ends by shredding and snapping all the impositions of fashion, advertising and patriarchal oppression, breaking things up 'in the cave she will claw out of – / a woman giving birth to herself' (2011: 70). Like her plays, these poems are didactic in intention, sometimes horrific in what they reveal, often unpredictable in structure and movement, comprehensively human and as wild as the ballads or MacDiarmid at his best. If Lochhead is understood to be not only a major writer but also a valued and vitalising influence on later generations, the significance of this work cannot be underestimated. In this sense, then, Gothic poetry is here to stay. And surely there is need of it.

References

Buchanan, Robert (1884), *The Poetical Works*, London: Chatto & Windus.

Child, Francis James (ed.) (1965), *The English and Scottish Popular Ballads*, 5 vols, New York: Cooper Square Publishers.

Coles, Cecil (2002), 'Fra Giacomo', on *Music from Behind the Lines*, CD, London: Hyperion CDA67293.

Davidson, John (1973), *The Poems*, ed. Andrew Turnbull, 2 vols, Edinburgh: Scottish Academic Press.

Geddes, James Young (1879), *The New Jerusalem and Other Verses*, Dundee: James P. Matthew.

— (1886), *The Spectre Clock of Alyth and Other Selections*, Alyth: Thomas McMurray.

Gifford, Douglas and Alan Riach (eds) (2004), *Scotlands: Poets and the Nation*,

Manchester: Carcanet and Edinburgh: Scottish Poetry Library.

Groom, Nick (2012), *The Gothic: A Very Short Introduction*, Oxford: Oxford University Press.

Kiberd, Declan (2009), *Ulysses and Us: The Art of Everyday Life in Joyce's Masterpiece*, New York: Norton.

Leonard, Tom (1990), *Radical Renfrew: Poetry from the French Revolution to the First World War*, Edinburgh: Polygon.

Lochhead, Liz (2011), *A Choosing: Selected Poems*, Edinburgh: Polygon.

MacCaig, Norman (2005), *The Poems*, ed. Ewen McCaig, Edinburgh: Polygon.

MacDiarmid, Hugh [1926] (1987), *A Drunk Man Looks at the Thistle*, ed. Kenneth Buthlay, Edinburgh: Scottish Academic Press.

McEwen, John Blackwood (1993), 'The Demon Lover', on *Three Border Ballads*, CD, Colchester: Chandos Records.

McGuire, Edward (1995), 'Cruel Mither', on *Saltire Quartet: Under the Hammer*, [music by] Kenneth Dempster, Ronald Center, David Ward and Edward McGuire, CD, Leeds: Mirabilis Records MRCDA961.

Mâle, Émile [1913] (1972), *The Gothic Image: Religious Art in France of the Thirteenth Century*, trans. Dorothy Nussey, New York: Harper & Row Icon Editions.

Manlove, Colin (1994), *Scottish Fantasy Literature: A Critical Survey*, Edinburgh: Canongate.

Morgan, Edwin (1990), 'Dunbar and the Language of Poetry', in *Crossing the Border: Essays on Scottish Literature*, Manchester: Carcanet.

Orage, Alfred Richard (1906), *Friedrich Nietzsche: The Dionysian Spirit of the Age*, London: T. N. Foulis.

Rideout, Bonnie and John Purser (2011), *Harlaw: Scotland 1411 Ancient Music and Stories Commemorating the Legendary Battle*, CD, Alexandria, VA: Tulloch Music.

Smith, G. Gregory (1919), *Scottish Literature: Character and Influence*, London: Macmillan.

Thomson, James [1880] (1993), *The City of Dreadful Night*, intro. Edwin Morgan, Edinburgh: Canongate Classics.

Watson, Roderick (1972), 'The Symbolism of *A Drunk Man Looks at the Thistle*', in Duncan Glen (ed.), *Hugh MacDiarmid: A Critical Survey*, Edinburgh: Scottish Academic Press.

Whyte, Hamish (1983), *Noise and Smoky Breath: An Illustrated Anthology of Glasgow Poems 1900–1983*, Glasgow: Third Eye Centre and Glasgow District Libraries Publication Board.

Chapter 7

Calvinist and Covenanter Gothic
Alison Milbank

We don't need mair doubles, oor haill fuckin culture's littered wi them. If it's no guid versus evil it's kirk elders versus longhairs, heid versus hert, Hieland and Lowland, Glasgow and Edinburgh, drunk men and auld wifies, Protestants and Catholics ... Holy Willies and holy terrors, you name it Scotland's fuckin had it.

(Robertson 2001: 25)

So the protagonist of James Robertson's novel of nation-building and history, *The Fanatic*, declaims to his mirror in 1997, the year of the vote for devolution. Nationalism, then as now, provides a fantasy of a hope of unitary identity for Scotland, which will put to rest the warring dualities of its past. The irony of Robertson's Daniel Carlin raging against duality lies in the words immediately following this extract: 'I am talkin tae you, by the way', to which his mirror responds, 'I ken' (2001: 25). Carlin may dream of an escape from the complexities of history, but the past forms a hole in the back of his mind through which the 'Killing Times' of the Covenanter Wars of the late seventeenth century invade the present-day Edinburgh world of ghost tours, tourists and dossers.

In examining the long engagement of Scottish fiction with the Covenanters and Calvinist duality from Walter Scott to James Robertson, this chapter argues that there is indeed no escape from such narrative patterns, but that, rather than a nightmare from which an enlightened nation seeks to awake, the double has the potential to provide a productive episteme through which to think, allowing its multiple identities to be acknowledged. Moreover, the Covenanter conflict becomes, as it were, a macrocosmic version of the individual's struggle, and even here, the most effective fictional treatments are those that acknowledge and dramatise the multiplicity of perspectives and loyalties at play in society and in the self.

The Reformation is the founding myth upon which the fear so central to Gothic writing is engendered, in which a Protestant nation escapes from the priestly thrall of the Roman Catholic past, which is represented both by what John Galt terms 'fat friars' or the 'prelatic dragon' (1899, vol. 1: 34) – tyrannical clerics who cause the death and imprisonment of the just – and by their monastic powerhouses, such as St Andrews, where the salacious Archbishop feasts with his concubine in Galt's *Ringan Gilhaize* of 1823. This novel narrates the entire Reformation from the destruction of Catholicism after the Parliament of 1560, through the Covenant to the 'Killing Times'. It focuses on the career of Ringan, third-generation Calvinist and a Covenanter fleeing persecution after the restoration of Charles II, and culminates in his killing of Claverhouse at the Battle of Killiecrankie in 1689. The tale is told in the first person, as a family chronicle that becomes something much more like religious testimony:

> I took off my bonnet, and kneeling with the gun in my hand, cried, 'Lord, remember David and all his afflictions;' and having so prayed, I took aim as I knelt, and Claverhouse raising his arm in command, I fired. In the same moment I looked up, and there was a vision in the air as if all the angels of brightness, and the martyrs in their vestments of glory, were assembled on the walls and battlements of Heaven to witness the event, – and I started up and cried, 'I have delivered my native land!' (Galt 1899, vol. 3: 369)

Unlike Galt's other novels in which there is a strong sense of ironic distance, here history is made to validate Gilhaize's estimation of his own action. Although the battle went to the Jacobites, it would be the Presbyterians who would ultimately triumph under the Protestant rule of William III. Calvinist assurance of covenantal grace is therefore allied here with a proto-democratic nationalism. In making his fictional character a national saviour, Galt enacts an uncanny yoking of Calvinist perseverance of the saints with Scottish history in a manner quite natural to the Covenanters themselves. Gilhaize sees himself as a David, the true king, against Saul, who has lost the Lord's favour. The Covenant of Grace wins against the Covenant of Works, and Gilhaize appropriately has recourse to Psalm 115 to ascribe praise for the act to God rather than himself.

Galt wrote in deliberate challenge to Walter Scott's *Old Mortality* of 1816, which sought the very critical distance Galt's text eschewed. 'Old Mortality' travels the country to restore Covenant memorials. His pious motive is the maintenance of national memory, yet such an antiquarian activity safely embalms the past it preserves. Lacking the assurance of Gilhaize, Scott's main protagonist Henry Morton is conflicted and, at different times, is under threat of execution from Covenanters and their opponents. Charity in hiding the wounded saviour of his father's life and family piety lead him to the Covenanters' side, but his allies are suspicious of such natural affections. Morton is unable, in the seventeenth-century clash of political and religious ideologies, to maintain this middle way. He stands out as an anomaly in the period, which has no way to accommodate him or his hope of 'a union of the good, wise and moderate of all parties' (Scott 1886: 242).

Although both Galt and Scott are writing historical fiction, each employs a Gothic rhetoric of historiography to different ends. Galt evokes the violence and repressive cruelty of the Stuart regime as a way of celebrating and enacting a native progressive love of political liberty. Scott makes the double Gothic gesture of resistance to entrapment by the past, yet also nostalgia for what is lost. At the end of *Old Mortality*, Morton returns to his native glen where he encounters the extreme Cameronian Balfour, now living like an ornamental hermit in a grotto across a rushing torrent. With a clasped Bible in one hand and a sword in the other, Balfour literally holds up the future by withholding a paper that would allow the legal (but papistical Episcopalian) heir of the Bellenden estates to inherit. Although struggling with Balfour to gain the document, Morton refuses to fight, and leaps to safety with athletic grace over the chasm. While historical change is presented through ideological struggle, Scott can see no way of this engagement itself producing a synthesis. The future comes, paradoxically, from tradition and the affection-devoted past, represented by Morton. As Burke wrote:

> to be attached to the subdivision, to love the little platoon we belong to in society, is the first principle . . . of public affections. It is the first link in the series by which we proceed towards a love to our country, and to mankind. (Burke 2009: 47)

For Burke, as for Morton, revolution was a truly Gothic spectacle of theatrical violence but, as spectacle, only static. Paradoxically, one must cling, like Morton, to traditional loyalties so that a 'leap' to national renewal can be achieved.

Scott includes among his many forays into Scottish history a pair of novels that chart the progress of the Reformation in even more explicitly Gothicised terms: *The Monastery* and *The Abbot*, both published in 1820. Unlike Galt, he presents a variety of perspectives on Reform: two brothers, Protestant Halbert and Edward, the latter of whom becomes a monk to resolve their love rivalry, and two clerics, Father Eustace, the conscientious subprior of St Mary's Monastery, and his college friend, Henry Warden, a Protestant preacher. The novel is marked by an uneasy mixture of social realism and irony, mixing comedy with Gothic in the form of the ghostly White Lady of Avenel. Conceived by Scott as an astral spirit attached to the Avenel family, the White Lady's role is that of enabler of religious and historical change: she is indeed a principle of historical development. Her main role is to ensure that the Reformist tendencies of Lady Alice Avenel are embraced by her daughter, Mary. To this end the White Lady twice removes Alice's 'black book' from the hands of monks. On one occasion she nearly drowns Father Philip in the River Tweed, chanting 'the black book hath won' as she snatches the volume (Scott 1871: 89). In Scott's *The Lay of the Last Minstrel* (1805), the black book at Melrose had been a collection of spells belonging to the magician Michael Scott. Here the Bible itself is rendered an uncanny object. Scott even has Protestant Halbert taken down by the White Lady to a cave reminiscent of the crystalline hall of Eblis in Beckford's *Vathek*, so that he may rescue the Bible from its protective flames through the power of truth. Perhaps the Episcopalian Scott wished to present the Bible as an ancient and dangerous possession given that it required interpretation. Knox's Reformation and the Covenanters advocated a doctrine of *sola scriptura*, whereby all that was needed for salvation was the Bible. Protestant biblical interpretation in terms of the two covenants of works and grace tended to collapse the historical and theological distinction between Old and New Testaments, so that the killing of the Archbishop of St Andrews by Covenanters such as Balfour was justified by the massacring of Israel's opponents in Joshua or Judges. By making the Bible 'Gothic', Scott removes this easy Protestant sense of appropriation and ahistorical interpretation; his Bible comes historically and even supernaturally mediated.

The Monastery is an artistic failure in its uneasy blend of comedy with supernatural machinery but that same grotesque mixture would lead to the greatest example of Calvinist Gothic: *The Private Memoirs and Confessions of a Justified Sinner* by James Hogg, which was published in 1824 in the wake of this series of Covenanter narratives, and is set in 1703 when the Scottish Parliament's Act of Security marked the success of the Covenanters in preventing English interference with Presbyterianism. Two sons are born to an ill-matched couple, an easy-going Episcopalian laird and his fervent Calvinist wife. Robert, the younger, may well be the illegitimate son of Lady Dalcastle and her preacher friend Wringhim, who spend all night together in prayer. George, the elder and legitimate brother, plays tennis with his upper-class friends while Robert interposes himself as an antagonist on multiple occasions, a 'devilish-looking youth' who haunts George like a shadow (Hogg 2001: 84). Robert, attentive to the sermons of Wringhim, has no doubt that 'his father and brother were cast-aways, reprobates, aliens from the church and the true faith, and cursed in time and eternity' (2001: 73). Wringhim's creed causes him to view everyone in the dualist frame Robertson's Carlin regards with such derogation, for he adheres to the doctrine of double predestination whereby all are under the curse of sin and predestined to damnation while God elects some to salvation, not for any good they do but of his own gratuitous mercy. The elder Wringhim prays for vials of God's wrath to be poured on the reprobate, justifying this with verses from Psalm 109:

> Set thou the wicked over him,
> *And upon his right hand*
> *Give thou his greatest enemy,*
> *Even Satan leave to stand.*
>
> (Hogg 2001: 73)

The younger Wringhim applies this malediction to his own family. The reader learns, however, from Robert's own memoirs, that he had earlier been quite unsure of his own election. Indeed, if in Calvin's system salvation is purely by the imputed righteousness of Christ and not by the individual's good actions or by his faith, how can someone know he is of the Elect? Such dubiety opens a space of self-conscious inner examination whereby the subject potentially splits, divides and doubles itself.

Calvin indeed recognises this, stating that in the act of self-scrutiny, the ego is revealed as 'an empty image' (1960, vol. 1: 37). We are all hypocrites, but only when we look on God will we see our foulness and be struck with 'dread and wonder' – '*horror ille et stupor*' (1960, vol. 1: 38). Such a revelation casts the soul into despair at its own corruption and it is at this point that one should look beyond the self to God's grace. Yet such horror can indeed immobilise, as the word *stupor* suggests, and trap the self in despair. In a schema of double predestination, the self is in a state of constant spiritual warfare to dispel the shadow self of reprobation.

This is the underlying logic of Hogg's novel, in which young Wringhim lives in 'a hopeless and deplorable state of mind' unable to prevent himself sinning until finally, the elder Wringhim announces his 'effectual calling': 'I am assured of your acceptance by the Word and Spirit of him who cannot err, and your sanctification and repentance unto life will follow' (Hogg 2001: 131) .The problem is that Robert has not yet looked fully within himself in either the mirror of the law or Christ's commandments. He has not faced up to his duality at all, believing he has only broken four commandments. For Calvin, as for Luther, understanding of one's total depravity is essential.

At the very point of Robert's ecstatic certainty of election, the mysterious Gil-Martin appears and quickly helps him to break the other six commandments, including committing murder and bearing false witness. The Covenanters 'resisted to blood' against those they thought tyrannical, but Robert kills his own mother and brother. His reward is indeed 'double': it is to have an actual doppelgänger, Gil-Martin or Satan, stand over him as in the psalm and direct all his actions to suicide and damnation. It is he who is the 'man of sin', what Calvin called the 'shadow-shape' of faith, and not because he has a double, since we all have that and are porous to demonic influence, but because Wringhim never discerns his own duality.

The novel is thus an exercise in a religious mode of irony in which the terrors of hell and the usurper Satan form the fearful tropes, and the duality of self the Gothic arena. As in the Catholic mode of the psychomachia play *Everyman*, all registers from tragic to comic have their metaphysical place in this drama of the soul. The final document takes the form of an exhumation of the body of poor Robert Wringhim in the present day, and adverts to a letter by Hogg himself in *Blackwood's Edinburgh Magazine* of the previous year, presented as if written by another person. The editor discounts the truth of the account found on the mummified corpse but with equivocation, making it both impossible to believe from a modern perspective while at the same time saying that its account 'corresponds minutely with traditionary facts' (2001: 232), thus rendering it quite credible. The corpse both appears and is minutely described, yet falls to dust, apart from parts of the thighs, when exposed to the air. The reader is thus left in a position of hesitation, unable to discount or to believe, this awkward position mirroring the awkwardness of the actual magazine article intruding into a fictional narrative and also parodying Calvinist doubt.

There is more, however, to Hogg's novel than a tale of tortured duality. The editor's narrative seeks a way in which the very duality that is such a problem for Robert and the brother he shadows can be rendered productive. The problem with Calvin's model of redemption is that it is wholly extrinsic: he denies any mediation save the legal stamp of imputed righteousness. Before such justification is effected, not even God's creation can bring us to love and know him, for we have lost the vision by which to read it, while God himself is wholly mysterious. Charity itself has no role in our justification, nor can it be an episteme, since that again would be to rely on works rather than unmerited grace. The logic of such a position led to the antinomian controversy of the early eighteenth-century Church of Scotland, where some concluded from this that once justified, law had no power over them, nor sin, whatever they might do (Hogg 2001: 16–18).

The dangers of antinomianism and its remedy are played out in the first part of Hogg's novel. The brothers collide in the romantic environs of Arthur's Seat, a hill above Edinburgh. George, enjoying the blue haze of early morning, marvels at the 'fairy web' caught on his hat, 'composed of little spheres, so minute that no eye could discern any of them; and yet they were shining in lovely millions' (2001: 78). George is careful to preserve this industry of nature, which fills him with charity and delight, whereas to Robert, the dew is merely instrumental in allowing him to track his brother's footsteps. On reaching the summit, George is overcome by the wonder of a rainbow within a cloud and then terrified by what appears to be a gigantic monster gazing at him across the ravine, alternately advancing and retreating. This is, in fact, the natural effect known to Alpine explorers as the Brocken spectre. The monster is an actual shadow caused by the presence of Robert as he summons the courage to attack his brother. Nature thus saves her admirer, as terror causes George to turn round and grapple with his assailant. Robert too has a supernatural mediator, a white lady, who emerges close to St Margaret's Well and angrily upbraids him, but her words are powerless against the control of Gil-Martin. Neither natural nor supernatural mediation is accepted as Wringhim spurns the mutual forgiveness offered by his brother.

Human mediation is also offered by two women in the story, Arabella Logan and Arabella Calvert. Hogg portrays them as a comic version of the Marys of the Gospel who witness the Resurrection. They become the agents of justice, seeking to establish the truth about George Colwan's murder, out of charity and familial affection, since Arabella Logan was foster-mother to the young George. Not only are they doubled in name and role but they are graced with second sight, which Reverend Robert Kirk's *Secret Commonwealth* of 1815 defines as follows:

> They have seen at those meetings a double-man or the shape of a man in two places . . . this copy, Echo, or living picture goes at last to his own herd, or as a sportful Ape, to counterfeit all his actions. (Kirk 2001: 80)

Although Robert Kirk's treatise deals also with fairies, it aims to be a work of science, belonging to that period of the founding of the Royal Society when alchemy rubbed shoulders with natural science. He establishes second sight as an empirically observed phenomenon, as did Boyle and Glanvill in England and Fraser and Kirk in Scotland. Fairies are regarded as 'natural', possessing a mode of creaturehood, which is how Hogg himself presents them in his poem 'The Origin of the Fairies' (1832), in which they are the offspring of seven cursed women and a human knight. Both fairies and the doubles seen through second sight had become in the late seventeenth century a mode of religious apologetics against proto-Enlightenment rationalism. Arabella Logan sums up this empirical approach: 'as you once said before, we have nothing but our senses to depend on, and if you and I believe that we see a person, why we do see him' (Hogg 2001: 110). The two Arabellas share a common charity and ethic and a unified common sense in the manner of Thomas Reid's riposte to Humean scepticism, which in questioning the external world denies the truth of something demanded by our human constitution: common sense. When they get their hands on Robert Wringhim, they beat him up in a form of poetic justice shared by the equally energetic fury of the wives of Windsor against Sir John Falstaff. There is no malice in the Arabellas but a strong humane sympathy of which Hogg has much to say in his *Lay Sermons* (1834). There he argues, against Deists, the importance of the mediation of Christ that engenders all sorts of charity and sympathy and friendship (Hogg 1997). The two women in Hogg's novel represent the reconcili-ation, in comic mode, denied by Robert to George. While they begin as enemies, as Arabella Calvert burgles Mrs Logan's house, they unite in charity, putting their second sight to effective use for the common good.

Hogg often uses the supernatural in his other fiction, as well as the Radcliffean explained supernatural, to promote mediation between extreme dualities. In 'The Brownie of the Black Haggs' (1828), a laird's wife who violently persecutes pious Presbyterian servants is punished by what proves to be a supernatural agent. The Brownie of the title exer-cises a terrible fascination over her, so that she leaves home with him only to be tormented to death. The fairies here seem to be on the side of Scottish Covenanters rather than Catholics so that in 'The Origin of the Fairies' we learn that 'when the psalms and prayers are nightly heard / from the mossy cave or the lonely sward', and 'the mountain burns have a purple stain' with the blood of the persecuted Covenanters, then the fairies are to leave for a better land (Hogg 2007: 168).

In Hogg's novel *The Brownie of Bodsbeck* (1818), the grotesque form of the Brownie is popularly supposed to haunt the land around the Laidlaw home in the Scottish Borders amidst the 'Killing Times' when the Covenanters were persecuted by Claverhouse and his troops. Laidlaw's own daughter Katharine is accused of consorting with this Brownie and of practising witchcraft. The local cleric who sits up with her to prevent further magical activity attempts to rape Katharine, but the Brownie intervenes:

> In a moment the outer-door that entered from the bank was opened, and a being of such unearthly dimensions entered, as you may never wholly define. It was the Brownie of Bodsbeck ... small of stature, and its whole form utterly mis-shaped. Its beard was long and grey, while its look, and every line-ament of its face, were indicative of agony – its locks were thin, dishevelled, and white, and its back hunched up behind its head. . . . Katharine, stretching forth her hands, flew to meet her unearthly guardian; – 'Welcome, my watch-ful and redoubted Brownie,' said she; 'thou art well worthy to be familiar with an empress, rather than an insignificant country maiden.'
> 'Brownie's here, Brownie's there
> Brownie's with thee every where,'
> said the dwarfish spirit, and led her off in triumph. (Hogg 1818, vol. 1: 201–2)

What eventually is revealed is that Katharine is far from being a witch but rather a protector of the oppressed Cameronians, the extreme Covenanting party, some of whose members were hiding in the wild caves and mosses of Ettrick. The Brownie is revealed not to be super-natural, but one John Brown who had been grievously wounded at the Battle of Bothwell Bridge, resulting in a deformed shoulder. The Covenanters are, therefore, the guarantors and enablers of Scottish tra-dition and Christian charity.

Two later Scottish writers show the enduring fascination with the Covenanter heritage: Robert Louis Stevenson and John Buchan. Stevenson grew up hearing a great deal of Covenanter tales from his nurse, and his father had his sixteen-year-old son's account of the Pentland Rising published on the two-hundredth anniversary of the event. In *Catriona* (1893), David Balfour is imprisoned on the Bass Rock for a while, where he hears tales of the time it was a gaol for 'sants and martyrs, the saut of the yerd, of which it wasna' worthy' (Stevenson 1995: 171). Again, the Covenanters are associated with the uncanny, as Peden the prophet rounds on a girl who laughs at his prayers with a prophecy of what proves to be her death, and the guard considers the whole rock '*an unco place*' (1995: 170). He tells a tale of second sight in which the disappointed rival for his father's appointment in charge of the Bass Rock takes the form of a solan bird to peck and kill Tam Dale. He is seen by witnesses at his loom where he dies with the very bullet through his chest that was shot at the solan bird. As in Hogg, the second sight is presented as both natural and supernatural, or rather a mode of mediation between them, just as the Covenanters themselves have become for Stevenson mediators of Scottish identity and tradition, which in the person of David Balfour, who shares the name of Archbishop Sharp's killer, unites with the Highland tradition of Catriona, granddaughter of Rob Roy.

Stevenson's *Strange Case of Dr Jekyll and Mr Hyde* of 1886 is the most celebrated tale of duality in literature but is rarely connected to its Calvinist origins. Jekyll's motive for creating an alternate persona, however, is to deal with his pre-existent duality. He is disturbed by

> the two natures that contended in the field of my consciousness . . . If each, I told myself, could but be housed in separate identities, life would be relieved of all that was unbearable; the unjust might go his way, delivered from the aspirations and remorse of his more upright twin; and the just . . . no longer exposed to disgrace and penitence by the hands of this extraneous evil. (Stevenson 2002: 56)

Jekyll is experiencing the inner warfare of the Calvinist divided self and seeks to resolve it, not through acceptance of Christ's imputed righteousness, but by an avoidance of penitence. Instead of the productive duality of sanctification, in which conscience acts as a second self to produce good deeds, he chooses a murderous unitary division of two autonomous selves. The 'elect' Dr Jekyll does indeed devote himself to charity and increased religious practice, but the 'reprobate' Hyde grows in strength. Eventually, during a moment of self-satisfaction that he is better than other men, Jekyll spontaneously transforms into Hyde and, from that time forward, his neat separation explodes into warring internal enmity, which ends with Jekyll denying Hyde as a part of himself. His attempt to gain holiness by denying the need for repentance mirrors Wringhim's, and the same damnation is realised in self-slaughter. Far from rejecting the Presbyterianism of his upbringing, Stevenson yokes modern ideas of repression and the subconscious with a thoroughly Calvinist anthropology.

Duality is also the theme of John Buchan's novel of the Covenanter period, *Witch Wood* (1927). Like Deacon Brodie of Stevenson's play, the pious Presbyterian elders of Woodilee have a secret double life, in which they take to the ancient wood of Melanudrigill for Satanic rituals. Covenanter extremism is seen to produce a demonic shadow-self and Chasehope, the coven leader, is finally rendered mad by it after engineering the excommunication of the moderate minister, David Semphill, who had sought to unmask him. The Presbytery solemnly deliver David over to Satan *'for the destruction of the flesh that the spirit may be saved'* (Buchan 1993: 285; original emphasis) but it is Chasehope whose body ends up dead after devilish pursuit over the rocks of Garple Linn in an exact parallel of the curse of Wringhim in Hogg's *Confessions*, which rebounds on Robert. Chasehope had relied on 'the imputed righteousness of his Redeemer' and the Calvinist doctrine of the perseverance of the Saints whereby once justified, the Elect cannot fall: 'I aye ettled to repent, for I was sure o' the Mercy Seat' (1993: 276). As in Hogg, it is antinomian ideas that allow such a double life, refusing to acknowledge the participation in the divine through the process of sanctification, which would involve an intrinsic change in the character and actions of the justified Christian, and taking to a bizarre extreme the liberty of the soul.

As in Hogg, it is nature that is the arena of mediation. Woodilee's extreme Calvinists fear the woods as pagan and even demonic, associating them with the 'high places' of Old Testament idolatry. They lack, therefore, any way of responding to nature in religious terms, and are vulnerable to the violence of the pagan past. As the charitable minister, Mr Fordyce, advises: 'we're apt to treat the natural man as altogether corrupt, and put him under over-strict pains and penalties, whereas there's matter in him that might be shaped to the purposes of grace' (1993: 119). Such a Catholic view of grace allows a cooperative element and an intrinsic habit of holiness. It is represented in the novel by the 'fairy' heroine, Katrine Yester, who delights in a glade in the wood that she terms 'Paradise', where David Semphill learns to love nature and humanity. Buchan elides the Garden of humanity's first innocence in Genesis with Dante's Earthly Paradise in *Purgatorio*, where he meets Beatrice and is made ready for heaven. For both Dante and Buchan, such a place represents the possibility of a human life of integration with the natural world. There, Semphill finds love and peace, but the fanaticism of the Presbytery drives him out. Buchan draws upon legends about Robert Kirk in making Semphill a minister popularly believed to have been taken by the fairies, while the novel ends with his assumed exile as a soldier, so that his uncanny presence remains an emblem of a lost opportunity for religious integration.

In contemporary Scottish literature, James Robertson writes as an inheritor of this Calvinist Gothic tradition, not only in the covenanting hero of *The Fanatic* (2000), but in *The Testament of Gideon Mack* (2006), his reworking of Hogg's *Confessions*. In *Gideon Mack*, the hypocritical Wringhim has become a weak, atheistic minister who encounters the devil and ends up as a pile of bones on Ben Alder. Gideon Mack is haunted by his 'double or even triple life' and it may appear that his choice of ordination as an unbeliever embraces that duality. His friend John Moffatt attests that Gideon has not done so: 'Pascal said if your choice is heads God exists, tails he doesn't, you're as well to call heads. . . . If you're right you hit the jackpot. If you're wrong you lose nothing.

But you're calling tails' (Robertson 2006: 105). Mack bets on God's *non-existence*, which is why the Devil tempts him by magicking a standing stone in a forest where Gideon runs regularly. Thus is he taunted by a natural object rendered uncanny by its separation from any metaphysical foundation.

Rescuing a dog from a ravine, Mack falls into the Black Jaws and is rescued by a smartly dressed man in black, who accepts the appellation 'devil': 'that's who I must be. A miserable devil. So now we understand each other' (2006: 282). Like Hogg's Gil-Martin, this Satan returns his prey to society and Mack plays tricks on the pious elders of Monimaskit by organising an unconventional funeral, complete with marijuana, for an atheist. Although this carnivalesque event is presented positively, it fails to help Mack reconnect, since it is too sentimental to address the chasm of despair and hollowness inside him. There is, however, some sense in which the Satanic encounter has the productive duality of another Stevenson tale, 'Markheim' (1885), in which the demonic double pushes the protagonist towards redemption. The Devil helps Gideon to see that secular modernity is locked into dualist modes of thought as deadly as Calvinism. Indeed, it is its mirror-image:

> 'I do like Scotland,' says the Devil. 'I like the miserable weather. I like the miserable people, the fatalism, the negativity, the violence that's always just below the surface. And I like the way you deal with religion. One century you're up to your lugs in it, the next you're trading the whole apparatus in for Sunday superstores.' (Robertson 2006: 283)

As the Devil suggests, he is the outcome if one holds to this murderous dualism. Robertson's novel, however, does attempt some mediation – the stone itself stands for the Pictish memorials of Fife and Angus, which combine pagan and Christian symbols. Robert Kirk's *Secret Commonwealth* had been given by the Devil to Mack's own father, and was there to read. Kirk himself, in the legend of his entrapment in a tree above Aberfoyle by the fairies, is invoked as a mediating presence between Christianity and the fairy world. As an Episcopalian, Kirk would be called in Scottish parlance a 'piskie', suggesting something fairy-like, and, as seventh son, a double-seer. Furthermore, the novel ends with a direct imitation of the dewy Arthur's Seat scene in Hogg, as a journalist looks down to the Black Jaws:

> There's this permanent mist of water droplets in the air like an almost invisible veil or film . . . the light plays on it, there are fragments of rainbow everywhere, and through them you see shapes shifting among the projecting trees and shadows of the cliffs. (Robertson 2006: 386–7)

He then sees a man fall and feels as if it were part of himself going to his death. Yet as so often in Gothic representations of self-division, the embrace of duality is not so much a death as an opening to the possibility of self-knowledge, and a way forward *through*, rather than an entrapment *in*, the Calvinist past. Scottish Calvinist Gothic is very often a protest against a murderous dualism, whether in the psyche or the nation, and embodies the insight that, while we are all, in Jekyll's words, 'multifarious, incongruous and independent denizens' (Stevenson 1999: 76), we are a 'polity' nonetheless.

References

Buchan, John [1927] (1993), *Witch Wood*, ed. James C. G. Greig, Oxford: Oxford University Press.

Burke, Edmund [1790] (2009), *Reflections on the Revolution in France*, ed. L. G. Mitchell, Oxford: Oxford University Press.

Calvin, Jean [1536] (1960), *Institutes of the Christian Religion*, ed. John McNeill, trans. Ford Lewis Battles, 2 vols, Louisville, KY: John Knox Press.

Galt, John [1823] (1899), *Ringan Gilhaize, Or: the Covenanters*, intro. George Douglas, 3 vols, London: Greening.

Hogg, James (1818), *The Brownie of Bodsbeck and Other Tales*, 2 vols, Edinburgh: Blackwood.

— [1834] (1997), *Lay Sermons on Good Principles and Good Breeding*, ed. Gillian Hughes and Douglas S. Mack, *Collected Works of James Hogg*, Edinburgh: Edinburgh University Press, vol. 5.

— [1824] (2001), *Private Memoirs and Confessions of a Justified Sinner*, ed. Adrian Hunter, Peterborough, ON: Broadview.

— [1832] (2007), *A Queer Book*, ed. Peter Garside, Edinburgh: Edinburgh University Press.

Kirk, Robert [1815] (2001), *The Secret Commonwealth*, in Michael Hunter (ed.), *The Occult Laboratory: Magic, Science and Second Sight in Late Seventeenth-Century Scotland*, Woodbridge: Boydell Press.

Robertson, James (2001), *The Fanatic*, London: Fourth Estate.

— (2006), *The Testament of Gideon Mack*, London: Hamish Hamilton.

Scott, Sir Walter [1820] (1871), *The Monastery*, Edinburgh: Adam and Charles Black.

— [1816] (1886), *Old Mortality*, Edinburgh: William Paterson.

Stevenson, Robert Louis [1893] (1995), *Catriona*, intro. George MacDonald Fraser, London: Harvill.

— [1888] (2002), *The Strange Case of Dr Jekyll and Mr Hyde and Other Tales of Terror*, ed. Robert Mighall, Harmondsworth: Penguin.

Chapter 8

Gothic Scott
Fiona Robertson

For record numbers of viewers in the summer of 2015, Scottishness and Gothic were provocatively juxtaposed in the exhibition *Alexander McQueen: Savage Beauty* at the Victoria and Albert Museum in London (first staged at New York's Metropolitan Museum of Art in 2011). McQueen's collections, *Highland Rape* (1995) and *The Widows of Culloden* (2006), while distinct from his more overtly macabre uses of Gothic, dramatise not only a personal family identity but also an interrogative, sometimes confrontational, approach to Scottish history and 'heritage' (with all the ironic inflections of that term): 'I like to challenge history', McQueen stated in 2008 (Wilcox 2015: 51). The grandeur and poignancy of the exhibition's staging of pieces from *The Widows of Culloden*, in particular, invite reflections on where Scottish 'history' most strongly emerges as a construct of narrative and design – as something which possesses creative and intellectual coherence but which explicitly opens itself up to question, to 'challenge'. It is not only McQueen's use of the MacQueen tartan and his circling round the cultural aftermath of the definitive Jacobite defeat at Culloden in 1746 which should bring those interested today in Scottish Gothic back to Sir Walter Scott. Scott's first novel, *Waverley; or, 'Tis Sixty Years Since* (1814), convincingly reanimated the uprising of 1745–6 for generations of readers, but did so in a narrative of complex and pervasive disempowerment. As Edward Waverley experiences before the Battle of Prestonpans, being caught up in a deep cultural past can generate not the reassuring connectedness traditionally expected of historical fiction, but difference and alienation:

It was at that instant, that looking around him, he saw the wild dress and appearance of his Highland associates, heard their whispers in an uncouth and unknown language, looked upon his own dress, so unlike that which he had worn from his infancy, and wished to awake from what seemed at the moment a dream, strange, horrible, and unnatural. (Scott 1993–2012, vol. 1: 236)

(This analysis is already haunted by the words of the Ghost of Hamlet's father for his murder – 'foul, strange, and unnatural' – in *Hamlet* I, v, 28.) The allusions and misalignments in McQueen's two major Scottish collections seem simultaneously more lyrical and more abrasive than anything offered by Scott but, as technical constructions in entirely different media, their works have much in common. This chapter seeks to add to existing scholarship on Scott's place in Scottish Gothic by emphasising the techniques of his approach to what is agreed to be one of the dominant preoccupations of Scottish Gothic, the problem of a broken and self-alienated national history. It highlights the thresholds of his fictions, in different genres, and the significance of his strongly architectural ways of approaching conflicting pasts.

Assessments of Scott's role in a specifically Scottish Gothic have focused on the problems of history, on what Ian Duncan has called 'the uncanny recursion of an ancestral identity alienated from modern life' (2001: 70) and David Punter 'a history that is constantly under the threat of erasure' (2002: 105). Angela Wright has emphasised Gothic's centrality to the 'careful excavation of Scotland's past' (Wright 2007: 76) during a period in which, as Meiko O'Halloran explains, Britain was 'in the midst of the uneasy building of a collective national identity for the four nations' (2015: 277). One of the agreed spurs to Scottish Gothic is the lack of a unitary national culture, a persistent emphasis on division that has been variously theorised and historicised (as the results of linguistic, religious and political differences, the effects of the Union and a history of civil war). Importantly, this construct of Scottish history, with all its implications for Scottish Gothic, is deeply indebted to Scott's fictions, in prose and verse. The 'unknown' Gaelic alluded to in the passage from *Waverley* is a constant presence in this novel, and is central to the conflicts of *Rob Roy* (1818) and 'The Highland Widow' (1827). Displaced and disconnected figures circle all Scott's fictions – the gypsies of *Guy Mannering* (1815), the outlaws of *The Lady of the Lake* (1810), *Rokeby* (1813) and *Ivanhoe* (1820), the Glee Maiden and orphan Conachar in *The Fair Maid of Perth* (1828). Traces of undead, culturally unassimilable pasts are found across Scott's Scottish novels: clan superstitions in *Waverley* and *A Legend of the Wars of Montrose* (1819), borderlands strongholds and crypts in *The Black Dwarf* (1816), the dark plots of Edinburgh in *The Heart of Mid-Lothian* (1818), the priories and island prisons of *The Monastery* and *The Abbot* (both 1820), denying father-figures in *The Pirate* (1822) and *The Surgeon's*

Daughter (1827), and the most viscerally realised of all the various levels of psychological and imagined horror in all Scott's fictions, *The Fair Maid of Perth*.

Scott's fictions, in poetry and prose, were central to developing and popularising an identifiably Scottish Gothic. However, they participated in an early nineteenth-century Gothic field that was complex, and shifting. Commenting on Ann Radcliffe's first novel, *The Castles of Athlin and Dunbayne* (1789) – which he considered, on the whole, not 'worthy of her pen' – Scott wrote in 1824: 'The scene is laid in Scotland, during the dark ages, but without any attempt to trace either the peculiar manners or scenery of the country' (Scott 1869–71, vol. 3: 341). The comment is just a little self-conscious for, by 1824, Scott's works had established aesthetic expectations that Radcliffe's early foray into the Scottish past could no longer meet. Some critics have separated Scott from Gothic, situating his turn to antiquarianism and historical documentation as part of a critical unease about Gothic in the 1810s and 1820s (see, most persuasively, Gamer 2000: 163–200). Others have seen Gothic as a continuing narrative feature of his works, especially in relation to the romance tradition (Duncan 1992; Robertson 1994). Scott's earliest publications were translations from Goethe and German balladry – *An Apology for Tales of Terror* (1799), and ballads contributed to M. G. Lewis's *Tales of Wonder* (1801). Reflecting on his literary debts to Lewis in his 1830 'Essay on Imitations of the Ancient Ballad', he called the publication of *The Monk* (1796) 'an epoch in our literature' (Scott 1833–4, vol. 4: 51). When he was contributing to *Tales of Wonder*, however, Scott felt privately that this style of writing was becoming outdated and that 'we shall overstock the market' (Scott 1932–7, vol. 12: 158).

Although Gothic conventions became a central part of the literary currency of Scott's times, writers were aware of their potential subversiveness. Coleridge's 'Christabel' (1797; 1800) and 'The Mad Monk' (1800), Keats's 'Isabella' (1818) and 'The Eve of St Agnes' (1819) with their consciously, implicative, Gothicised erotics, the imprisoning convents and madhouses of Percy Shelley's 'Epipsychidion' (1821) and 'Julian and Maddalo' (1818–19), De Quincey's psychological architecture of imprisonment and abyss, all redirected Gothic conventions, as did experimental works in prose fiction, notably those by Charles Robert Maturin, Mary Shelley and James Hogg. In his critical prose as well as in his poems and novels, Scott helped shape understandings of the modalities of Gothic. Both Maturin and Mary Shelley wrote to Scott for advice on subsequent works after he praised their work in prominent reviews (for the *Quarterly Review* in 1810 and for *Blackwood's*

Edinburgh Magazine in 1818). With Maturin Scott maintained a twelve-year correspondence, and he was closely involved in the composition of Maturin's 1816 play *Bertram*. Scott's works and Hogg's touched and reacted at many points during a long friendship, from their different experiments in Borders balladry to divergent political fictions (the contrast between *The Brownie of Bodsbeck* (1818), and *The Tale of Old Mortality* (1816), for example), which we can see retrospectively as contesting the boundaries of Scottish Gothic's openness to folk tradition and the supernatural. In his 'Prefatory Memoirs' of Walpole, Reeve and Radcliffe in *Ballantyne's Novelist's Library* (1821–4), Scott commented acutely on individual fictions and on differentiated varieties of the narratology of fear. Emphasising Walpole's originality as one 'who led the way in this new species of literary composition', he contrasted Walpole's and Radcliffe's approaches to the supernatural (a contrast commonly now expressed as the 'explained' versus the 'unexplained' supernatural) (Scott 1869–71, vol. 3: 317, 368). He protested 'against fettering the realm of shadows by the opinions entertained of it in the world of realities' in his essay on Reeve (1869–71, vol. 3: 329). Noteworthy in the genealogy of Scottish Gothic are comments in his essay on Smollett. The episode in the robbers' hut in *The Adventures of Ferdinand Count Fathom* (1753) is 'a tale of natural terror which rises into the sublime' while, in weighing up the merits of Fielding and Smollett, Scott argues that 'the northern novelist soars far above [Fielding] in his powers of exciting terror' (1869–71, vol. 3: 137–8).

As these critical observations suggest, Scott was a pivotal figure in the development of a Gothic mode in Scottish writing. Sophisticated in his understanding of the techniques as well as the more obvious motifs of previous fictions, Scott was able to complicate and extend the repertoire, making new forms of it available to later writers and readers in ways that often proved too textually overburdened to assimilate. One of the key ways in which he did this was in his development of the formal and imaginative thresholds so important in the works of Walpole and Radcliffe, in particular. Throughout Gothic tales, readers hesitate between the natural and supernatural, history and magic. These fictions thrive on generic instability, existing in-between, rather than alongside, other literary forms, and frequently highlight, to the point of fetishisation, architectural analogues for this instability. Chapter 2 of Ann Radcliffe's *The Romance of the Forest* (1791) opens with an especially telling series of entrance-portals. An epigraph quotes lines about 'the suspended soul' from Walpole's play *The Mysterious Mother* (1768; 1791); La Motte approaches 'the Gothic remains of an abbey', ruinous, but with an entire Gothic gate, from which he enters a chapel, then the nave of a great church, before coming to a door, through which is another door. This enshrinement of entrances occupies the first five long paragraphs of the chapter (Radcliffe 1986: 15–16). In Scott's work, proliferating frame narratives and other forms of authorial paratext – appendices, explanatory notes, Dedicatory Epistles, antiquarian editors who flit from one work to the next – keep readers in-between fictitious and historical worlds, in that state of uncertainty Freud sought to define as the uncanny and which Keats put at the centre of all creativity as an ability to remain in uncertainties, or negative capability. In the hide-and-seek of the anonymous publication of his novels, Scott created a mystery beyond the plots and secrets of individual novels, a meta-mystery of authorship.

From the start of his career, too, Gothic architectural structures were central to the appeal of Scott's fictions. Later illustrations (including the series of engravings after J. M. W. Turner that were commissioned for Scott's 1833–4 *Poetical Works*) testified to the importance of the buildings Scott helped make iconic, including Melrose, Roslin, Norham and Tantallon. For all its rapid narrative pace, Scott's first long narrative poem, *The Lay of the Last Minstrel* (1805), subordinates both action and inset balladry to atmospheric architecture. At its narrative heart is the buried book of the magician, Michael Scott. The 'dark Abbaye' (1833–4, vol. 6: Canto I, xxxi) and 'the dark words of gramarye' (1833–4, vol. 6: Canto III, xiv) link the spells of architectural setting and sorcery, while the opening-up of the Wizard's tomb in Canto II potently combines the quest for a buried knowledge with sacrilege-narrative. Although it ends with a sentimental image of social and aesthetic reintegration, the *Lay* as a whole exposes the fragility of the ways in which stories survive. In *Marmion; A Tale of Flodden Field* (1808), Scott pushes further the technical rifts between past and present and uses what he calls in the introduction to Canto I, his 'Gothic harp' to evoke both the springs of his own imagination in Scottish history and scenery and the lasting national scars of Flodden. The six cantos are introduced by epistles to friends on questions of national decay and revival, forcibly interrupting the reader's desire to enter a consistently fashioned historical realm; and the tale, too, moves through dark and oppressive structures (the castles of Norham and Tantallon; Lindisfarne with its 'secret aisle'). Throughout *Marmion*, Scott explores Gothic conventions as a contract between writer and reader, implicitly inviting reflection upon the aesthetic vocabulary through which the past is imagined. This is clearest in the trial and death of Constance de Beverley in Canto II, in passages involving the mysterious Palmer, who tells of 'the strange pageantry of Hell, / That broke our secret speech' (1833–4, vol. 7: Canto VI, viii), and in the Lady Clare's appearance on the battlements of Tantallon (1833–4, vol. 7: Canto VI, iii).

Scott creates another 'double' romance narrative in *The Bridal of Triermain* (1813), but his poems after *Marmion* experiment with simpler poetic and narrative forms, and move away from the enclosing structures of ancient architecture. *The Lady of the Lake* swerves from the architectural preoccupations of its predecessors and, at the same time, from the elaborate architecture of paratexts, presenting instead Scott's most enticing 'natural' abode, Ellen's Isle, and displacing ruins to the psychological states of Brian the Hermit and Blanche of Devan. *Rokeby* is also a more psychologically focused work, though it culminates in the destruction of an ancient house while celebrating the demesne of Scott's friend, J. B. S. Morritt of Rokeby Hall, Teesdale. In *The Lord of the Isles* (1815), the opening three stanzas of Canto IV, which (unlike most of the poem) are Spenserian stanzas, formalising the element of romance, evoke 'the northern realms of ancient Caledon' as sublime and lonely spaces of 'savage grandeur', none more so than 'that dread shore / That sees grim Coolin rise, and hears Coriskin roar' (Scott 1833–4, vol. 10: 109–10). Over the course of Scott's long narrative poems, architectural Gothic gives way to haunted, but also possibly just empty, scenery; the focus moves from borderlands to Highlands; the narrative form becomes more direct.

Although this does not fully show itself until the first series of *Tales of My Landlord* (1816, encompassing *The Tale of Old Mortality* and *The Black Dwarf*), Scott's turn to prose fiction from 1814 is a return to the narrative layers and complications of the *Lay* and *Marmion*. My analysis considers two novels which show very different aspects of his aesthetic vocabulary of Gothic (*The Tale of Old Mortality* and *The Bride of Lammermoor*, 1819), then moves to *Redgauntlet* (1824) and a non-Scottish novel, *Woodstock* (1826), which Scott's publisher, James Ballantyne, feared would be castigated as an imitation of Radcliffe. It concludes with a discussion of Scott's most important non-fictional contribution to the stock of Scottish Gothic, *Letters on Demonology and Witchcraft* (1830), a volume contributed to John Murray's series of works of popular instruction, 'Murray's Family Library' (eventually 80 vols, 1829–47). First, however, it continues the sense of dialogue with the poems displayed in Scott's third novel, *The Antiquary* (1816).

In chapter 25 of *The Antiquary*, in the moonlit ruins of St Ruth's Priory, the German adept Dousterswivel, who has been digging for treasure in an ancient grave, witnesses a secret burial performed in accordance with the rites of the Roman Catholic Church, at that time illegal in Scotland. Scott reports:

> Dousterswivel, the place, the hour, and the surprise considered, still remained uncertain, whether what he saw was substantial, or an unearthly representation of the rites, to which, in former times, these walls were familiar, but which are now rarely practised in Protestant countries, and almost never in Scotland. (Scott 1993–2012, vol. 3: 208)

Set in north-east Scotland in 1794, *The Antiquary* is, historically and geographically, close to the time of its publication, and also full of intertextualities with the first great decade of Gothic fiction – the decade, too, of Scott's first forays as a writer. As well as the actual ruins and claustrophobic aristocratic mansions of *The Antiquary*, and the collected treasures jumbled in Oldbuck's *sanctum sanctorum*, reached via 'a labyrinth of inconvenient and dark passages' (1993–2012, vol. 3: 20), Scott explores the ruins of the mind, notably those of the decayed servant, Elspeth Meiklebackit, likened by Edie Ochiltree to 'some of the ancient ruined strengths and castles that ane sees amang the hills', some parts decayed but others 'the stronger, and the grander, because they are rising just like to fragments amang the ruins o' the rest' (1993–2012, vol. 3: 228). Ancient architecture here is a way of articulating psychological ruin, and also a ruined cultural heritage.

Among Scott's fictions, *The Tale of Old Mortality* (1816) has always been celebrated as an especially brilliant and fully realised work of historical imagination, embodying Scott's profound knowledge of seventeenth-century Scottish history. Most of the novel is set in the summer of 1679 after the assassination of Archbishop Sharp by a group of extreme Covenanters; it ends in 1689, after the so-called Glorious Revolution. The threat of insurgency linked 1679 to Scott's present: in 1815, radicals had gathered on the battlefield of Loudoun-hill to celebrate the Covenanters' victory there in 1679 and also to celebrate Napoleon's escape from exile and imprisonment in Elba (as Douglas Mack notes (Scott 1993–2012, vol. 4b: 433–4)). In the frame narrative, a memorial of memorialisation, Old Mortality toils to preserve Covenanters' gravestones, and the novel that develops from this questioning beginning is open to several different ways of engaging with the past, emotionally and nationally. Unlike some of the other fictions Scott was composing at this time (notably its companion-tale, *The Black Dwarf*), *The Tale of Old Mortality* is free of standard Gothic motifs and situations. Instead, Scott's historical writing confronts and reconfigures the psychological language of fear and loss, making it implicitly national and cultural as well as personal. The language of loss and alienation in *The Tale of Old Mortality* emerges, cumulatively, from the young hero's experiences, rather than being a form of shorthand for them from the outset. Henry Morton can emerge from his dependency on a miserly uncle only by accepting the control of his father's symbolic substitute, Balfour of Burley, who demands an obedience approaching subjection. Unlike heroes like Edward Waverley before him and Wilfred of Ivanhoe after him, Morton is active, resourceful, a leader and strategist in the Covenanting army and the decisive rescuer of others from Burley's clutches. After the Battle of Bothwell Bridge, however, Morton's psychological language changes, a shift first marked when he finds himself at the mercy of extremists in the lonely house of Drumshinnel. Morton has one nightmare prior to his involvement in the rebellion, described as a 'blended vision of horror' in which his beloved, Edith Bellenden, seems to be crying out to him for help which, in a nightmare paralysis familiar in Gothic, he is unable to give (1993–2012, vol. 4b: 44). After Bothwell Bridge, he has daylight nightmares. Stripped of the new sense of identity he has won as a leader in the Covenanting army, at Drumshinnel Morton awaits execution after the strike of midnight in a far more disordered frame of mind than when condemned to death many chapters before, at Tillietudlem, on the orders of the royalist Claverhouse. This time, his rational equanimity dissolves into violent hallucination:

> His destined executioners, as he gazed around on them, seemed to alter their forms and features, like the spectres in a feverish dream; their figures became larger, and their faces more distorted; and, as an excited imagination predominated over the realities which his eyes received, he seemed surrounded rather by a band of demons than of human beings; the walls seemed to drip with blood, and the light tick of the clock thrilled on his ear with such loud, painful distinctness, as if each sound were the prick of a bodkin inflicted on the naked nerve. (Scott 1993–2012, vol. 4b: 264)

In this single sentence, authorial judgement, firmly allocating Morton's impressions to 'an excited imagination', vies with a strange combination of physical immediacy and the substitution of one type of sensory experience for another. When he is rescued by the timely arrival of Claverhouse and his troops, and taken prisoner for a second time, Morton accepts his new fate as if it were a form of seduction. From this point, he becomes silent and complicit, his customary role as questioner of rights and authorities ceded to others, notably during the trial and torture of the young zealot, Ephraim Macbriar. Symbolically, what ought to have been Morton's death is displaced onto Macbriar; while Habakkuk Meiklewrath, formerly presented as occupying the lunatic fringe of the novel's Covenanters ('the maniac' (1993–2012, vol. 4b: 260)), becomes their inspired voice after Claverhouse has rescued Morton. The confrontation between Morton and Burley at the Black Linn of Linklater, a fierce fall of 'tortured waters', is a concentratedly symbolic conclusion to their struggle throughout the novel, ending with an emancipation, but also with a deferred and displaced resolution. (An unnamed Dutch soldier grapples to the death with Burley in the Clyde.) In the scenes that follow Morton's return from exile, compensatory fantasy has to work hard to undo the tragic implications of his engagement with history. Scott signals the fictionality of this resolution by creating a novel-reading milliner's miss, Martha Buskbody, to comment on the ending and to request more details of the wedding. Though they seem to occupy different worlds, both Old Mortality and Martha Buskbody are devoted to an image of what they want to find in the past. The inability of a sentimental modern reader to attend to the historical import of the tale is the modern equivalent of the decline of impassioned remembrance into the committed, but pragmatic, culture of preservation.

In contrast to the resisted but cumulatively internalised Gothic of *The Tale of Old Mortality*, *The Bride of Lammermoor* is Scott's most porous Gothic story, and also the one which most influenced subsequent experiments in Gothic. It is a short step to Emily Brontë's *Wuthering Heights* (1847) from the scene in which Edgar Ravenswood, the night before his death in the quicksand of the Kelpie's Flow, instructs his ancient retainer that he wishes to spend the night in 'The room in which SHE slept' (Scott 1993–2012, vol. 7a: 266), and from the Kelpie's Flow to the Shivering Sand of Wilkie Collins's *The Moonstone* (1868). Like all Scott's fictions, *The Bride* tells a larger national and cultural story, in this case tracing the decline of an older aristocratic order at the hands of a manipulative professional class drawing power from new political affiliations in the royal court in London. Scotland's rival claims are reduced to the mangy Jacobitism of Craigengelt and the second-hand sorceries of the three local witches, stiflingly cross-referenced to William Shakespeare's *Macbeth* (1606). The self-conscious belatedness of these elements hangs heavily on the novel.

One episode in *The Bride* brings into focus the issues of narrative and architecture that are key to Scott's ways of suggesting the divisions and discontinuities of the past. In chapter 5, Lucy Ashton and her father are imperilled by the charge of a wild bull, which is killed by a shot from her father's sworn enemy. Lucy faints, and is gathered up by Ravenswood:

> He raised Lucy from the ground in his arms, and conveying her through the glades of the forest by paths with which he seemed well acquainted, stopped not until he laid her in safety by the side of a plentiful and pellucid fountain, which had been once covered in, screened and decorated with architectural ornaments of a Gothic character. But now the vault which had covered it being broken down and riven, and the Gothic front ruined and demolished, the stream burst forth from the recess of the earth in open day, and winded its

way among the broken sculpture and moss-grown stones which lay in confusion around its source. (Scott 1993–2012, vol. 7a: 38–9)

At this point, two long paragraphs tell the story of an earlier Lord of Ravenswood who is brought to doubt, test and destroy a beautiful but mysterious lover, and in penance builds the now-broken ornamented vault. The narrator offers other explanations for the legend: that the aristocratic Ravenswood had murdered his lower-born lover, and that the fountain was a site of pre-Christian myth. This aside from an already-charged erotic narrative takes place within the period of Lucy's unconsciousness, both replicating the structure of 'protection' around her and occupying an imagined space in her desires. The narrative resumes:

> It was in this ominous spot that Lucy Ashton first drew breath after her long and almost deadly swoon. Beautiful and pale as the fabulous Naiad in the last agony of separation from her lover, she was seated so as to rest with her back against a part of the ruined wall, while her mantle, dripping with the water that her protector had used profusely to recal her senses, clung to her slender and beautifully proportioned form. (Scott 1993–2012, vol. 7a: 40)

In this unsettlingly arranged position, Lucy's form seems unconsciously complicit in ruin, propped against the remnants of a broken protective, or guarding, structure. At the same time, she has almost vampirically drawn strength. The scene plays to some well-worn conventions of women in peril, but also suggests male sexuality, constrained in vain, and a broader creative danger that affects both writer and reader. Scott's paratextual setting for *The Bride of Lammermoor* is especially complex, emphasising story within story, hearsay and aesthetic accretion. After Lucy's death, the narrator reveals that 'those who are read in the private family history of Scotland' will see through his 'disguise' 'AN OWER TRUE TALE' (1993–2012, vol. 7a: 262), later elaborated on in the 'Magnum Opus' introduction to the *Bride* as the story of Janet Dalrymple. The scene of the natural spring set amid an architectural ruin is suggestive far beyond its erotic context.

The uncanniness of historical fiction as imagined by Scott emerges strongly in *Redgauntlet*, in which Jacobitism comes back from the dead in a fictitious rebellion of 1765. It is, by this historical moment, an old story, reanimated by the zealous Jacobite Hugh Redgauntlet and aggressively imposed on his unknowing grandson, Darsie Latimer, who spends the novel in a search for his true identity and who must confront that identity's embroilment in an undead national past. Scott creates a double narrative, following the adventures of the anchorless Darsie and his close friend Alan Fairford, by contrast anchored all too firmly in the legal profession and in the mazes of the legal culture of Edinburgh. The obsessive litigant, Peter Peebles, whose ancient case Alan must try to resolve, echoes the accreted complexities of the Jacobite cause, creating a complex fragmentation of Scottish history and its rights and wrongs. The present, as Scott suggests, is haunted not so much by the past as by determined and partial obsessions with the past – an uncanny of the mind and of a culture continually seeking to claim its modernity and (like Darsie and Alan) its rights of self-determination.

In *Woodstock*, architectural form is more explicitly tied to narrative approach than anywhere else in Scott's fictions. The hunting lodge at Woodstock formalises the approach to a hidden past; it is character-ised by sliding panels, secret passageways, portraits that conceal secret entrances. The narrative, like the house and its setting, offers labyrin-thine approaches which are simultaneously deferrals, and where the central point at issue is the preservation of the royal line (in the disguised figure of Charles II). *Woodstock* draws on Gothic staples and uses points of imaginative reference from Scott's earlier fictions (most pertinently to the present discussion, an echo of the Mermaiden's Well from *The Bride of Lammermoor* in Rosamund's spring, a 'fountain of old memory' now 'gushing out amid disjointed stones, and bubbling through fragments of ancient sculpture' (1993–2012, vol. 19: 197)). The source of the spring is legitimate power; its course now dispersed by the broken relics of an older culture. The labyrinthine structuring principle reflects not only on narrative approaches and frustrations, but also on the nature of his-torical processes of progression and retardation, continuity and fracture; and on human psychology, which is appropriate in a novel that makes extended and self-conscious use of the fake supernatural.

Scott was interested in witchcraft and local legend throughout his writing life, as many passages in the poems and novels, as well as histori-cal notes appended to them, demonstrate. He periodically considered writing histories of witchcraft, and, according to Archibald Constable, proposed a novel called *The Witch* (*Redgauntlet* ensued instead (Scott 1993–2012, vol. 17: 381)). Although his *Letters on Demonology and Witchcraft* ranges widely, both historically and geographically – taking in the demonology of ancient European tribes, South and North American traditions, and tracing historical change from Old Testament times to the seventeenth century – it is especially authoritative on Scottish lore and shows first-hand knowledge of the historical legal records in Scotland. Letters VIII (on England and New England) and IX (on Scotland), in particular, develop from a legal conscience about the nature of evidence in witchcraft trials. As in *The Heart of Mid-Lothian*, 'The Two Drovers' (1827) and *Anne of Geierstein* (1829), Scott's legal training, as well as his interest in storytelling, quickens his writing about persecution and false witness, bringing added focus to the heavy investment of Gothic in disbelieved voices and rigid social systems of marginalisation and exclusion. At the end of Letter VIII he writes that 'The system of witchcraft, as believed in Scotland ... is different in some respects from that of England, and subsisted to a later period, and was prosecuted with much more severity' (Scott 1869–71, vol. 29: 272). *Letters on Demonology and Witchcraft* has a reassuring narrative structure, in which the most troubling questions about the psychology of superstition and the borderlines between supernatural report and mental disturbance are raised in Letter I, lightened by elf- and fairy-lore (Letter IV and part of Letter VI), and ending in Letter X with remarks on astrology and ghosts. The perspective is, throughout, rational, while always attentive to historical and cultural difference. But this moderating structure exists to present individual stories told powerfully and with evident horror at the unstoppability of collective credence and legal process.

As Ian Duncan has suggested, Scott became in himself a Gothic figure in Scottish writing, an 'Eidolon', representative or shadow, of the Author found in the subterranean chambers of Edinburgh publishing, 'the core of a capitalist mode of literary production' which is also 'an underworld of occult procreative powers' (Duncan 2007: xiii). In Sarah Green's fiction *Scotch Novel Reading; or, Modern Quackery: A Novel Really Founded on Facts* (1824), Britain was possessed by a 'Caledonian Mania' in which no Scottish writer was likely to emerge as distinguishable from 'Scott' (himself, at that stage, still anonymous). In subsequent Scottish writing, and in the wider cultural contexts represented at the start of this chapter by Alexander McQueen, Scott's works have sometimes come to seem authoritatively historical – as, in themselves, a form of the historical uncanny, in Sigmund Freud's terms 'something repressed which *recurs*' (1955: 241). They preoccupy the varieties of nineteenth-century Scottish Gothic produced by J. G. Lockhart, Hogg, Margaret Oliphant and Stevenson; and, among contemporary Scottish writers, the historical fiction of James Robertson (whose PhD thesis was on Scott) and the crime fiction of Ian Rankin. As fast as Scott's prolific fictions weave the fabric of imaginable pasts, however, 'repeatedly, he constructs the past as Gothic trauma that rises and resurfaces through his works' – as Catherine Spooner has written not of Scott, but of McQueen (Wilcox 2015: 154). Like McQueen, Scott draws on different aspects of existing Gothic experimentation, and with different inflections and ironies, in the various styles and phases of his work. His writing invites us to reflect on the cultural potency, and instability, of echoes and allusions of the past, and in the past. Central to the articulation and dissemination of a distinctively Scottish Gothic, Scott's fictions, in all their genres, keep readers in states of uncertainty, hesitating between 'historical' and 'imagined' worlds and between contingencies and interpretative contexts in the desired consumption of 'Scottishness'.

References

Duncan, Ian (1992), *Modern Romance and Transformations of the Novel: The Gothic, Scott, Dickens*, Cambridge: Cambridge University Press.

— (2001), 'Walter Scott, James Hogg and Scottish Gothic', in David Punter (ed.), *A Companion to the Gothic*, Oxford: Blackwell, pp. 70–80.

— (2007), *Scott's Shadow: The Novel in Romantic Edinburgh*, Princeton: Princeton University Press.

Freud, Sigmund [1919] (1955), 'The "Uncanny"', in *The Standard Edition of the Complete Psychoanalytic Works of Sigmund Freud*, ed. and trans. James Strachey, London: Hogarth Press, vol. 17, pp. 219–52.

Gamer, Michael (2000), *Romanticism and the Gothic: Genre, Reception, and Canon Formation*, Cambridge: Cambridge University Press.

O'Halloran, Meiko (2015), 'Gothic Borders: Scotland, Ireland and Wales', in Angela Wright and Dale Townshend (eds), *Romantic Gothic: An Edinburgh Companion*, Edinburgh: Edinburgh University Press, pp. 277–98.

Punter, David (2002), 'Scottish and Irish Gothic', in Jerrold E. Hogle (ed.), *The Cambridge Companion to Gothic Fiction*, Cambridge: Cambridge University Press, pp. 105–23.

Radcliffe, Ann [1791] (1986), *The Romance of the Forest*, ed. Chloe Chard, Oxford: Oxford University Press.

Robertson, Fiona (1994), *Legitimate Histories: Scott, Gothic, and the Authorities of Fiction*, Oxford: Clarendon Press.

Scott, Walter (1833–4), *The Poetical Works of Sir Walter Scott, Bart.*, ed. J. G. Lockhart, 12 vols, Edinburgh: Robert Cadell.

— (1869–71), *The Miscellaneous Works of Sir Walter Scott, Bart.*, 30 vols, Edinburgh: A. and C. Black.

— (1932–7), *The Letters of Sir Walter Scott*, ed. H. J. C. Grierson et al., 12 vols, London: Constable.

— (1993–2012), *The Edinburgh Edition of the Waverley Novels*, gen. ed. David Hewitt, 30 vols, Edinburgh: Edinburgh University Press.

Wilcox, Claire (ed.) (2015), *Alexander McQueen: Savage Beauty*, London: V&A Publishing.

Wright, Angela (2007), 'Scottish Gothic', in Emma McEvoy and Catherine Spooner (eds), *The Routledge Companion to the Gothic*, London and New York: Routledge, pp. 73–83.

Chapter 9

Gothic Hogg
Scott Brewster

As Angela Wright has noted, in Scottish Gothic literature, graves and manuscripts are 'warmly contested sites of authenticity and authority' (2007: 76). The burial ground excavated at the end of James Hogg's *The Private Memoirs and Confessions of a Justified Sinner* (1824) is just such a contested memorial: the grave that harbours an uncanny tale of religious fundamentalism, or diabolical possession, does not readily give up its secrets. Robert Wringhim's corpse preserves a manuscript whose provenance, and legacy, cannot be determined. The exhumed body releases its enigmatic text into circulation, and this final resting place becomes an opening to future readings. In his antiquarian or archaeological – and thus typically Gothic – effort to authenticate Wringhim's memoir, the Editor's narrative draws on 'history, justiciary records, and tradition' (Hogg 2002c: 64) to frame the 'singular' document whose 'drift' (2002c: 174) he cannot comprehend. Yet the 'sequel' to these narratives (it is actually a beginning) returns us to Hogg's home territory of the Borders. The field trip to Wringhim's grave is prompted by a letter published in *Blackwood's* from 'James Hogg', concerning the excavation of the corpse of a suicide discovered in a miraculous state of preservation. Keen to examine these 'wonderful remains personally', the Editor tracks down Hogg at the ewe fair in Thirlestane, but the taciturn Shepherd has no interest in exhuming this 'Scots mummy': 'I hair mair ado than I can manage the day, foreby ganging to houk up hunder-year-auld bones' (2002c: 170). Hogg refuses the role of Wordsworthian 'rustic' (Pope 1992: 223), eager to tell the story of the bones to a stranger (which is, precisely, ironically, what the 'real' James Hogg is doing). The Shepherd's letter has initially triggered the Editor's curiosity, but it warns against further disturbance of the grave, which will cause the flesh to 'fall to dust' (Hogg 2002c: 169). His resistance to the enterprise may suggest guilt at exposing old bones to the modern gaze, but equally the desire to see the found text trouble and perplex the enlightened reader. This ambivalent encounter between urban modernity and rural tradition, and the failure to establish an agreed account of the Scottish past and present, exemplify Hogg's brand of Gothic.

Hogg's Gothic emerges from the vernacular storytelling tradition of Lowland Scotland, a form acknowledged as central to the modern nation. As James Kelly has shown, Burns's deployment of superstition and dialect speech shaped a 'folk Gothic' that became popular in Scotland in the 1820s, and had 'a profound effect on subsequent Scottish fiction dealing with the uncanny'. The supernatural trappings of this fiction 'could be presented as part of a wider anthropological project of understanding the survival of primitive cultural remains in the present day' (Kelly 2014: 46). Hogg grants renewed life to the oral culture of Ettrick Forest, a tradition he perceived as 'under assault in the contemporary drive to modernity' (Bold and Gilbert 2012: 14), but this revivifying of an earlier age is far from nostalgic. As Scotland continued to negotiate its place in the Union, the importance of oral culture for Hogg must be read against the gradual bifurcation of orality 'into an acclaimed ideal and a disparaged social condition' (Fielding 1996: 22). Hogg was sceptical of the Whig master-narrative of historical development established by Adam Smith, which fostered assumptions that 'the law-abiding and commerce-based modern Lowland Scotland of the Enlightenment era was well on its way to becoming a fully evolved society – one in which civilized values and high culture could be expected to thrive' (Mack 2012: 64). Hogg's interweaving of oral and literary forms can be seen as resisting the discourse of improvement and cultural Anglicisation, by counterposing the secular rationalism of Edinburgh with the popular folk culture of the Borders. Early Gothic stages this confrontation between enlightenment and superstition, but the primitive and the periphery are typically tamed. In contrast, through what Antony Hasler has termed his 'cloven fiction', Hogg presents this clash as an unfinished process (Hogg 2002b: xxiv).

Alongside Hoffmann, Poe, Stevenson and Wilde, Hogg's *Confessions* occupies a prominent place in the Gothic tradition of doubling, possession and live burial. (The most striking recent expression of this tradition in Scottish Gothic – at a time when Scotland's place within the Union was far from settled – is James Robertson's *The Testament of Gideon Mack* (2006): its narrative structure and preoccupations self-consciously mirror those of Hogg.) As Peter Garside observes, *Confessions* tends to be regarded as exceptional, a view that obscures its links with Hogg's 'far less regarded work' (2002: xii). Hogg displays a consistent fascination with unquiet graves, destructive passions, doubtful appearances and unresolved pasts, concerns imbricated with the political and religious conflicts that shaped Scottish history since the mid-seventeenth century. Affinities with *Confessions* can be traced across his short fiction, and perhaps the most striking counterpart in terms of diabolical ambivalence and disturbed ground is 'The Brownie of the Black Haggs' (1828). Set in the 1680s when Covenanters were harried and the law was entirely on the side of the 'true loyal subject' (Hogg 2002a: 243), the story is both supernatural tale and political allegory. The deadly embrace between Lady Sprot of Wheelhope and the Brownie Merodach resembles the affinity between Wringhim and Gil-Martin. The 'delirium of hatred and vengeance' (2002a: 246) that Merodach provokes in Lady Sprot, a vehement and unrelenting Anti-Covenanter, mirrors the persecutory climate of the age. Significantly, in the end, her mangled and tormented body is found by fugitive Covenanters, those she had condemned and who, in turn, had cursed her. In this final instance of strange affinity, she is interred 'like a dog' with 'three huge stones upon her grave' (2002a: 254), the same rough burial reserved for the very men she had opposed in life. Bound to each other by excessive passion, these antagonists may share common ground in death, but the grave remains a site of contention rather than reconciliation.

Hogg's historical narratives *The Brownie of Bodsbeck* (1818), *The Three Perils of Man* (1822) and *The Three Perils of Woman* (1823) exploit a range of Gothic scenarios and effects and, crucially, present Scottish history as haunted by the 'uncanny recursion' of old and long-familiar elements (Duncan 2012: 123). They contest, in varying ways, Walter Scott's version of the Scottish national tale, as epitomised in novels such as *Waverley* (1814) and *Old Mortality* (1816). To a major extent, Scott's fiction settles historical accounts and brings a rational, modern sensibility to bear on the fanaticism and 'primitive modes of belief' of a previous age (Duncan 2007: 29). Katie Trumpener has argued that the *Waverley* novels 'represent the triumph of the single-focus narrative history', with the trauma and jaggedness of historical experience relegated to footnotes and antiquarian interest (Trumpener 1993: 710). Hogg's Gothic recaptures this 'jaggedness', unleashing the uncanniness contained by Scott's fiction.

The Brownie of Bodsbeck challenges Scott's portrayal of Covenanters in *Old Mortality*, in which graves play a significant role. Old Mortality's dedication to renewing the inscriptions on Covenanting gravestones can be viewed as melancholia rather than proper mourning, a traumatic repetition that sustains the memory of suffering. This nostalgic reanimation of the past is in sharp contrast to the narrator Peter Pattieson's view of the graves, which seem to him 'softened and deprived of their horror by our distances from the period when they have been first impressed' (Scott 1999: 61). The novel, which portrays the Covenanters as dangerous fanatics akin to Jacobin revolutionaries in France, functions as a Tory warning against radicalism in the early nineteenth century. Douglas Mack has stressed that the memory of the Covenanters' rebellion against the Stuarts was still strong in Lowland Scotland in the early nineteenth century (Mack 2012: 68). Hogg's intimate familiarity with oral culture and connection to the demotic Presbyterian tradition of the Borders gave him 'a more democratic and grass-roots view' (Tulloch 2012: 127) of the Covenanters' persecution than Scott's version. Hogg draws on his father's account of this history, itself informed by Robert Wodrow's *The History of the Sufferings of the Church of Scotland* (1721), to accentuate the voices of the sympathetic local population that helps the Covenanters in Ettrick Forest. *The Brownie of Bodsbeck* is a tale of common folk and individual suffering as much as it is a tale of the Scottish nation. This is borne out by its narrative form: the novel is episodic, evocative of oral storytelling, weaving together high and low matter, and featuring the deceptions and revelations typical of the historical romance, compositional principles repeated in *The Three Perils of Man* and *The Three Perils of Woman*.

The novel is set in the autumn of 1685, at the height of the 'Killing Times'. During this period, the Covenanters suffered persecution that 'raged in its wildest and most unbridled fury', making this 'the most dismal and troublous time that these districts of the south and west of Scotland ever saw, or have seen since' (Hogg 2009, vol. 1: 9). The central protagonist, Walter Laidlaw, is a loyal subject of the crown and one who 'loved his king and country' (2009, vol. 1: 49), but he is liberal rather than nakedly partisan in a time of religious extremism. Laidlaw's household and the text waver between adherence to prelatic principles and sympathy for Covenanters, and his daughter Katharine becomes a secret, ministering 'angel o' light' (2009, vol. 2: 34) to this desperate community, regardless of its political or religious allegiance. One of Laidlaw's servants, Nanny Elshinder, observes that Katharine's conviction banishes the storm of delirium and unrestrained tyranny that turns the world upside down, a world in which the righteous are not saved and the certainties of faith are overturned (2009, vol. 2: 32).

While Laidlaw and the unnamed narrator appear to maintain a scrupulous fairness to all sides in the conflict, the long, ameliorating view endorsed by Scott in *Old Mortality* is countered by the sadistic violence meted out in Hogg's text by forces serving Charles II, whose claim to absolute authority Dissenting Scottish Presbyterians fiercely opposed. Whereas Scott depicts John Graham of Claverhouse as a principled, gentlemanly royalist, Hogg depicts his wanton brutality and flagrant disregard for the law in his pursuit of the Covenanters after the Battle of Bothwell Bridge in 1679. Scattered groups of Covenanters hiding near Laidlaw's farm at Chapelhope are pursued relentlessly by Clavers and Highland regiments, who punish any perceived assistance that these fugitives receive from the local population. Clavers thus exhibits the same fanatical commitment attributed to his enemies. One of the elderly Covenanters hiding out in Chapelhope recalls the execution of his two sons with a voice 'wildly solemn, but his looks were mixed with madness' (2009, vol. 1: 32). This may, however, betray a mind distracted by shocking personal loss rather than fundamentalist beliefs. The impact of such traumatic events is evoked by the brutal treatment of old John of Muchrah 2009, vol. 1: 60), and by the 'strange soliloquy' (2009, vol. 1: 43) of Nanny Elshinder, who recalls a Covenanting trial and the threat of torture she faced.

This violent history is explored through dissenting voices. When Laidlaw, his equable temperament provoked by intemperate times, denounces the injustice of Clavers, his vernacular speech is corroborated by the third-person narrator's unambiguous declaration that Clavers 'traversed the country more like an exterminating angel, than a commander of a civilized army' (2009, vol. 1: 49). Folk memory 'corrects', or at least challenges, the historical record, as when it recounts Clavers as 'one of the infernals' in his harrying of stragglers. While the historically informed narrator must resist fanciful immersion in local lore, and not believe that the visible traces of hoofprints are made by 'the devil's foot', his witnessing of these 'deep green marks' (2009, vol. 1: 68) does not discard tradition.

The text deploys the 'explained supernatural', but this accentuates rather than cloaks the stark reality of historical crisis. In these 'momentous' times, the dead are 'astir' (2009, vol. 2: 38). The Brownie is revealed to be flesh and blood and not a creature of native superstition, confirming the scepticism of Laidlaw, but the plight he embodies still makes his appearance a thing of terror. The secretive, nocturnal presence of John Brown, goodman of Caldwell and Nanny Elshinder's husband, is explained by his responsibilities to the outlawed community of Covenanters. He resembles the Brownie of folk tradition due to injuries he sustained at Bothwell Bridge, and he performs tasks customarily associated with the unearthly creature. Chad T. May remarks that Scott uses the uncanny figure of the ghost to generate a form of 'empathetic unsettlement' in his fiction (2005: 112), but this term may be equally applicable to Brown and those he protects, who inhabit wild areas and are often mistaken for ghosts and spirits. The text unobtrusively discloses a fugitive past, with few monuments to commemorate it. The hidden cavern where the Covenanters live in seclusion, reminiscent of the anchorite caves in Scott's *The Antiquary* (1816), represents the lingering trace of a forgotten, or superseded, age. This 'horrid den', containing a coffin 'raised a little on two stones' (Hogg 2009, vol. 2: 69), constitutes at once a memorial and the active recovery of a shrouded history.

Set in 'the days of chivalry and romance' (Hogg 1996: 1), *The Three Perils of Man* presents a more obliquely Gothicised history, but one in which differing forms of belief vie for supremacy. Graham Tulloch comments that none of the characteristic tropes of the national tale emerge in the novel: there is no dirt, no transformation of the traveller and no symbolic union that heals divisions (Tulloch 2012: 125). The military struggle over Roxburgh Castle between Sir Thomas Musgrave, Earl of Northumberland, and James, Earl of Douglas and Mar, high-lights the cultural diversity within, rather than between, Scotland and Northern England; Musgrave perceives Douglas's forces, which contain Highlanders and Lowlanders, to be drawn from 'two different nations' (Hogg 1996: 71). Hogg's recourse to folk tradition, his unorthodox treatment of a captive heroine, and the absence of the 'self-contained, literary supernatural' of Walpole or Radcliffe also leads Tulloch to con-clude that *The Three Perils of Man* is 'not a Gothic romance' (Tulloch 2012: 123–4). The novel may be read, however, as a self-reflexive exam-ination of Gothic conventions, where every step is anticipated. This is suggested by the story's origin: the Editor acquires the manuscript of an old curate, Isaac, who begins – and presumably continues – in a 'notable tell-tale manner' (Hogg 1996: 2). The quest to Aikwood Castle is also shadowed by Gothic tradition. It is a 'dark-looking pile' (1996: 162), full of eldritch laughter and cruel sport, whose supernatural trappings veil the capricious exercise of feudal power. It serves equally as a Gothic visitor attraction, replete with vaults and a skeleton on display (1996: 168). The storytelling contest presided over by Sir Michael Scott is a sim-ilarly self-conscious exercise: telling tales, or watching a magic-lantern show, while stranded in a Gothic castle is romance in the making. When Charlie Scott later regales the Queen and her maidens of honour with stories of witchcraft at Aikwood (1996: 477–8), this may be an ironic comment on the Gothic's predominantly female readership.

There is more serious purpose in the novel's deployment of Gothic tropes, however, as this work stages the typical early Gothic confronta-tion between reason and superstition, enlightenment and barbarism. John Plotz argues that *The Three Perils of Man* is an example of Hogg's polydoxy, a practice that orchestrates 'the intersection of profoundly disjunctive belief systems within a single piece of fiction' (2012: 115).

Historical and supernatural events co-exist at a time when wanton cruelty vies with honour, and the 'demon of animosity and revenge' (Hogg 1996: 87) is easily conjured. The military and political actors of the period are as susceptible to the supernatural as the ordinary population: 'none of that age were exempt from the sway of an overpowering superstition' (1996: 107). The Borders are a lawless and violent region where the Cross on a sword or spear is more trusted than 'that hanging at the pouch of a priest' (1996: 119). In Ettrick, doors are protected by holy water against fairies, but these native denizens of folklore have been overtaken by the witchcraft of Michael Scott, whose charts are written in red letters. This great enchanter, conjuring monsters and controlling the elements, is a Faustian overreacher who has changed the land with his black arts, learned from 'colleges abroad' (1996: 376). In Aikwood, supernatural and spiritual, but also magical and scientific, powers jostle for supremacy. The Friar, Scott's rival in the narrative, has himself been 'persecuted as a necromancer' in southern Europe due to his interest in chemistry (1996: 206). His knowledge, and feats of natural 'magic', are construed as 'black arts' by his companions, especially when his understanding of gunpowder enables him to blast the enchanter's seneschal skyward.

Perceptions of Michael Scott's demise, and his legacy, are also subject to 'disjunctive belief systems'. Local people, well versed in Scott's abilities, nonetheless explain the supernatural forces unleashed by his sublime conflict with Satan as an 'uncommon' thunderstorm (1996: 535). According to Gilbert Jordan who witnesses the events, this prodigious battle is provoked by Scott's desire to remove the Devil's 'usurped and tyrannic sway over the mighty energies of nature' (1996: 528). A complicated figure of enlightenment, the enchanter will not be enslaved. His prophecies have inspired political action in the Borders, but he 'wad refuse the king o' France' when not 'i' the key for human conversation' (1996: 110), and only belatedly foretells the outcome of the siege of Roxburgh. Thus he stands apart from all forms of spiritual and temporal hierarchy. Jordan claims that Scott's fate is a 'good lesson to all those who form combinations inimical to the laws or authority of the land in which they reside' (1996: 530), a conservative conclusion that suggests 'supernatural terror will always be vanquished by true faith' (Bloedé 1992: 84). Disputed authority once again turns on a grave. At the king's behest, Scott's body is interred like a saint in Melrose Abbey, his black book and golden rod deposited with him as 'dangerous relics' (Hogg 1996: 536). The Master is both the 'most profound scholar of the age' (1996: 535) and its agitating spirit, and his burial lays to rest threatening allegiances. The Border conflict is temporarily ended, Aikwood is never inhabited again, and the supernatural becomes the stuff of palace entertainment. In the uneasy move toward quiescence, the power of the Gothic, like the power of darkness, drains away.

The Three Perils of Woman places this progressive trajectory in question: the transition to modernity provokes turmoil rather than tranquillity, and history is recursive. Gatty Bell's marriage to the Highland gentleman Diarmid M'Ion in the First Peril heals the wounds left by the Second Jacobite Rebellion of 1745–6, a crisis recounted in the subsequent Perils. M'Ion's broken inheritance is restored through his uncle's honourable treatment, thus assuring his lineage and his worthiness for Gatty's hand. As such, the union of the Lowlands and the Highlands constitutes an allegory of national renewal, which is paralleled by Gatty's return to health from her death-like state. Hogg, however, writes this national tale in reverse: the romance of the present becomes the muted echo, rather than the triumphant overcoming, of a bitter past. Domestic stability emerges from traumatic beginnings. The very night that Gatty conceives her son Colin, she is transformed into a 'ghastly automaton' (Hogg 2002b: 201), an uncanny figure neither living nor dead:

> The body sprung up with a power resembling that produced by electricity. It did not rise up like one wakening out of a sleep, but with a jerk so violent that it struck the old man on the cheek, almost stupefying him; and there sat the corpse, dressed as it was in its dead-clothes, a most appalling sight as man ever beheld. The whole frame appeared to be convulsed, and as it were struggling to get free of its bandages. (Hogg 2002b: 200)

This horrifying state of suspended animation, in which it appears 'as if an angel and demon had been struggling for possession of her frame' (2002b: 207), lasts for three years before Gatty sufficiently recovers to move to the Highlands with her husband.

The marriage between Gatty and M'Ion is compromised by a disrupted temporality that finds an analogue in contemporary events. *The Three Perils of Woman* was published the year after the 'King's Jaunt' in 1822, an event stage-managed by Walter Scott. As Antony Hasler comments, George IV's visit to Edinburgh, ostensibly celebrating the stability of the Union, presented a 'spectacular fiction' of a unified Britain (Hogg 2002b: xxxiv). The Hanoverian monarch, dressed in tartan, reviewed Highland troops who now enjoyed privileged status as a result of their contribution to victory at Waterloo. This moment of pageantry masked an awkward historical fact: the ancestors of those troops may have fought Crown forces during the Jacobite rebellion of 1745–6, and the final Peril charts the savage aftermath of its defeat. Scott's *Waverley* shows, post-Culloden, 'the carefully sentimentalized relationship that Anglo-Scottish

Lowlanders felt towards Gaelic Highland culture' (Trumpener 1993: 690), but *The Three Perils of Woman* is neither sentimental nor triumphant in its attitude towards Northern Scotland. Gatty initially views it as 'a country where all the people are Papists, rebels, and thieves' (Hogg 2002b: 22), and her brother Joseph positively compares the 'individual character' of Borderers to the feudal dependency of Highlanders (2002b: 99). Gatty's father Daniel Bell, a sheep farmer, believes he will exploit M'Ion's estate far better than any 'farmed in the auld way' (2002b: 127). (Hogg himself had tried to invest in Highland sheep farming.) Yet this change from the 'auld way' is unfinished business in more than one sense. Bell's desire to reintroduce sheep farming alludes to the Clearances in the wake of Culloden and, as Douglas Mack notes, the Sutherland evictions of 1814–15 would also have been part of the shared experience of the novel's first Scottish readers (Hogg 2002b: 427). In the closing Circle of the text, the dying MacKenzie recalls his family poet's vision of an angel pronouncing 'the exterminating curse on the guilty race of Stuart, and a triple woe on all that should support their throne' (2002b: 389). While this clearly echoes Walpole's 'sins of the fathers' message in *The Castle of Otranto*, it also has specific resonance for Lowland Scotland, as Highland regiments had been billeted in Covenanting areas during the reign of James VII, Charles Edward Stuart's father.

This prophecy of ruin for the Jacobite cause would seem to be fulfilled in the novel's present: accounts are settled, old antagonisms surmounted. Yet the narrative's backward look casts doubt on this resolution. Hogg's ambivalent perspective on this historical legacy is suggested by his reflections, during a journey to the Highlands in 1803, on Charles's hiding places following his final defeat: 'While traversing the scenes, where the patient sufferings of the one part, and the cruelties of the other were so affectingly displayed, I could not help being a bit of a Jacobite in my heart' (Hogg 2010: 81). This could be construed as the sentimental identification of the tourist, who imbibes local atmosphere before passing on, just as the spectral procession of Highland troops on Lewis and Uig is witnessed in 'Basil Lee' (Hogg 2004: 50–2). More strikingly, however, visiting these sites of loss and departure is an act of commemoration. As David Punter comments, 'Gothic in general is strewn with ruins' and its recapitulation of the past 'is never neutral' (Punter 2002: 122). Throughout Hogg's fiction, sites of remembrance are local, improvisatory or lacking in official inscription; they do not present a monumental history, but testify to 'a problematically ruined memory' (Hogg 2002a: 106) that *The Three Perils of Woman* excavates. In a sardonic aside on the antiquarianism associated with Scott, the narrator admits his motivation for tampering with the past:

> There were many things happened to the valiant conquerors of the Highlands in 1746 that were fairly hushed up, there being none afterwards that dared to publish or avow them. But there is no reason why these should die. For my part, I like to rake them up whenever I can get a story that lies within twenty miles of them, and, for all my incidents, I appeal to the records of families, and the truth of history. (Hogg 2002b: 332)

This opportunistic or exploitative, if figurative, raking up of old bones nevertheless constitutes a different, unfinished form of historical reckoning than that written by the victors. When visiting the rudimentary graves of the last Culloden men slain in the Highlands, the narrator notices that the ground 'appeared a little hollowed, as though some one had been digging in it' (2002b: 406).

This disturbed burial site epitomises the novel's preoccupation with restless corpses. The parallel romance narrative, in which Sally Niven follows her lover Peter Gow north to join the Jacobite forces, is framed by a graveyard scene and moonlight burials. The ghoulish farce of the gravedigger David Duff becoming trapped in a grave underneath a dead body, foreshadows the reanimation of Peter, presumed to have been buried by Duff on Culloden field. In this Gothic comedy of errors, Peter accidentally shoots a man in the graveyard but is exonerated of murder because he 'respects and venerates the ashes of his kindred' (2002b: 305). This dark inversion of romance tradition leads to no satisfactory union or resolution: Sally and Peter accept marriages of convenience, and Sally's journey ends with her husband MacKenzie and Peter mortally wounding each other. In the devastated Highlands, scarred by atrocity and fear after Culloden, Sally is mistaken for a ghost, and in their lurid fascination with the abjected body, the superstitious Duff and the physician Frazer become counterparts. Frazer perceives in Duff a 'rude' copy of himself, and they wander together, 'the one relating what deaths, pinings and ravings, he had seen during the summer; and the other, what miserable corpses he had found and interred in the wastes' (2002b: 393). The dead have no rest in this ruined land, and the novel closes at another graveside some months later, with Sally glimpsed by a young shepherd cradling her dead infant daughter. When he returns with his brothers, 'the mother and child were lying stretched together in the arms of death, pale as the snow that surrounded them, and rigid as the grave-turf on which they had made their dying bed' (2002b: 407). The novel rehearses one form of the national tale, whereby female socialisation is connected to plots concerning national identity, but in Hogg's macabre variation, it is the stricken female bodies of Gatty and Sally that figure the birth of modern Scotland.

The gothicised body of the nation also lies at the heart of *Confessions*.

Robert Wringhim's totalising vision leads us to no resolving truth. The attempts by Wringhim, and the Editor, to lay to rest a past full of contention, and to settle the future, end in a 'nauseating disintegration' (Duncan 2008: 263) of textual, psychological and corporeal integrity. Many psychoanalytic readings have been offered of Wringhim's 'condition', particularly in terms of schizophrenia or psychosis (Bloedé 1984; Brewster 2005), and Megan Coyer has recently argued that the medico-scientific culture of Edinburgh in the early nineteenth century could have enabled Hogg to depict 'a purely hallucinatory experience deeply connected to the mind and body of the individual' (2014: 1). An emphasis on the psychological, however, tends to detract from the historical and topographical aspects of *Confessions*, aspects that shape the fissured consciousness of Wringhim (Campbell 2002: 200). Just as the novel is concerned with doubling and internal divisions, so its settings reveal Scotland to be the unruly sum of its disparate parts. The storeys in Dalcastle, the Colwan family seat in the West of Scotland, are inhabited by different domestic factions that reflect wider political tensions. In a reversal of the romance structure, the novel begins with a union doomed by irreconcilable differences from the outset: a familial, domestic conflict becomes a doctrinal struggle. The narrative threads its way from this fractious arena through the mazes of Edinburgh, an enlightened space nonetheless conducive to riot and murder, until it finally becomes tangled in the looms and hayricks of the Borders, where the inhabitants are ready to believe the Devil has come calling with his 'cloven cloots' (Hogg 2002c: 160).

James Kelly suggests that it is religious and historical conflict that creates the 'second self' in Hogg's *Confessions*, as Robert Wringhim possesses the 'supernatural ability to step outside of the chronological confines of a progressive periodisation to trouble the living present' (2014: 48, 41). The novel is a reminder of 'the rage of fanaticism in former days' (Hogg 2002c: 64), a rage that Hogg's fiction consistently rekindles. Wringhim's narrative spans two contentious, and foundational, moments in Scottish history, the Revolution Settlement of 1689–90, which re-established Presbyterianism and the Act of Union in 1707. It is a period in which 'Reformation principles' (2002c: 3) have taken only partial hold, but also when memories of the 'Killing Times' are still raw. George Colwan and Robert Wringhim are born either side of 1688–9, and personify differing political and religious dispositions that clash in the Scottish Parliament and in the streets of Edinburgh. Wringhim's memoir justifying his election reflects this time of strong convictions, but his faith in God's grace is based upon the strange scripture of two father figures, Reverend Wringhim and his shape-shifting, diabolical familiar Gil-Martin, who reads a 'bible' 'all intersected with red lines' (2002c: 85). Antinomianism is a fundamentalist 'heresy' that eliminates doubt and brooks no opposition, and leads Robert to silence the moderate voice of Mr Blanchard, who warns about the dangers of extremism, which wrests religious principles 'beyond their due bounds' (2002c: 90–1). Immune from human judgement, the justified sinner transcends history and the vagaries of mutable meanings. Robert sees the truth through 'a cloudy veil' (2002c: 95), however, and his flawed interpretation leaves him enmeshed in his own narrative, just as he becomes tangled in the weaver's looms (2002c: 148–9). Despite the benefit of historical perspective, however, the reader is similarly ensnared by the riddle of this memoir. The Editor asserts that it is a 'bold theme for an allegory' but concludes that 'this writer' must be conceived as

> not only the greatest fool, but the greatest wretch, on whom was ever stamped the form of humanity; or, that he was a religious maniac, who wrote and wrote about a deluded creature, till he arrived at that height of madness, that he believed himself the very object whom he had been all along describing. (Hogg 2002c: 175)

It is unclear whether 'this writer' refers to the Editor or to Wringhim, but the height of madness may be to believe that the unruly fragments in Wringhim's grave can be authoritatively reassembled. The unearthing of Wringhim's confession, which lays bare a fractured past, also unsettles the present. Hogg's historical fiction leads persistently to the spatial and temporal terminus of the burial site, but it is an open rather than closed space that does not allow the final word to antiquarians or 'self-appointed narrators of the nation' (Wright 2007: 76). Here lies Hogg's Gothic: a place of cleaving, contested legacies and loose ends, where the dead do not stay still.

References

Bloedé, Barbara (1984), '*The Confessions of a Justified Sinner*: The Paranoiac Nucleus', in Gillian Hughes (ed.), *Papers Given at the First Conference of the James Hogg Society*, Stirling: James Hogg Society, pp. 15–28.
— (1992), 'The Gothic Antecedents of *The Three Perils of Man*', *Studies in Hogg and His World*, 3, 76–86.
Bold, Valentina and Suzanne Gilbert (2012), 'Hogg, Ettrick, and Oral Tradition', in Ian Duncan and Douglas Mack (eds), *The Edinburgh Companion to James Hogg*, Edinburgh: Edinburgh University Press, pp. 10–20.
Brewster, Scott (2005), 'Borderline Experience: Madness, Mimicry and Scottish Gothic', *Gothic Studies*, 7: 1, 79–86.
Campbell, Ian (2002), 'Afterword', in James Hogg, *The Private Memoirs and*

Confessions of a Justified Sinner, ed. Peter Garside, Edinburgh: Edinburgh University Press, pp. 177–94.

Coyer, Megan (2014), 'The Embodied Damnation of James Hogg's Justified Sinner', *Journal of Literature and Science*, 7: 1, 1–19.

Duncan, Ian (2007), *Scott's Shadow: The Novel in Enlightenment Edinburgh*, Princeton: Princeton University Press.

— (2008), 'Scotland and the Novel', in Richard Maxwell and Katie Trumpener (eds), *The Cambridge Companion to Fiction in the Romantic Period*, Cambridge: Cambridge University Press, pp. 251–64.

— (2012), 'Walter Scott, James Hogg and Scottish Gothic', in David Punter (ed.), *A New Companion to the Gothic*, Oxford: Wiley-Blackwell, pp. 123–34.

Fielding, Penny (1996), *Writing and Orality: Nationality, Culture, and Nineteenth-Century Scottish Fiction*, Oxford: Oxford University Press.

Garside, Peter (2002), 'Introduction', in James Hogg, *The Private Memoirs and Confessions of a Justified Sinner*, ed. Peter Garside, Edinburgh: Edinburgh University Press, pp. xi–xcix.

Hogg, James [1822] (1996), *The Three Perils of Man*, ed. Douglas Gifford, Edinburgh: Canongate.

— [1819–29] (2002a), *The Shepherd's Calendar*, ed. Douglas S. Mack, Edinburgh: Edinburgh University Press.

— [1823] (2002b), *The Three Perils of Woman*, ed. Antony Hasler and Douglas S. Mack, Edinburgh: Edinburgh University Press.

— [1824] (2002c), *The Private Memoirs and Confessions of a Justified Sinner*, ed. Peter Garside, Edinburgh: Edinburgh University Press.

— [1820] (2004), *Winter Evening Tales*, ed. Ian Duncan, Edinburgh: Edinburgh University Press.

— [1818] (2009), *The Brownie of Bodsbeck*, Charleston, SC: BiblioLife.

— [1802–4] (2010), *Highland Journeys*, ed. H. B. de Groot, Edinburgh: Edinburgh University Press.

Kelly, James (2014), 'Gothic and the Celtic Fringe, 1750–1850', in Glennis Byron and Dale Townshend (eds), *The Gothic World*, London: Routledge, pp. 38–50.

Mack, Douglas S. (2012), 'Hogg's Politics and the Presbyterian Tradition', in Ian Duncan and Douglas Mack (eds), *The Edinburgh Companion to James Hogg*, Edinburgh: Edinburgh University Press, pp. 64–72.

May, Chad T. (2005), '"The Horrors of My Tale": Trauma, the Historical Imagination, and Sir Walter Scott', *Pacific Coast Philology*, 40: 1, 98–116.

Plotz, John (2012), 'Hogg and the Short Story', in Ian Duncan and Douglas Mack (eds), *The Edinburgh Companion to James Hogg*, Edinburgh: Edinburgh University Press, pp. 113–21.

Pope, Rebecca A. (1992), 'Hogg, Wordsworth and Gothic Autobiography', *Studies in Scottish Literature*, 27: 1, 218–40.

Punter, David (2002), 'Scottish and Irish Gothic', in Jerrold E. Hogle (ed.), *The Cambridge Companion to Gothic Fiction*, Cambridge: Cambridge University Press, pp. 105–23.

Robertson, James (2006), *The Testament of Gideon Mack*, London: Hamish Hamilton.

Scott, Walter [1816] (1999), *Old Mortality*, ed. Jane Stevenson and Peter Davison, Oxford: Oxford University Press.

Trumpener, Katie (1993), 'National Character, National Plots: National Tale and Historical Novel in the Age of *Waverley*, 1806–1830', *ELH*, 60: 3, 685–731.

Tulloch, Graham (2012), 'Hogg and the Novel', in Ian Duncan and Douglas Mack (eds), *The Edinburgh Companion to James Hogg*, Edinburgh: Edinburgh University Press, pp. 122–31.

Wright, Angela (2007), 'Scottish Gothic', in Catherine Spooner and Emma McEvoy (eds), *The Routledge Companion to the Gothic*, London: Routledge, pp. 73–82.

Chapter 10

'The Singular Wrought Out into the Strange and Mystical': *Blackwood's Edinburgh Magazine* and the Transformation of Terror

Robert Morrison

When Lord Byron decided in May 1819 to publish his Gothic fragment, 'Augustus Darvell', *Blackwood's Edinburgh Magazine* seemed to him the obvious choice (Byron 1973–94, vol. 6: 126).[1] Though founded only eighteen months earlier, the magazine had quickly established itself as one of the leading periodical publications of the day, and one that specialised in terror. Led by its editor, William Blackwood, and key contributors such as John Wilson and J. G. Lockhart, *Blackwood's* routinely used variously aestheticised forms of violence and fear as a method of engagement with a host of social, critical and cultural issues, and as a means of promulgating its virulent version of High Toryism, as seen most clearly in its bellicose attacks on Whig enemies such as the *Edinburgh Review*, and its literary assassinations of 'Cockney School' writers like John Keats and Leigh Hunt (Schoenfield 2013). The magazine's finest fictive offerings were part of this much broader campaign of terror, and unlike its politics, which looked decisively to the past, its tales of dread and the macabre pioneered a new form of Gothic fiction that rejected not only the long and anxious narratives of late eighteenth-century Gothic novels and romances by English authors such as Ann Radcliffe, Matthew 'Monk' Lewis and William Godwin, but profoundly altered the distinctively Scottish tradition of the Gothic as it had emerged in the poetry of James Macpherson and Robert Burns. *Blackwood's*, as Byron realised, was especially interested in short, unnerving terror fiction like 'Augustus Darvell', and over the course of William Blackwood's seventeen-year editorship the magazine's most characteristic tales of terror set new standards of concentrated dread and precisely calculated alarm that had a powerful influence on writers such as Charles Dickens, Robert Browning, the Brontës and, of course, Edgar Allan Poe.

William Blackwood was the force behind the magazine that bore his name, and the one primarily responsible for making it the era's most influential and exciting periodical publication (Morrison 2006: 21–48). Born in Edinburgh in 1776, he was apprenticed as a bookseller in both Scotland and England before returning in 1804 to Edinburgh, where he established a shop specialising in the sale of rare books and began to experiment in publishing. By 1811 his business was flourishing, and he became the Edinburgh agent for the eminent London publisher John Murray, a connection that linked his name to authors such as Byron, Jane Austen, George Crabbe and Robert Southey, and that reached its high point in 1816 when he and Murray co-published Walter Scott's *Tales of My Landlord*. In April 1817, Blackwood founded the *Edinburgh Monthly Magazine*, and while it contained work by Wilson, Lockhart, Scott and James Hogg, it also opened – irritatingly – with an article praising Francis Horner, arch Whig and one of the founders of the *Edinburgh Review*. Decidedly unimpressed, Blackwood gave his editors, Thomas Pringle and James Cleghorn, two more numbers to give his magazine a clear direction and a distinct identity, but they failed to deliver, and by October he himself was in the editor's chair when a reconstituted effort, *Blackwood's Edinburgh Magazine*, exploded onto the British literary scene with an issue that contained a scathing review of Samuel Taylor Coleridge's *Biographia Literaria* (1817), the first indictment of the 'Cockney School of Poetry', and the 'Chaldee Manuscript', an allegorical attack by Hogg, Lockhart and Wilson on prominent Edinburgh Whigs that left many gasping and others threatening legal action. Blackwood's conservative politics were an essential factor in the magazine's success. Scotland, in the eyes of Tories like him, was not a parochial nation struggling to make an impact from the margins of English political and cultural life, but a nation at the heart of the Unionist ideology and the Anglo-British empire, a nation of two distinct but compatible identities in which local loyalties flourished within an imperial community (Craig 1996: 11–30). 'It is quite right that the Scotch should glory . . . in the name of Britain', Archibald Alison declared pointedly in the July 1819 issue; but 'it is equally indisputable that . . . an independent nation, once the rival of England, should remember, with pride, the peculiar glories by which her people have been distinguished' (qtd in Duncan 2007: 17). *Blackwood's* commitment to what Susan Manning labels 'a bifocal national identity, at once Scottish and British' gave it a purpose and a swagger that permeated it at every level, and that often led it to poke fun at the English as themselves marginal when set against *Blackwood's* exuberant celebration of both its native and its imperial aims (Manning 2007: 54). 'The truth must be told', Wilson wrote gleefully in *Blackwood's* for April 1822. '*London is a very small insignificant place.* Our ambition is, that our wit shall be local all over the world' (Wilson 1822: 488; original emphasis).[2]

Despite these high levels of confidence in Scotland's political identity and Britain's colonial mission, Blackwood and his key writers typically represented the world as corrupt and deeply unstable, especially in the late 1820s and early 1830s, as liberals and radicals pushed hard for Catholic Emancipation and then Reform, and *Blackwood's* shot back with increasingly hysterical – and ineffectual – defences of the status quo. 'Reformers ... are utterly irreclaimable', Alison ranted characteristically in January 1832; 'they will live and die Reformers, though the Jacobin dagger were at their throat, the revolutionary halter about their necks, or the torch of anarchy in their dwellings' (Alison 1832: 4–5). Similarly, *Blackwood's* pursuit of the 'Cockney School' writers reads very much like a Gothic tale of paranoia and revenge, for it recognised in a poet such as John Keats a radical and defiant originality that profoundly threatened the political and cultural hierarchies it cherished, and in response it attacked him as a vulgar mediocrity with ideas far above his social station (Wheatley 1992). Lockhart, the prime mover in the assaults, wrote under the pseudonym 'Z', and set his sights especially on the 'King of the Cockneys', Leigh Hunt, whom he threatened to 'probe ... to the core', while forever haunting his mind 'like an avenging shadow' (Lockhart [?] 1818: 197, 201, 199). John Scott, editor of the rival *London Magazine*, was also singled out by *Blackwood's* for persecution, and the bitter conflict between the two magazines led eventually to a duel and Scott's death in February 1821 at the hands of Lockhart's ally Jonathan Christie (Cronin 2010: 1–17). The incident provoked outrage, but *Blackwood's* was unrepentant. Less than two months after Scott's death, it cheerfully referred to 'Z' as 'wet with the blood of the Cockneys', and cited the magazine's fictional editor 'Christopher North' as a man who had 'slain' many with his 'trenchant and truculent falchion' (Maginn 1821: 62). Across Blackwood's editorship, his magazine remained on the warpath, and his writers were regularly 'looking about for some person or other to immolate to our fury – some victim to break upon the wheel, and to whom we might give, with soft reluctant amorous delay, the coup-de-grace' (Wilson [?] 1823: 321).

It is, however, *Blackwood's* publication of original fiction that constitutes its most thoroughgoing and enduring exploitation of the Gothic mode. Blackwood relished above all 'the exciting, the terrible, and the grisly', and his magazine regularly featured short, terrifying tales that reworked various well-established Gothic tropes while also taking the genre in dramatic new directions (Kilbourne 1966: 67–8). The *Blackwood's* terror tale varied in length from 1,000 to 15,000 words, but could almost invariably be read in one sitting, for it was Poe's understanding of these *'tales of effect'* that led directly to his theorisations on 'the short prose narrative, requiring from a half-hour to one or two hours in its perusal', as the best way to communicate terror and produce 'the immense force derivable from *totality*' (Poe 1984b: 573, 572; original emphasis). The *Blackwood's* tale of sensation usually focuses on a protagonist who has inadvertently trapped himself in some horrible, strange or grotesque predicament that threatens him both bodily and mentally, inducing terrifying forms of confusion, delirium and hysteria that drive him steadily toward either madness or death. The usual tone of these stories is 'first-hand yet detached, factual yet involved', in Tim Killick's characterisation, as the narrator 'reports' or unflinchingly 'witnesses' accidents, disasters, suicides, assassinations, executions and death-ravings (Killick 2008: 21). The tales are most clearly indebted to the eighteenth-century tradition of 'true crime' narrative found in chapbooks, broadsheets, broadsides, newspapers and, most famously, *The Newgate Calendar* (1773). The narrator of Henry Thomson's tale 'Le Revenant' (1827) seems to speak for many of the *Blackwood's* terror writers when he confesses that his 'greatest pleasure, through life, has been the perusal of any extraordinary narratives of fact', such as 'an account of a shipwreck in which hundreds have perished', or 'a plague which has depopulated towns or cities', or 'anecdotes and inquiries connected with the regulation of prisons, hospitals, or lunatic receptacles' (Thomson 1995: 73–4).

The realism and brevity of *Blackwood's* terror fiction marked a decisive break from the Gothic tradition inaugurated by Horace Walpole in *The Castle of Otranto* (1764), with its assemblage of dungeons, castles, subterranean passageways, virtuous maidens and tormented villains. Later writers variously and more successfully reimagined these materials, including Matthew Lewis in *The Monk* (1796), a three-volume extravagance of brutality, supernaturalism and sexual prurience, and Ann Radcliffe in *The Romance of the Forest* (1791), *The Mysteries of Udolpho* (1794) and *The Italian* (1797), all of which feature the leisurely construction of foreboding and anxiety, and all of which include brave lovers threatened by appalling fates that they eventually elude. Radcliffe's romances, and those of her many imitators, held sway in the circulating libraries for two decades. Further, they spawned an entire sub-tradition of Gothic 'fragments' and 'tales' that recapitulated the basic elements of her plots but at breakneck speed and in a fraction of the space, as in the anonymous 'Ruins of the Abbey of Fitz-Martin' (1801) or Isaac Crookenden's 'The Vindictive Monk' (1802) (Baldick 1992: xvi–xviii).

Blackwood's terror fiction clearly has much more in common with the heavily redacted versions of Radcliffean Gothic, as opposed to its full-blown evocations. One of the finest *Blackwood's* tales, William Mudford's 'The Iron Shroud' (1830), echoes Radcliffe in its historical setting in a medieval Italian castle, its brutal villain the Prince of Tolfi, and its sublime Sicilian landscapes visible to the hero Vivenzio only through the windows of his prison. But Mudford strips away Radcliffean sentimentalism, 'atmosphere' and light relief, and replaces it with a dread that is both concentrated and distending: in his tale there is no love interest, no subsidiary plots or minor characters and, most importantly, no escape. Vivenzio is trapped in a contracting prison, and his physical fear and mental anguish grow in inverse proportion to the shrinking size of the cell, until after a week of terror his time finally runs out: 'on, and on, and on came the mysterious engine of death, till Vivenzio's smothered groans were heard no more! He was horribly crushed by the ponderous roof and collapsing sides – and the flattened bier was his *Iron Shroud*' (Mudford 1995: 114). Mudford's tale highlights the differences between the Radcliffean and Blackwoodian representations of terror, vast in the case of her novels, and still sharp as regards the countless 'fragments' and 'tales' of her imitators.

Blackwood's similarly responded to another important mode in late eighteenth-century Gothic fiction, and with the same tactic of compression. William Godwin's *The Adventures of Caleb Williams* (1794) is a novel of isolation, persecution and despair centring on the relationship between the aristocratic Falkland and the eponymous hero, his servant. In *Frankenstein* (1818), Godwin's daughter, Mary Shelley, transforms central features of *Caleb Williams*, for as Chris Baldick remarks, the 'dynamic principle of the narrative' in both novels 'is one of endless flight and ineluctable pursuit, as the roles of accuser and accused exchange between "father" and "son" figures' (1987: 26). Then, in *Blackwood's* for February and March 1832, Godwin's only son, William Godwin Junior, publishes 'The Executioner', which draws heavily on *Caleb Williams* and *Frankenstein*, but which is also a pointed condensation of both – in effect, a Godwinian novel in the form of a Blackwoodian tale. Like Mary Shelley's monster, Godwin Junior's unwitting executioner Ambrose enters the world full of hope but meets only violence and scorn. 'I felt that my heart was gradually changing within me', Ambrose broods:

> I had brought it into the world of men, with its offering of love and kindness, but none would accept it. . . . As I laboured along in solitude, misery, and neglect, I demanded of myself a thousand times, 'Why am I to have love for man, when mankind has none for me?' (Godwin Junior 1995: 141)

Like Godwin's Caleb, Godwin Junior's Ambrose ends up in a prison cell on the verge of insanity: 'My story is told! My confessions are numbered!' he exclaims. 'Why, I know not – but so it is; even as surely as I am now the inmate of a melancholy cell, and am counted by my fellow-men among the maniacs of the earth. – Mad! Oh no, I am not mad!' (1995: 179).

Yet as engaged as they were with the various manifestations of the Gothic emanating from England, the separate Scottish tradition had a much deeper hold on Blackwood and his writers, and was given far more space in his magazine. 'The thematic core of Scottish Gothic consists of an association between the *national* and the *uncanny or supernatural*', argues Ian Duncan, and is best traced back to the 'elegiac hold of a dead past over a living present' in the Ossianic poetry of James Macpherson, and the 'subversive outburst of energies of popular "superstition"' in Robert Burns's poems such as 'Tam o' Shanter' (2000: 70, 73; original emphasis). In *Blackwood's*, several writers take up these concerns, including Walter Simson in 'Anecdotes of the Fife Gypsies' (1817–18), R. B. Cunninghame in 'Fergusson and Burns' (1822), David Campbell in 'Popular Superstitions, &c. of the Highlanders of Scotland' (1823) and Allan Cunningham in his 'Recollections of Mark Macrabin, the Cameronian' (1819–21).

James Hogg, though, was of course *Blackwood's* most important and prolific writer of traditional Scots Gothic, in series such as 'Tales and Anecdotes of the Pastoral Life' (1817) and 'The Shepherd's Calendar' (1819–29), as well as in a host of stand-alone tales. 'A Scots Mummy', for example, was published by Hogg in *Blackwood's* for August 1823, and then retrieved by him a year later for incorporation into his terror novel, *The Private Memoirs and Confessions of a Justified Sinner* (2001: 165–9, 248). For Hogg, supernatural legends of witches, fairies, goblins, wraiths and brownies could not be consigned to the past, but were part of a living rural culture, and in his finest *Blackwood's* tales the 'uncanny' and the 'unaccountable' both defy all attempts at rational explanation, and provoke the extremes of paranoia and obsession. Perhaps most revealingly, in 'The Mysterious Bride' (1830), Hogg opens by chiding those who are 'beginning broadly to insinuate that there are no such things as ghosts, or spiritual beings visible to mortal sight', and declares himself particularly aggrieved with 'Sir Walter Scott', a rationalising 'renegade' who is 'trying to throw cold water on the most certain, though most impalpable, phenomena of human nature' (1995: 115). In the tale itself, the Laird of Birkendelly feels an intense sexual attraction to a mysterious young woman in white and green who haunts a specific stretch of road, and who finally marries and then murders him as the last descendant of the man who murdered her. The following morning the Laird's body – 'his skin . . . of a livid colour, and his features terribly distorted' – is found on the exact spot where he first saw his mysterious bride, and when the villagers dig down far below the road they find her corpse. The Scottish countryside, Hogg affirms, is still alive with potent supernatural agencies that write their lessons 'on Divine justice . . . in lines of blood' (1995: 127, 130).

Many of the most powerful *Blackwood's* tales of terror, however, responded neither to the English nor the Scottish Gothic traditions, but used the strategies of immediacy and concision to initiate a new variation that set, rather than reformulated, Gothic trends, and that was shamelessly commercial and modernist – the product of an 'age which, if ever any *did*, idolatrises the tangible and the material', as Thomas De Quincey observed in *Blackwood's* in 1830 (2000: 46–7; original emphasis). John Wilson was the magazine's first important terror fiction writer, as seen especially in his 'Extracts from Gosschen's Diary' (1818), a disturbing tale of just over 2,000 words in which a priest visits an incarcerated lunatic and listens in horrified silence as he confesses to his bloody crime. 'I murdered her', the prisoner calmly declares:

> Who else loved her so well as to shed her innocent blood? . . . I grasped her by that radiant, that golden hair, – I bared those snow-white breasts, – I dragged her sweet body towards me, and, as God is my witness, I stabbed, and stabbed her with this very dagger, ten, twenty, forty times, through and through her heart. . . . I laid her down upon a bank of flowers, – that were soon stained with her blood. I saw the dim blue eyes beneath the half-closed lids, – that face so changeful in its living beauty was now fixed as ice, and the balmy breath came from her sweet lips no more. My joy, my happiness, was perfect. (Wilson 1995: 21)

Wilson's tale – representative in its explicitness, savagery and psycho-logical extremism – suggested the principal incident in Bryan Waller Procter's *Marcian Colonna, an Italian Tale* (1820), and is a probable source for Robert Browning's first dramatic monologue, 'Porphyria's Lover' (1836), where a woman with 'yellow hair' and 'blue eyes' is strangled to death by her lover, who issues the final, chilling words, 'And all night long we have not stirred, / And yet God has not said a word!' (Mason 1974: 255–66; Browning 2009: 124).

John Galt produced his best fiction for Blackwood, including a terror tale called 'The Buried Alive', which he published in the magazine in October 1821 as an independent narrative, and then folded into his novel *The Steam-Boat*, which he serialised in *Blackwood's* in 1821, and then published in volume form a year later. 'The Buried Alive' exploits contemporary fears about premature burial, grave-robbers and the shortage of suitable corpses for anatomical dissection in the medical schools, and was one of several early *Blackwood's* tales to record the acute psychological effects of being trapped, incarcerated or even entombed in unbearable conditions of confinement and panic. In Galt's tale, an apparently dead man is still fully conscious:

> I heard the sound of weeping at my pillow – and the voice of the nurse say, 'He is dead.' – I cannot describe what I felt at these words. – I exerted my utmost power of volition to stir myself, but I could not move even an eyelid. ... The world was then darkened, but I still could hear, and feel, and suffer. (Galt 1995: 35)

Charles Dickens, a great admirer of the new *Blackwood's* terror fiction, emulated Galt's insertion of 'The Buried Alive' into *The Steam-Boat* when he produced his own Blackwoodian tales of terror, including 'The Convict's Return' and 'A Madman's Manuscript', for incorporation into *The Pickwick Papers* in 1836–7 (Sucksmith 1971).

William Maginn was a voluminous contributor to *Blackwood's*, and produced one of the most original of its early tales, 'The Man in the Bell' (1821), in which the narrator finds himself stuck within inches of a huge church bell as it tolls deafeningly over him. Physically, he feels himself to be in danger, but mentally the strain is far worse:

> the roaring of the bell confused my intellect, and my fancy soon began to teem with all sort of strange and terrifying ideas. The bell pealing above, and opening its jaws with a hideous clamour, seemed to me at one time a ravening monster, raging to devour me; at another, a whirlpool ready to suck me into its bellowing abyss. ... Every object that was hideous and roaring presented itself to my imagination. (Maginn 1995: 63)

For Poe, tales like Maginn's exemplified the intensification – the ramping up – at the crux of *Blackwood's* innovation: they depicted, as he explained in an 1835 letter to his editor Thomas W. White, 'the ludicrous heightened into the grotesque: the fearful coloured into the horrible: the witty exaggerated into the burlesque: the singular wrought out into the strange and mystical' (1966, vol. 1: 57–8). In 'How to Write a Blackwood Article' (1838), Poe has Mr Blackwood explain to a potential contributor, Miss Psyche Zenobia, that 'The Man in the Bell' is ideally suited to his magazine because

> sensations are the great things after all. Should you ever be drowned or hung, be sure and make a note of your sensations – they will be worth to you ten guineas a sheet. If you wish to write forcibly, Miss Zenobia, pay minute attention to the sensations. (Poe 1984a: 281)

Poe returned again to Maginn's tale when, together with 'The Iron Shroud', he reimagined it in one of his greatest excursions into short terror fiction, 'The Pit and the Pendulum' (1842).

Blackwood's most popular terror series was *Passages from the Diary of a Late Physician*, serialised in the magazine from August 1830 through August 1837, and written by Samuel Warren, who announced at the beginning of the first instalment that, whereas 'the bar, the church, the army, the navy, and the stage, have all of them spread the volumes of their secret history to the prying gaze of the public', he intended to exploit the 'rich mine of incident and sentiment' surrounding the 'medical profession', which has 'remained hitherto – with scarcely an exception – a sealed book' (Warren 1830a). Warren's tales are a striking advance on the *Blackwood's* mode in that they are typically from 10,000 to 15,000 words long, rather than only 2,000 to 3,000 words as in the earlier tales of Wilson, Galt, Maginn and others. Moreover, while he prizes the same kinds of graphic realism and unyielding dread, he elaborates upon them at much greater length, 'overdosing the reader with horrors', as Henry Crabb Robinson put it in 1835 (1938, vol. 2: 453). Warren's fictional doctor is both a voyeur and an expert witness who is called to death chambers from across the social spectrum, and who reports on all manner of physical and mental horrors in patients whose suffering he frequently turns into spectacle. The tales borrow at times heavily from contemporary medical and scientific discourse to validate the sources of the suffering and the possibilities of a cure, but they also indulge liberally in moralising, euphemism and – especially – sentimentality, as Warren lurches between clinical observation and overwrought emotionalism. Deformity, abnormality, lunacy, suicide, disease, depravity, imprisonment and martyrdom are among his favourite subjects, and throughout the series he displays an almost erotic obsession with the sensational and the bizarre: 'I have seen many hundreds of corpses, as well in the calm composure of natural death, as mangled and distorted by violence', the physician notes in 'Death at the Toilet' (1830); 'but never have I seen so startling a satire upon human vanity, so repulsive, unsightly, and loathsome a spectacle, as a *corpse dressed for a ball!*' (Warren 1830b: 940; original emphasis).

'A "Man About Town"' is one of his most characteristic and unnerving tales. Blending lurid descriptions with sanctimonious moralising, it tells the story of the Honourable St John Henry Effingstone, brilliant and aristocratic, but an 'abandoned profligate', a 'systematic debauchee' and an 'irreclaimable reprobate' who is clearly suffering from venereal disease, and who endures excruciating spiritual and physical pains until his body actually begins to rot: 'The flesh of the lower extremities – the flesh – Horrible! All sensation had ceased in them for a fortnight! He describes the agonies about his stomach and bowel to be as though wolves were ravenously gnawing and mangling all within' (Warren 1995: 184, 205). The attending nurse soon requests that she be relieved of her duties, while the physician's own health begins to give way. Effingstone briefly believes himself to be recovering, but it is of course not to be, and he dies in rented rooms in an obscure part of London after refusing yet again the consolations of religion. As in several other tales from the *Passages*, in 'A "Man About Town"' Warren orchestrates his melodramatic and gruesome materials to remarkable effect, primarily through his ability to create a sustained atmosphere of terror and despair. When the tale appeared, he wrote to Blackwood that it was 'exciting a sensation among the Clubs, and elsewhere. "Horrible", "ghastly", "frightful", "lamentable", are some of the expressions to which I have listened' (qtd. in Oliphant 1897, vol. 2: 31). Anne Brontë seems to borrow from 'A "Man About Town"' for the deathbed scene of Arthur Huntingdon in *The Tenant of Wildfell Hall* (1848), while other tales from the *Passages* may have influenced Dickens in *The Pickwick Papers* and Poe in 'The Fall of the House of Usher' (1839) (Winnifrith 1973: 92–3; Sucksmith 1971: 149–50; Alterton 1965: 26–7). Throughout the series, Warren ghoulishly delights in documenting the genuinely terrifying ways in which death and decay make fierce incursions into our quotidian lives. By blurring the lines between fiction and fact, science and romance, and the personal and the professional, he elevates the *Blackwood's* terror tale to new levels of intricacy and intensity, and creates what Meegan Kennedy labels 'Gothic medicine', a mode that looks back to Shelley's *Frankenstein*, and extends forward to include Charles Reade's *Hard Cash* (1863), Robert Louis Stevenson's *Strange Case of Dr Jekyll and Mr Hyde* (1886), Charlotte Perkins Gilman's 'The Yellow Wall-Paper' (1892), Bram Stoker's *Dracula* (1897) and Henry James's *The Turn of the Screw* (1898), among many others (Kennedy 2004: 342, 345).

William Blackwood published and edited his magazine from 1817 until his death in 1834, and from shaky beginnings he turned it into the most important literary-political journal of its day, rooted in the intellectual and cultural achievements of Edinburgh but with an international reach and reputation. Belligerently pro-Unionist, *Blackwood's* borrowed extensively from the rhetoric of the Gothic in its campaigns against Whigs, radicals, cockneys and Tory deserters, and across a host of parodies, reviews, squibs, satires and quasi-fictive histories. The magazine's deepest and most original engagement with the Gothic, though, came in its terror fiction, which broke decisively from the diverse traditions of the genre that had emerged in Britain from the mid-eighteenth century onward. Grim, graphic and materialist, the *Blackwood's* tales transformed representations of terror in the early nineteenth century by revealing the potency of the short prose narrative to horrify and dismay. *Blackwood's* concentrated on new, modern and often bizarre subject matter, and approached it with an evolving series of strategies and techniques, setting the pattern for shorter terror fiction for decades to come, and, more broadly speaking, establishing the groundwork for the emergence of the modern short story as an internationally significant form in the writings of Nikolai Gogol, Aleksandr Pushkin, Honoré de Balzac, Prosper Mérimée and Arthur Conan Doyle (Morrison and Baldick 1997: xxi–xxii).

Notes

1. I acknowledge with gratitude a grant from the Social Sciences and Humanities Research Council of Canada for research into *Blackwood's Magazine*.
2. The attributions of articles in *Blackwood's Magazine* are based on Strout 1959; Houghton 1966–89, vol. 1: 7–209; and Murray 1967. A question mark in square brackets following the name of the author indicates that the attribution is uncertain.

References

Alison, Archibald (1832), 'Remote Causes of the Reform Passion', *Blackwood's Magazine*, 31, 1–18.

Alterton, Margaret (1965), *Origins of Poe's Critical Theory*, New York: Russell.

Baldick, Chris (1987), *In Frankenstein's Shadow: Myth, Monstrosity, and Nineteenth-Century Writing*, Oxford: Oxford University Press.

— (1992), 'Introduction', in Chris Baldick (ed.), *The Oxford Book of Gothic Tales*, Oxford: Oxford University Press, pp. xi–xxiii.

Browning, Robert [1836] (2009), 'Porphyria's Lover', in Adam Roberts and Daniel Karlin (eds), *Browning: The Major Works*, Oxford: Oxford University Press, pp. 122–4.

Byron, Lord [1819] (1973–94), *Letters and Journals*, ed. Leslie A. Marchand, 13 vols, London: Murray.

Craig, Cairns (1996), *Out of History: Narrative Paradigms in Scottish and British Culture*, Edinburgh: Polygon.

Cronin, Richard (2010), *Paper Pellets: British Literary Culture After Waterloo*, Oxford: Oxford University Press.

De Quincey, Thomas [1830] (2000), 'Kant in His Miscellaneous Essays', in Robert Morrison (ed.), *The Works of Thomas De Quincey, Volume Seven*, London: Pickering and Chatto, pp. 45–78.

Duncan, Ian (2000), 'Walter Scott, James Hogg and Scottish Gothic', in David Punter (ed.), *A Companion to the Gothic*, Oxford: Blackwell, pp. 70–80.

— (2007), *Scott's Shadow: The Novel in Romantic Edinburgh*, Princeton: Princeton University Press.

Galt, John [1821] (1995), 'The Buried Alive', in Robert Morrison and Chris Baldick (eds), *Tales of Terror from Blackwood's Magazine*, Oxford: Oxford University Press, pp. 35–8.

Godwin Junior, William [1832] (1995), 'The Executioner', in Robert Morrison and Chris Baldick (eds), *Tales of Terror from Blackwood's Magazine*, Oxford: Oxford University Press, pp. 131–79.

Hogg, James [1830] (1995), 'The Mysterious Bride', in Robert Morrison and Chris Baldick (eds), *Tales of Terror from Blackwood's Magazine*, Oxford: Oxford University Press, pp. 115–30.

— [1824] (2001), *The Private Memoirs and Confessions of a Justified Sinner*, ed. Peter Garside, Edinburgh: Edinburgh University Press.

Houghton, Walter (gen. ed.) (1966–89), *The Wellesley Index to Victorian Periodicals*, 5 vols, Toronto: University of Toronto Press.

Kennedy, Meegan (2004), 'The Ghost in the Clinic: Gothic Medicine and Curious Fiction in Samuel Warren's *Diary of a Late Physician*', *Victorian Literature and Culture*, 32: 3, 327–51.

Kilbourne, William (1966), *The Role of Fiction in Blackwood's Magazine from 1817 to 1845*, unpublished PhD thesis, Northwestern University.

Killick, Tim (2008), *British Short Fiction in the Early Nineteenth Century: The Rise of the Tale*, Aldershot: Ashgate.

Lockhart, J. G. [?] (1818), 'Letter from Z to Leigh Hunt, King of the Cockneys', *Blackwood's Magazine*, 3, 196–201.

Maginn, William (1821), 'Hymn to Christopher North', *Blackwood's Magazine*, 9, 59–64.

— [1821] (1995), 'The Man in the Bell', in Robert Morrison and Chris Baldick (eds), *Tales of Terror from Blackwood's Magazine*, Oxford: Oxford University Press, pp. 61–6.

Manning, Susan (2007), 'Post-Union Scotland and the Scottish Idiom of Britishness', in Ian Brown (gen. ed.), *The Edinburgh History of Scottish Literature*, 3 vols, Edinburgh: Edinburgh University Press, vol. 2, pp. 45–56.

Mason, Michael (1974), 'Browning and the Dramatic Monologue', in Isobel Armstrong (ed.), *Robert Browning*, London: Bell, pp. 231–66.

Morrison, Robert (2006), 'William Blackwood and the Dynamics of Success', in David Finkelstein (ed.), *Print Culture and the Blackwood Tradition, 1805–1930*, Toronto: University of Toronto Press, pp. 21–48.

Morrison, Robert and Chris Baldick (1997), 'Introduction', in Robert Morrison and Chris Baldick (eds), *The Vampyre and Other Tales of the Macabre*, Oxford: Oxford University Press, pp. vii–xxii.

Mudford, William [1830] (1995), 'The Iron Shroud', in Robert Morrison and Chris Baldick (eds), *Tales of Terror from Blackwood's Magazine*, Oxford: Oxford University Press, pp. 101–14.

Murray, Brian (1967) 'The Authorship of Some Unidentified or Disputed Articles in *Blackwood's Magazine*', *Studies in Scottish Literature*, 4: 3/4, 144–54.

Oliphant, Margaret (1897), *Annals of a Publishing House: William Blackwood and His Sons*, 2 vols, Edinburgh: Blackwood.

Poe, Edgar Allan [1835] (1966), *The Letters of Edgar Allan Poe*, ed. John Ward Ostrom, 2 vols, New York: Gordian.

— [1838] (1984a), 'How to Write a Blackwood Article', in Patrick F. Quinn (ed.), *Poetry and Tales*, New York: Library of America, pp. 278–97.

— [1842] (1984b), '*Twice-Told Tales*. By Nathaniel Hawthorne', in G. R. Thompson (ed.), *Essays and Reviews*, New York: Library of America, pp. 569–88.

Robinson, Henry Crabb [1835] (1938), *On Books and Their Writers*, ed. E. J. Morley, 3 vols, London: Dent.

Schoenfield, Mark (2013), 'The Taste for Violence in *Blackwood's Magazine*', in Robert Morrison and Daniel Sanjiv Roberts (eds), *Romanticism and Blackwood's Magazine: 'An Unprecedented Phenomenon'*, Houndmills: Palgrave, pp. 187–200.

Strout, Alan Lang (1959), *A Bibliography of Articles in Blackwood's Magazine: Volumes I Through XVIII, 1817–1825*, Lubbock: Texas Technological College.

Sucksmith, H. P. (1971), 'The Secret of Immediacy: Dickens's Debt to the Tale of Terror in *Blackwood's*', *Nineteenth-Century Fiction*, 26: 2, 145–57.

Thomson, Henry [1827] (1995), 'Le Revenant', in Robert Morrison and Chris Baldick (eds), *Tales of Terror from Blackwood's Magazine*, Oxford: Oxford University Press, pp. 73–87.

Warren, Samuel (1830a), 'Passages from the Diary of a Late Physician', *Blackwood's Magazine*, 28, 322.

— (1830b), 'Death at the Toilet', *Blackwood's Magazine*, 28, 938–40.

— [1830] (1995), 'A "Man About Town"', in Robert Morrison and Chris Baldick (eds), *Tales of Terror from Blackwood's Magazine*, Oxford: Oxford University Press, pp. 181–213.

Wheatley, Kim (1992), 'The *Blackwood's* Attacks on Leigh Hunt', *Nineteenth-Century Literature*, 47: 1, 1–31.

Wilson, John (1822), 'Noctes Ambrosianae, No. II', *Blackwood's Magazine*, 11, 475–89.

— [?] (1823), 'Love, A Poem, in Three Parts', *Blackwood's Magazine*, 13, 321–3.

— [1818] (1995), 'Extracts from Gosschen's Diary', in Robert Morrison and Chris Baldick (eds), *Tales of Terror from Blackwood's Magazine*, Oxford: Oxford University Press, pp. 19–24.

Winnifrith, Tom (1973), *The Brontës and Their Background*, London: Macmillan.

Chapter 11

Gothic Stevenson
Roderick Watson

When Stevenson tackled Scottish subjects for the first time in his fiction it was, as Stephen Arata has observed, 'by way of the Gothic' (2010: 59). 'Thrawn Janet', 'The Body Snatcher' and 'The Merry Men' were all written on the author's return to Scotland from North America, during a sojourn in Pitlochry and Braemar in the wet summer of 1881. This chapter will propose that from these Scottish roots Stevenson went on to develop the Gothic genre to explore his sense of the nature of human identity and, beyond that, the conditions of material existence itself. It will trace such mutations at work in three specifically 'Gothic' texts, 'Thrawn Janet' (1881), *Strange Case of Dr Jekyll and Mr Hyde* (1886) and 'Olalla' (1885), in order to demonstrate Stevenson's evolving engagement with the genre, and its importance to any critical understanding of his work.

A 'Gothic' approach to identity and being was not unique to Stevenson for literary critics have noted how Scottish culture in general in the late eighteenth and nineteenth centuries tended to play the more 'rational' claims of modernity and the Enlightenment against older discourses from traditional culture, oral lore and superstition. Ian Duncan has argued that 'the thematic core' of Scottish Gothic grows from the disjunctions created when an increasingly modern and urban population seeks its national identity by turning to a 'cultural otherness designated as pre-modern' (2012: 123). Arata agrees that this disjunction produced 'an intimate estrangement' in the relationship between Scottish writers and the icons of national culture in the nineteenth century, and argues that Stevenson, growing up in a respectable family of civil engineers, haunted by his nurse's tales of Covenanting martyrs and eerie folklore, was especially subject to 'psychic splittings and fragmentations' (2010: 60).

Gothic writing is characterised by its engagement with what has been or should be repressed, and the suspicion that dreams and fancies, or the cellar and the dusty attic (metaphors for the unconscious) may contain more than we suspect, working in unforeseen ways. Prompted by the many readers who asked about the genesis of *Strange Case of Dr Jekyll and Mr Hyde*, Stevenson produced 'A Chapter on Dreams' for *Scribner's Magazine* in 1887, to recount the dream that generated his tale, and to reflect on the workings of his own unconscious. It is no accident that he chose the brownies, supernatural figures from Scottish folklore, to make his point, recognising that they are without conscience, and can be both helpful and malevolent by turns. His dream of the brown dog eating a fly and winking at him is a small masterpiece of the uncanny, and almost as disturbing is an overtly Oedipal dream of parricide, recounted in detail and suffused with shadowy guilt, but never quite recognised for what it is: a young man murders his father and finds himself more and more deeply entangled with his young stepmother (Stevenson 1924a: 47–9). These brownies are the real thing.

Stevenson's early engagement with supernatural lore, Covenanting history and Calvinist belief (he had planned *A Covenanting Storybook* at the age of eighteen) marked him for life. Given Scottish Calvinism's core concept of election, which is to say salvation or damnation regardless of merit, not to mention its insistence on original sin and the literal presence of the demonic in everyday life, it is not surprising that Stevenson's early Gothic fictions should have taken the ideological form they did. One might go so far as to say that – in its Scottish manifestations at least – the wilder reaches of Calvinism were *always already* Gothic. In this sense, the undoubted masterpiece of Scottish Gothic uncertainty and psychological fragmentation is James Hogg's *The Private Memoirs and Confessions of a Justified Sinner* (1824), particularly notable for its use of what Arata calls the 'fractured narrative structures and multiplication of perspectives that characterise the genre' (2010: 54). Hogg's use of oral Scots as the 'unreliable' narrative voice in many of his supernatural tales adds even more to the uncertainties of perception and subjectivity so characteristic of Gothic writing, as if older forms of discourse and dread were constantly erupting into the text.

Such disjunctions illustrate what Arata calls an 'intimate estrangement' at the heart of Scottish Gothic (2010: 60), and that intimacy can never quite be thrown off. This is the final meaning of Stevenson's extraordinary polysemous fable 'The House of Eld', which imbricates the inescapability of old times, doctrinal religion, inheritance, belief and (again) parricide. This disturbing fable, published posthumously in 1896, merits serious consideration as a key to Stevenson's dark playfulness, and serves to reveal some of the unconscious drives of his psyche, not least regarding the recurring claims of authority, tradition, and the relationship between fathers and sons (Abrahamson 2007). It begins, 'So soon as the child began to speak, the gyve was riveted', and when young Jack asks why strangers do not share this handicap, his uncle, 'the catechist', replies, 'do not complain about your fetter, for it is the only thing that makes life worth living. None are happy, none are good, none are respectable, that are not gyved like us' (Stevenson 1924b: 86). When Jack finally frees himself and his community from the burden of these (literal) shackles, he finds that he has only shifted the fetters to everyone's other leg and killed his family in the process. The fable ends with a bleak moral that stresses its deep origins in the unconscious:

> Old is the tree and the fruit good
> Very old and thick the wood.
> Woodman, is your courage stout?
> Beware the root is wrapped about
> Your mother's heart, your father's bones;
> And like the mandrake comes with groans.
>
> (Stevenson 1924b: 92)

Stevenson's first and most straightforward engagement with orality, hard-core Calvinism and the Scottish Gothic appears in 'Thrawn Janet', a tale that might indeed have been told by James Hogg himself (see Massie 2003). Stevenson had already drafted a 'Story of Thrawn Janet' for his *Covenanting Storybook*, and by 1881 he was planning a complete collection of supernatural stories, to be called *The Black Man and Other Tales*, drawing heavily on books that had thrilled his imagination when he was younger, most notably George Sinclair's seventeenth-century text *Satan's Invisible World Discovered* (see Swearingen 1980: 59). The connection is significant for the mine runs deep, as Stevenson was to say of *Jekyll and Hyde*: 'the gnome is interesting, I think, and he came out of a deep mine, where he guards the fountain of tears' (Stevenson 1924c: 67). Thinking of Scottish identity at large, Ian Duncan has argued that 'Scottish Gothic narrates a parody or critique of [the] nationalist project of romance revival, in which the reanimation of traditional forms is botched or nightmarish, rather than restorative' (2012: 123–4), and 'Thrawn Janet', while properly nightmarish, does seem to be possessed of what might be called a complex spirit of reanimated 'Scottishness' that is full of relish, blackly comedic and even vengeful.

The scene is set by a diegetic narrative voice, but the most and best part of the tale is delivered in broad Scots just as 'one of the older folk would ... recount the cause of the minister's strange looks and solitary life' (Stevenson 1924d: 110). We learn that the parish of Balweary in the vale of Dule (sorrow, lamentation) contains the Hanging Shaw (overhanging wood), the Water of Dule, the De'il's Hag, and the Black Hill (Stevenson is enjoying the trappings of the genre). The Reverend Soulis's parishioners, pious and level-headed in their own eyes, are soon revealed as uncharitable bigots presaging both the Kailyard school of sentimentality at the turn of the century and George Douglas Brown's bitter attack on it in *The House with the Green Shutters* (1901). It is these stoutly familiar 'worthies' who persecute Janet M'Clour (known for her sharp tongue and reputed to have had an illegitimate child in her youth), giving her a stroke (as the reader suspects and the minister believes) and her 'thrawn' twisted or surly features. We are told that 'Janet was mair than suspeckit by the best folk in Ba'weary', but now the godly are even more convinced that she has been possessed by the devil: 'she couldna speak like a Christian woman, but slavered an' played click with her teeth like a pair o' shears; an' frae that day forth the name of God cam' never on her lips' (1924d: 113). Stevenson creates memorable scenes of terror as his tale sets about dismantling the minister's rational act of charity. Soulis encounters a large black man surrounded by crows in the old graveyard on the hill and suffers feverish nights in a month of exceptional heat, until the vision of Janet suspended on a single nail by a single thread, and her slow descent of the stairs like a walking corpse, shatters his sanity, vindicates folk belief, justifies superstitious bigotry and brings the tale to an end.

In keeping with the conventions of Gothic fiction, the narrative seems to allow for a rational explanation, even as the folk-voice of the main text establishes itself as an unreliable narrator full of its own rectitude and utterly convinced of supernatural presence. Stevenson's relish for the traditional details of the bogey tale is evident, and there is a hint of parody in his tone when he retails the ghastly and gloomy piety of his antinomian parishioners. More to the point, however, 'Thrawn Janet' explicitly enacts the disjunction between enlightenment rationality and folk belief as noted by Ian Duncan and others. Fresh from university, Soulis is immediately identified by his new flock as a young man full of book learning, but 'nae leevin' experience in religion'. Worse than this, he reads from a large library of books, 'when the hail o' God's Word would gang in the neuk o' a plaid', and is revealed as doubly suspect and socially ambitious when he accepts the laird's advice to hire Janet M'Clour as a servant, for 'in thae days he wad hae gane a fair gate to pleesure the laird' (1924d: 111). The tale is thus revealed as a parable of folk-revenge against modernity, rationality and any authority other than the harsh creed of individual faith and election. Stevenson's final twist is to show us, in the text's opening pages, that Soulis himself, like Janet before him, has become an object of dread, as he wanders and howls in the night with an eye that had 'pierced through the storms of time to the terrors of eternity' (1924d: 109).

As Stevenson's simplest and most traditionally 'Gothic' tale, 'Thrawn Janet' clearly understands the essence of the genre as a site through which repressed fears and unconscious drives erupt, as the Presbyterian godly of Balweary oversee their atavistic and misogynist revenge upon modernity, womankind and ambitious university-educated young ministers. Stevenson understands, enjoys and exposes the congregation's unholy satisfaction. And yet, confirmed in an 'iron composure' with a 'wild scared and uncertain eye' (1924d: 109), the Reverend Soulis (does his name evoke the soul?) has become a telling emblem of their own, their religion's and the genre's inner disjunction. By such means, at least one version of the national tradition is simultaneously recognised and satirised. By comparison, 'The Body Snatcher' (1884) is a lesser and much more conventionally gruesome tale.

In thinking of 'Thrawn Janet' in later years, Stevenson remarked that it had the defect of being 'true only historically, true for a hill parish in Scotland in old days, not true for mankind and the world' (1924d: xv). 'The Merry Men' (1882) was to take this on board and go a stage further. This second tale keeps to a historical setting, but its vision of guilt and terror is much wider. In enthusiastic letters to his editor Sidney Colvin and his friend W. E. Henley, Stevenson described 'a fantastic sonata about the sea and wrecks', insisting that these elements and their setting on a remote Scottish island were the essence of the story: 'I like it much above all my other attempts at story-telling; I think it is strange; if ever I shall make a hit, I have the line now, as I believe' (1924e: 158). Stevenson's 'line' was to push beyond the stagy Calvinism of 'Thrawn Janet' and its 'vale of Dule' to engage with a broader and ultimately existential vision of the terrors of the universe.

At the centre of the tale, but by no means its symbolic heart, is old Gordon Darnaway, an extreme Presbyterian – indeed, a Cameronian Calvinist who has looted a ship that was wrecked on the rocks and the deadly tidal rip (known as the Merry Men) off the coast of his lonely island in the Inner Hebrides. Tormented by guilt, for it transpires that he murdered a lone survivor, and yet convinced that the wrecks are nothing less than the work of divine justice, he has become greedy for gain and even more greedy for the sight of ruin. The tale is told by Darnaway's orphaned nephew Charles, who is equally given to the assumption that everything happens only according to God's will. He is not without his own ambivalent motives, however, for he hopes to restore his fortune and marry his uncle's daughter by finding treasure from a Spanish galleon, the *Espirito Santo*, sunk in the bay at the time of the Armada. Charles loses his taste for the quest when he stumbles on long-drowned bones, only to discover a much more recent grave on the shore – evidence of his uncle's crime. Nor is Charles alone in his search, for another boat appears with strangers seeking the same old galleon, only to be caught in a rising storm and destroyed by the Merry Men on a terrible night during which old Gordon Darnaway's last shreds of sanity are blown away as he exults in the disaster.

'The Merry Men' is a tale of considerable symbolic complexity by which the whole landscape – a world away from the conventionally spooky vale of Dule in 'Thrawn Janet' – speaks for ambivalence and the generation of theological or indeed metaphysical doubt. Nothing is certain on these shores, yet they encompass holy names, for we are told that the island 'Aros Jay' in Gaelic means 'the house of God'; the treasure galleon was the *Espirito Santo*; and the most recent wreck, with a defaced nameboard, is the *Christiana*, named after Christian's wife in *Pilgrim's Progress* or perhaps *Christiania* after the Norwegian city (1924d: 25). Old Darnaway, however, can only read it as '*Christ-Anna*', gloomily remarking, 'It's an awfu' name' (1924d: 12). If the wreck is a judgement in the eyes of Darnaway, and the Lord rides on the tempest, then surely the ocean deep is a measure of God's mighty works – at least according to the metrical psalms of David? Yet Darnaway has moments of doubt when he is 'temp'it to think it wasna the Lord, but the muckle, black deil that made the sea' and his vision of the fish and the crabs 'cauld-wamed, blind-ee'd uncanny ferlies', eating the dead in the underwater dark, leads him to cry out 'the horror – the horror o' the sea!' (1924d: 14, 16).

In part, of course, Darnaway's fears derive from a bad conscience for profiting (as an ex-seaman himself) from the deaths of others, and in a quieter moment his nephew Charles recognises that we are prone to read into the world what we are inclined to find there. He notes 'when it is calm, as it often is, there appear certain strange, undecipherable marks – sea runes, as we may name them – on the glassy surface of the bay' (1924d: 18). So it is that Gordon reads the letter 'C' for *Christ-Anna*, while Charles sees only his own name, and then again 'M' for his beloved Mary. His uncle is haunted by 'misery, mercy, marriage, money', all related to the themes of the story, and finally, of course, 'murder'. Nevertheless, despite the colourations of subjectivity and the dualisms of Darnaway's Calvinist guilt, it is Stevenson's invocation of the power and terror of the final storm that will become the central and controlling vision of the whole tale.

'The Merry Men' invokes a universe of all-engulfing noise, mindless and 'almost mirthful', as we find ourselves on the edge of a cliff, peering

> upon a world of blackness, where the waters wheel and boil, where the waves joust together with the noise of an explosion, and the foam towers and vanishes in the twinkling of an eye. . . . Thought was beaten down by the confounding uproar; a gleeful vacancy possessed the brains of men, a state akin to madness. (Stevenson 1924d: 41)

Charles is fated to watch the wreck of the mysterious schooner, and realises that it was on just such a night that his drunken uncle witnessed the death of the *Christ-Anna*, and all this on a little island named 'the house of God'. Charles may be caught between confoundingly dualistic accounts of a 'charnel ocean' and the 'great bright creature of God's ocean' (1924d: 29–30), but we recognise them, along with Stevenson, as one and the same thing, in the same singular and natural world – which is our world, not just the little island of Aros Jay. Quite what this world, and our place in it, ultimately *means*, however, is another question.

'The Merry Men' can be seen to have invoked a kind of existential Gothic, or indeed a Gothic existentialism, in its vision of the natural world as a whirl of energy and matter, always at risk of shipwreck in 'the roaring blackness' at the edge of an abyss. Stevenson was to return to the theme in his essay 'Pulvis et Umbra', which was first published in *Scribner's Magazine* in April 1888. The essay may model itself on Roman stoicism by taking its title (*pulvis et umbra sumus* – we are but dust and shadow) from Horace's *Odes* (IV, 7), but its position is much influenced and modified by contemporary advances in astronomical and evolutionary science. In fact, Stevenson called it his 'Darwinian Sermon': 'Of the Kosmos in the last resort, science reports many doubtful things and all of them appalling' (1924f: 60). He maintained that it was 'true' but 'touching and beneficial, to me at least' (1924c: 169); nevertheless, he presents an unforgettably grim vision of a rapacious universe:

> Meanwhile our rotatory island loaded with predatory life, and more drenched with blood, both animal and vegetable, than ever mutinied ship, scuds through space with unimaginable speed, and turns alternate cheeks to the reverberation of a blazing world, ninety million miles away. (Stevenson 1924f: 62)

This is not so far from Gordon Darnaway's experience on his own little island – except that this universe of dust and shadow is godless, and a Calvinist distrust of the flesh has mutated into a vision of all material phenomena, most especially the body itself, as something utterly abject in the Kristevan sense.

Julia Kristeva's theory of abjection argues that we expel and deny the things that remind us of our mortality, that threaten our sense of unique subjectivity, and ultimately even the symbolic order of language itself. This urge to abjection can be seen in our own and society's response to rotten food, excreta and most especially to the 'self' as a corpse subject to decay:

> Refuse and corpses *show me* what I permanently thrust aside in order to live. . . . If dung signifies the other side of the border, the place where I am not and which permits me to be, the corpse, the most sickening of wastes, is a border that has encroached on everything. It is no longer I who expel, 'I' is expelled. (Kristeva 1982: 3–4; original emphasis)

Thus Stevenson:

> This vital putrescence of the dust, used as we are to it, yet strikes us with occasional disgust, and the profusion of worms in a piece of ancient turf, or the air of a marsh darkened with insects, will sometimes check our breathing so that we aspire for cleaner places. But none is clean: the moving sand is infected with lice; the pure spring, where it bursts out of the mountain, is a mere issue of worms; even in the hard rock the crystal is forming. (Stevenson 1924f: 61)

Stevenson's position in 'Pulvis et Umbra' is to find comfort in the fact that we still manage to live and love despite the horrors of our physical condition. Nevertheless, it is his vivid and totally alienating account of those horrors that remains most forcibly with the reader:

> What a monstrous spectre is this man, the disease of the agglutinated dust, lifting alternate feet or lying drugged with slumber; killing, feeding, growing, bringing forth small copies of himself; grown upon with hair like grass, fitted with eyes that move and glitter in his face; a thing to set children screaming. (Stevenson 1924f: 62)

– A creature from the crypt, indeed (see Watson 2011). Passages such as these and old Gordon Darnaway's vision of life as a 'roaring blackness, on the edge of a cliff' (Stevenson 1924f: 42) begin, like Kristeva's encounter with abjection, to suggest an encounter with the 'real'. Kristeva cites Lacan's understanding of this term, which is not dissimilar in its properties from Stevenson's own account, in 'Pulvis et Umbra', of 'something called matter: a thing which no analysis can help us to conceive; to whose incredible properties no familiarity can reconcile our minds' (1924f: 61).

The abjection of the flesh had already appeared as a motif in Stevenson's writing in 1886, when he was seeking to convey the hidden horrors of human nature in *Strange Case of Dr Jekyll and Mr Hyde*. Far from Aros

Jay and far from the eighteenth century, Stevenson's most famous fable of the fragile and divided self has a modern urban setting, finding the smart avenues and lanes of London to be no less appropriately 'Gothic' than the De'il's Hag. The mark of Calvinism remains, however, for it is Jekyll's desire for singular virtue, against the multiple weaknesses of his own flesh, that leads him into his experiments, only to find that the despised drives of his repressed self, hidden in the form and revealed by the name of his alter ego, are powerfully addictive.

The text is famously polysemic, and contemporary anxieties about Darwinian evolution and degeneration co-exist with equally contemporary fears about drug addiction, urban crime and class inequality. Readers have identified a critique of upper-class homosocial complacency and privilege in its pages, as well as homosexual hints and anxieties and – with or without a prefiguring of Freud's theories of the unconscious – a significantly modern challenge to any notion of the unified self. As Jekyll confides in his 'Full Statement of the Case':

> I was no more myself when I laid aside restraint and plunged in shame, than when I laboured, in the eye of day, at the furtherance of knowledge or the relief of sorrow and suffering . . . I thus drew steadily nearer to that truth, by whose partial discovery I have been doomed to such a dreadful shipwreck: that man is not truly one, but truly two . . . and I hazard the guess that man will be ultimately known for a mere polity of multifarious, incongruous and independent denizens. It was the curse of mankind that these incongruous faggots were thus bound together. (Stevenson 1924b: 57–8)

Such an understanding is a clear development beyond the simple dualism of 'Thrawn Janet' or the more nuanced Dostoevskian psychological drama of 'Markheim'. In fact, Stevenson's subsequent work shows an increasingly subtle engagement with, and modification of, simplistic dualism leading to his masterpiece in this regard, *The Master of Ballantrae* in 1889 (see also Watson 2004).

Stevenson's vision of the horrors of materiality, one that he was to explore at length, as we have seen, with 'Pulvis et Umbra', is a significant factor in his understanding of what Hyde represents. No one can meet Hyde without experiencing a kind of existential nausea that defies rational explanation. Yet the experience of Hyde also brings a lighter step, a terrible energy, intoxicating like wine, with 'a more generous tide of blood' (1924b: 65). What is this surge, but the drive of the flesh, and beyond that the drive of every kind of physical embodiment, animal, vegetable and mineral, all inescapably part of our consciousness, and yet utterly, and – on a bad day – horribly alien to it? Jekyll himself comes to see this in the last pages of his 'Full Statement':

Hyde, for all his energy of life, [was] something not only hellish but inorganic. This was the shocking thing; that the slime of the pit seemed to utter cries and voices; that the amorphous dust gesticulated and sinned; that what was dead, and had no shape, should usurp the offices of life. And this again, that that insurgent horror was knit to him closer than a wife, closer than an eye; lay caged in his flesh, where he heard it mutter and felt it struggle to be born. (Stevenson 1924b: 73)

And yet Hyde *is* Jekyll, flesh of his flesh, closer than a wife, closer than a son. The 'good' Dr Jekyll has been overwhelmed by a vision of materiality as abjection, strikingly similar to Sartre's existential disgust, when the protagonist of *Nausea* is penetrated and sickened by existence itself, by the bark of a chestnut tree in the park, when the 'veneer' of things has 'melted, leaving soft, monstrous masses, in disorder, naked, with a frightening obscene nakedness' (Sartre 1965: 183). Stevenson has moved far beyond what might be called the native parody of Gothic Calvinism in 'Thrawn Janet'.

Stevenson was to explore the sickening and seductive drives of the material body one more time in 'Olalla', his revisionist vampire tale, written only a month or so after *Jekyll and Hyde*. As with 'Thrawn Janet', the author recruits the usual Gothic tropes, as his protagonist comes to convalesce in a remote and decaying ancestral pile, the *residencia* of an aristocratic Spanish family fallen on hard times. Stevenson's hero is a wounded soldier from the Peninsular War, but in the structure of the tale his role is a stereotypically feminine one, caught up in strange doings, rather like Catherine Morland in *Northanger Abbey* (1817), Jane Austen's parody of the genre. There is an unseen sister who may be a lunatic, and terrible cries in the night when his bedchamber has been locked from the outside.

Our soldier's aristocratic hosts may be fallen in more ways than one, for the story is quick to engage quite specifically with late nineteenth-century society's fears of atavistic decline and genetic degeneration. The lady of the house is the last of a long and exhausted bloodline, solitary and reclusive, whose half-wit son acts as a servant or general factotum about the place. Felipe is dog-like and ingratiating in demeanour, he is not above torturing squirrels and his quick animal movements are slightly feral: 'full of starts and shyings, as inconstant as a hare' (Stevenson 1924d: 138). Still more disturbing is Felipe's mother, the Señora, a woman of once great beauty, languorous, sensual, idling all day by the fire in her little alcove in the courtyard. Her copper hair is as luxurious as that of any Pre-Raphaelite beauty, yet her expression is replete, complacent and 'blankly stupid' (1924d: 135), relieved only by her large and uncanny golden eyes. Stevenson returns to this alienating image at every turn, haunted by those 'great, beautiful and meaningless orbs, wide open to the day, but closed against human enquiry' whose pupils 'expanded and contracted in a breath'. Nor can his hero explain the peculiar 'distaste that jarred along my nerves' (1924d: 149) in her company – a reaction more than reminiscent of how people responded to Edward Hyde.

Stevenson teases us with the vampire motif when his hero cuts his wrist and the Señora bites him, but the true core of the tale is somewhere else, as is evident when he meets Olalla. As if in expiation of her family's degeneration, Olalla lives the life of a penitent and indeed ends the tale in that role, standing by a wayside crucifix, as the protagonist flees. I would argue, however, that the story's Gothic trappings are only a preparation for a much more disturbing exploration of the truly uncanny nature of sexual desire. The tropes of vampire lore and the Petrarchan conventions of love poetry are duly acknowledged when they 'drink' each other in, and she follows him with her 'great thirsting eyes' (1924d: 147). But there is an almost blasphemous spin to how Stevenson describes a kind of transubstantiation at their first encounter, within seconds of meeting: 'Her eyes took hold upon mine and clung there, and bound us together like the joining of hands; and the moments we thus stood face to face, drinking each other in, were sacramental and the wedding of souls' (1924d: 146–7). The soldier's rather purple response has the force of a drug, or the religious ecstasy of St Teresa of Avila:

> I beheld this maiden on whom God had lavished the richest colours and the most exuberant energies of life, whom he had made active as a deer, slender as a reed, and in whose great eyes he had lighted the torches of the soul. The thrill of her young life, strung like a wild animal's, had entered into me; . . . She passed through my veins: she was one with me. (Stevenson 1924d: 147)

Can such a creature really be the sister of Felipe and the daughter of the Señora? Can this drug really be love? Determined to speak of his attraction, the hero approaches Olalla only to find himself struck dumb again:

> When I did indeed encounter her, the same force of passion descended upon me and at once submerged my mind; speech seemed to drop away from me like a childish habit; but I drew near to her as the giddy man draws near to the margin of a gulf. (Stevenson 1924d: 150)

No words can express such an abject capitulation and he reflects again on what is happening to him:

> Was this love? Or was it mere brute attraction, mindless and inevitable, like that of the magnet for the steel? We had never spoken, we were wholly stran-

gers; and yet an influence, strong as the grasp of a giant, swept us silently together. (Stevenson 1924d: 151)

This goes beyond a patriarchal distrust of (female) sexuality, for all volition is lost in this gravitational pull, in the rapture of disindividuation and letting go:

> I felt a thrill of travail and delight run through the earth. Something elemental, something rude, violent, and savage, in the love that sang in my heart, was the key to nature's secrets; . . . She seemed the link that bound me in with dead things on the one hand, and with our pure and pitying God upon the other; a thing brutal and divine, and akin at once to the innocence and to the unbridled forces of the earth. (Stevenson 1924d: 153–4)

In this forest of contradictions, Olalla, too, seems to recognise that the elemental force between them is not necessarily a kindly thing. Under its influence, the fortress of her identity has been shaken just as Jekyll's was shaken by his elixir, and the clamour of desire is utterly without conscience.

The true vampire in this text is the vampire of human desire. Stevenson has already invoked the ambiguous literary codes of romantic love and religious ecstasy, and he has used the story's Gothic tropes to reveal the drives of the id, and the uncanny loss of identity under the dizzying spell of uncontrollable sexual desire (see also Beattie 2005: 17–18). It is from this that our wounded hero flees; it is this that leads to the socially necessary and restabilising renunciation of their feelings. It is this that leaves Olalla standing under the image of a crucified Christ at the end of the tale. She can only understand her plight in terms of her Catholic religion: 'we must all bear and expiate a past which was not ours; there is in all of us – ay, even in me – a sparkle of the divine' (1924d: 167). It is Stevenson, however, who sees that the 'divine' in this case has more in common with the great god Pan than it does with the Man of Sorrows. Despite their renunciation, and despite Olalla's piety, the genie is out of the bottle, for the abject abyss of sexual desire has been recognised – even if it has been related in coded terms.

Under Stevenson's pen, familiar Gothic tropes and social certainties have been subverted and overthrown. The Calvinist dualisms of the parishioners in 'Thrawn Janet' have been replaced by the multiple indeterminacies and the intimate seductions of *Jekyll and Hyde*. In 'The Merry Men' and 'Olalla', the conventions of original sin and mystery romance have revealed material existence and human desire to be utterly abject in a physical world that is chaotic and absurd. From old Scottish roots, pursuing what is ultimately a metaphysical or indeed a proto-existential vision, Stevenson has given a disturbingly new dimension to the conventions of Gothic fiction.

References

Abrahamson, Robert Louis (2007), '"I never read such an impious book": Re-examining Stevenson's *Fables*', *Journal of Stevenson Studies*, 4, 209–26.

Arata, Stephen (2010), 'Stevenson and *Fin-de-Siècle* Gothic', in Penny Fielding (ed.), *The Edinburgh Companion to Robert Louis Stevenson*, Edinburgh: Edinburgh University Press, pp. 53–69.

Beattie, Hilary J. (2005), 'Dreaming, Doubling and Gender in the Work of Robert Louis Stevenson: The Strange Case of "Olalla"', *Journal of Stevenson Studies*, 2, 10–32.

Duncan, Ian (2012), 'Walter Scott, James Hogg and Scottish Gothic', in David Punter (ed.), *A New Companion to the Gothic*, Oxford: Wiley-Blackwell, pp. 123–34.

Kristeva, Julia (1982), *Powers of Horror: An Essay on Abjection*, trans. Leon S. Roudiez, New York: Columbia University Press.

Massie, Eric (2003), 'Scottish Gothic: Robert Louis Stevenson, *The Master of Ballantrae* and *The Private Memoirs and Confessions of a Justified Sinner*', in William B. Jones Jr. (ed.), *Robert Louis Stevenson Reconsidered: New Critical Perspectives*, Jefferson, NC: McFarland, pp. 163–73.

Sartre, Jean-Paul [1938] (1965), *Nausea*, trans. Robert Baldick, Harmondsworth: Penguin Modern Classics.

Stevenson, Robert Louis (1924a), 'A Chapter on Dreams' (1887), in *Further Memories*, London: William Heinemann, Tusitala edn, vol. 30, pp. 41–53.

— (1924b), *Strange Case of Dr Jekyll and Mr Hyde, Fables, Other Stories and Fragments*, London: William Heinemann, Tusitala edn, vol. 5, pp. 86–92.

— (1924c), *The Letters of Robert Louis Stevenson, Volume III*, London: William Heinemann, Tusitala edn, vol. 33.

— (1924d), *The Merry Men and Other Tales*, London: William Heinemann, Tusitala edn, vol. 8.

— (1924e), *The Letters of Robert Louis Stevenson, Volume II*, London: William Heinemann, Tusitala edn, vol. 32.

— (1924f), 'Pulvis et Umbra', in *Ethical Studies: Edinburgh Picturesque Notes*, London: William Heinemann, Tusitala edn, vol. 26, pp. 60–6.

Swearingen, Roger G. (1980), *The Prose Writings of Robert Louis Stevenson: A Guide*, London and Basingstoke: Macmillan.

Watson, Roderick (2004), '"You cannot fight me with a word": *The Master of Ballantrae* and the wilderness beyond dualism', *Journal of Stevenson Studies*, 1, 1–23.

— (2011), '"Ginger beer and earthquakes" – Stevenson and the terrors of contingency', *Journal of Stevenson Studies*, 8, 108–24.

Chapter 12

J. M. Barrie's Gothic: Ghosts, Fairy Tales and Lost Children

Sarah Dunnigan

In his obituary of J. M. Barrie, George Bernard Shaw called his plays 'terrifying'. Although *Peter Pan* (first performed in 1904) had long become a cherished children's fantasy and a staple of Christmas theatricals, Shaw seemed more perturbed than enchanted by it (1993: 151). Barrie is seldom described as a Gothic writer, although his own well-known and often reductively understood biography has been 'Gothicised' into a dark psycho-narrative. Rather than use the latter to suggest Barrie's election to the Scottish Gothic canon, this chapter takes its cue from recent work by R. D. S. Jack (2010), Valentina Bold and Andrew Nash (2014) and others, who demonstrate how Barrie is a writer of complexity and contradiction. The generic and thematic range of Barrie's writing means that he is not a consistent or fully fledged Gothic writer but nevertheless Gothicism still inks a recurrent pattern of motifs and ideas in his work. This chapter singles out three texts in particular from the first three decades of the twentieth century: the novella, *Farewell Miss Julie Logan* (1931); the play, *Mary Rose* (1920), which Alfred Hitchcock had a long, unrealised dream of filming (McBride 2001: 24); and *Peter Pan*, here discussed in its incarnations as both drama and prose text (1902; 1904; 1906). It suggests that Barrie's Gothicism most arrestingly coheres in the mode of the ghost story, retrospectively echoing the conventions of the classic late Victorian ghost story whilst mirroring the psychological complexities of contemporary Modernist supernatural fictions (see Briggs 1997; Riquelme 2008; Smith 2010; Thurston 2012). In its delicate yet complex obsession with themes of death and loss, memory and the past, his spectral writing provides evidence of an engagement with Scottish national Gothic, specifically in the persistent portrayal of historical and psychological 'pasts' which cannot be exorcised, and in the use of thematic and aesthetic motifs from traditional folkloric belief. This chapter suggests, however, that this engagement is subtly manifest as an ambivalence towards a past that is simultaneously feared and desired. In its imaginative obsession with loss – with the consequences of 'calling back' the missing or the vanished – and ultimately with the figure of the child beyond reach, Barrie's writing is an intensely 'affective' form of Gothic.

Farewell Miss Julie Logan

This novella, aptly called 'A Wintry Tale', was first published in 1931 as a supplement to the Christmas edition of *The Times* (Nash 2004). Its 'white wastrie of a world' is configured as a Gothic northern topography where winter periodically 'locks' the glen and its inhabitants, both living and ghostly, into snow-bound stasis – a time when, as the new young minister, Adam Yestreen, discovers, 'the stories that crawl like mists among our hills' come to life; 'White hillocks' resemble 'eggs'; and snow-laden branches ominously become 'white ropes' (Barrie 1989: 34–5). This northern supernaturalism is a trope with deep roots in Romantic Celticism or, in Matthew Wickman's phrase, 'Highlandism' (2007: 10), whilst 'the journey North' of the Lowland Presbyterian minister, evokes, as Kirsty Macdonald notes, a lineage of Scottish writing portraying the Highlands as 'Gaelic-speaking, primitive, often supernatural and certainly other' (2009: 2).

Varieties of 'otherness' are newly encountered and experienced by Yestreen, thus defying the 'pastness' into which his name (Scots for 'yesterday') symbolically locks him. His capacity for erotic desire is disclosed once the haunting by the titular spirit, Miss Julie Logan, has begun. Linguistic and cultural alterity is embedded in the environment on which Yestreen, literally and figuratively, trespasses. Seasonal English visitors intent on blood sports discomfort Yestreen, and make social and cultural estrangement the precondition for his haunting. The landscape is portrayed as a palimpsest, built up out of geological, historical and symbolic layers that are easily disturbed. This recalls Romantic and early nineteenth-century Scottish antiquarian writing about the Highlands and islands – such as W. G. Stewart's *Popular Superstitions and Festive Amusements of the Highlanders of Scotland* (1823) – that blends historical and topographical knowledge with accounts of traditional lore and 'superstition'. The terrains traversed by their writers are haunted by social, cultural and political memories and, in gothically charged moments, direct both curiosity and fear about what lies beneath in literal and symbolic terms. Barrie's glen, once the former 'hiding place' of Jacobites and now their haunting ground, can be placed in this tradition of Romantically stratified landscapes. These Jacobite ghosts also recall a trope of the Gothic Romantic novel of the Anglo-Protestant tradition which portrays Jacobitism as an alien, unassimilable force whose incursion into the present threatens to undo its politically and culturally achieved stability (see Groom 2012; Pittock 2012). Barrie's novella, then, echoes a tradition of 'political' Gothic which pathologises the threat posed by a resurgent identity – Stuart, Jacobite and Catholic – to a Unionist and Protestant Britain.

These rebel armies (evocatively called 'The Strangers') comprise the novella's 'undead', then, but Barrie's text does not really pursue the political and cultural associations of this strangely embodied historical past: why this particular return of the repressed, as it were, at this particular temporal juncture? The final encounter between Yestreen and Miss Julie is an odd exorcism which brings to the surface, without fully unravelling, the psychological and cultural implications of this incursion of past within present : '"Hold me closer," she said, "lest by some dread undoing you should let me slip." I held her closer. "Adam dear," she said, "it is this, I am a Papist." At that awful word I dropped her in the burn' (Barrie 1989: 77). Alistair McCleery describes this as the 'one dramatic instant difficult to swallow . . . ineffective, even allowing for the prejudices of the period' (1989: 94). By this time, however, Barrie's titular protagonist is a fusion of the text's multiple 'dark cause[s]': Jacobitism, Catholicism, femininity and malign enchantment. She combines the Gothic eroticism of the Victorian female vampire with Stuart iconography – blackberry wine stains Miss Julie Logan's throat 'which they say also happened with Mary Stewart' (1989: 57). In her strange delivery of a villager's baby, she also evokes traditional Scottish folkloric belief in the fairy woman who malevolently steals newborn children: 'I had a sinking that she was going to bite it [the baby]. I nippit it from her' (1989: 43).

Farewell, then, is a powerful but haphazard blend of traditional Gothic motifs. Its central protagonist is terrified by the ghosts of a hidden national history, a trope whereby, in Murray Pittock's terms, the 'irrational alterity' of 'rejected' political, religious and cultural realms resurfaces (2012: 243), particularly strong in Scottish (and Irish) Gothic writing. It even replicates the Gothic tradition of the 'found' text bearing witness to uncanny events, exemplifying the 'resurrection of textual antecedents' which Timothy C. Baker describes as a defining feature of the complex category of Scottish Gothic (2014: 5). But it also contains something of Barrie's own distinctive Gothicism that *Mary Rose* and *Peter Pan* deepen and intensify. Before she metamorphoses into a more rapacious and sexualised spirit, Miss Julie is fleetingly imbued with a 'sweet homeliness' (Barrie 1995: 55), and strikingly so within the space of the 'very unhomely manse' (1995: 57), a term replete with associations of the *unheimlich*, the Freudian uncanny (Freud 2003). In this respect, she exemplifies the '(un)homely' revenant of Barrie's ghost fictions who is at once cherished and frightening, familiar and unfamiliar; and, like the past itself, both feared and desired.

Mary Rose

By his own admission, Barrie called *Mary Rose*, first performed at the Haymarket Theatre in London on 22 April 1920, 'strange' (Ormond 1983: 59). In a play whose setting shifts between Sussex and the Hebrides – an English 'manor house' Gothic versus a 'misty, eerie' (Barrie 1995: 271) Scottish island Gothic – the titular heroine is, like Miss Julie Logan, a revenant. She, too, recalls those restless, anxious spirits who haunt the living in traditional Scottish ballad and folklore but also echoes the figure of the changeling, the child-victim of fairy abduction. Mary Rose vanishes and returns more than once: first, when aged eleven, on a remote Hebridean island with her father, but found twenty days later, 'sitting on the tree-trunk sketching' (1995: 259), unaware that she had been missing; then again, as a married woman, the island's 'call' (1995: 278) – its source never explicitly defined but suggestive of the fairies' call – comes once more; missing for twenty-five years, she again returns 'across the fields' to her supposedly bereaved elderly parents and husband; whilst in the final scene, now her son, Harry, returns from the war to that same Sussex manor in which her ghost has been locked. In that sense, both mother and son are revenants, returning visitants from another realm: the former otherworldly, the latter culturally, since Harry as a young child fled to Australia and has now returned as a soldier, conscious of his 'otherness'.

   Mary Rose is a classic example of 'domestic Gothic', a story full of secrets. We learn that her father never told his daughter that she had vanished: 'we were afraid to alarm her, to take the bloom off her' (1995: 259); her husband-to-be, Simon, says the event had 'no effect on her' except that sometimes he catches her 'listening for a sound' (1995: 261). A classic Gothic topographical motif, the house itself, having been 'long . . . for sale', sepulchrally embodies secrets within its rooms and staircases: in Barrie's detailed authorial prologue to the play's first scene, we are told that 'if a photograph could be taken quickly we might find a disturbing smile on the room's face . . . knowing only what the dead should know' (1995: 241). This is a suggestive metaphor: traces, echoes and memories of Mary Rose and the past inexorably seep through the materiality of the present – rooms, objects and natural emblems such as the 'apple tree' where we first encounter Mary Rose, entwined in its branches, summoned by her mother; a girl-child-woman about to be engaged but needing protection from '... myself ... Simon ... daddy' (1995: 252). When her father later wants the tree cut down, it is painful proof for his wife that he has forgotten Mary Rose, whilst to the returned Harry it is a vanished emblem of his own childhood. But the past is tenacious: the housekeeper informs Harry that the tree's 'root' survives. When Mary Rose's father assures Simon that his daughter's childhood vanishing is an event 'dead and done with' (1995: 261), we sense that its roots – its memory and significance – remain to be unearthed. As Baker observes, *Mary Rose*'s island 'stands for all that which cannot be explained or identified', 'a world without resolution' as well as 'a state of mind' (2014: 93–4).

Mary Rose expands the psychological and emotional parameters of the ghost story. In a drama ostensibly about how her disappearance(s) and loss impinge on those left behind, Mary Rose survives as a figure of empathy. Portrayed by others as 'odd', physically and emotionally delicate, and defined by 'innocence', Mary Rose has been compared to the similarly vanishing, spiritualised heroine of James Hogg's poem, 'Kilmeny' (1813) (Ormond 1983: 133). Her mother even suggests that 'It is as if Mary Rose was just something beautiful you and I and Simon had dreamt together' (Barrie 1995: 285). She is the girl who never grew up, a dream-child in the mould of Peter Pan, his feminine alter ego. Fascinatingly, as Ormond points out, in the first draft of the play, Barrie contrived a meeting between Mary Rose and Peter Pan on the island (Ormond 1983: 61). Like Peter, Mary Rose manifests fear of maturation and intimacy. She negotiates her impending marriage (Barrie 1995: 261) by resuming the role of a child in need of the 'safe place' that ironically she imagines her father once thought the island might be for her (1995: 263). Tellingly, it is described as being made to fit Mary Rose and vice versa (1995: 264), as if conjured up by herself; and she treats it as if it is an animated thing, in need of nurture. Marriage, sexuality and the island's dark allure are implicitly associated. Mary Rose's mother warns her husband that 'She can't marry, James, without your first telling the man. We agreed' (1995: 251), alluding to the event of the inexplicable childhood vanishing. This implies that only upon marriage will revelation of that secret or repressed knowledge be made to anyone outside the family. Since her earlier 'unnatural' experience is thus linked to another rite of passage (marriage), Mary Rose resembles a ballad heroine whose enchantment is invested with socio-sexual symbolism.

Though her portrayal has been seen as troublingly reductive, arguably it possesses more psychological nuance, for Mary Rose is a mother as well as the dream child. Poignantly, she glimpses her son, Harry, waving to her just as she herself once did 'from this very spot' to her father (1995: 266). Neither moment in this repetitive sequence is elaborated further by Barrie, except for Mary Rose's aside that this instance of distant but tender mutual recognition signified 'That was a happy time' (1995: 266). Ironically, twenty days after she disappears, it is the vision of her waving (and 'sketching') again which summons her father across to the island to fetch his 'same merry unselfconscious girl' (1995: 259). This simple gesture becomes a touchstone of both innocence and experience, a measure of both the love and distance that characterise the interlocking relationship of father–daughter–son. Before she vanishes again, Mary Rose worries whether she has 'been all right as a mother' (1995: 276); this seems prescient, as if she needs to find peace of mind before she leaves (1995: 276). Mary Rose's haunting might be best understood as an act of love, an answer to what she asks of her husband before vanishing:

> MARY ROSE: . . . Have I been the sort of mother a child could love and respect?
> SIMON: That is a very awkward question. You must ask that of Harry Morland Blake. (Barrie 1995: 276)

The play's extraordinary final scene, in which mother and son are tenderly and disconcertingly reunited, represents an act of completion acknowledged from the outset – a needful exorcism: 'The room is in a tremble of desire to get started upon that nightly travail which can never be completed till this man is here to provide an end' (1995: 247). Mary Rose is a ghost in mourning, grieving for the child whom she never saw growing up. Perhaps as a result of its myriad rewritings (Ormond 1985: 125–33), Barrie's handling of this scene makes it irresolute. Mary Rose takes Harry's knife in hand, angry that he might in fact be the abductor, 'The one who stole him from me' (Barrie 1995: 295). This misrecognition is painful to observe in the drama's final moments, founded on a reversal of the mother–child bond where *he* seemingly nurtures *her*. The final published version seems cruelly to withhold confirmation that Mary Rose recognises and thus 'finds' her lost son, but Ormond suggests that she is indeed 'released' or exorcised by him in the play-text's final ending which shifts to a more religious register (Ormond 1985: 131): 'The call is again heard, but there is in it now no unholy sound . . . the weary little ghost knows that her long day is done. Her face is shining' (Barrie 1995: 298).

Mary Rose's Gothicism helped make it a popular success but so too probably did its impulse towards wish-fulfilment – that the living and the dead are inseparable, that the missing can always come back. In that respect, it is a ghostly fairy tale that exemplifies Barrie's characteristically ambiguous portrayal of the incursive Gothic past. Jennifer Bann interestingly suggests that the empathically imaginative potential of the ghost story was partly fostered by the influence of the spiritualist movement. Spiritualism enabled writers to portray 'spectrality' as 'something inherently powerful and transformative', and to imply 'that the dead were willing and able to communicate with the living, and that what they had to say was worth listening to' (2009: 663, 665). Significantly, Barrie's post-war play, *A Well-Remembered Voice* (1918), features a seance as its central dramatic and emotional premise (Stevenson 2013: 81). Arthur Conan Doyle, a friend of Barrie's and famously fascinated by the occult, observed how spiritualism seemingly allowed the bereaved to be reunited with their loved ones in all their physical and emotional particularity:

> What is it to a mother if some impersonal glorified entity is shown to her? She will say, 'that is not the son I lost – I want his yellow hair, his quick smile, his little moods that I know so well.' That is what she wants; that, I believe, is what she will have. (Arthur Conan Doyle qtd. in Bann 2009: 673)

In Mary Rose, Barrie creates a tender, empathic spirit; elusive and ambiguous, she still possesses a definite emotional quest – a mother in search of her child. In turn, that child is seeking his missing mother. As a 'demobilised soldier' (Ormond 1983: 59), Harry is implicitly carrying his own traumatic burden from his experience of war. Shadowed in the relationship between Mary Rose and Harry are those other severed or lost relationships between sons and mothers in the Great War.

Peter Pan

In defining the experience of the uncanny in relation to Samuel Coleridge's poetry, David Punter observes that it resembles 'a coming home, a return to the familiar, in which nonetheless all is changed' (2002: 195). This is the case when we return to *Peter Pan* in the light of the Gothicism that has been traced in Barrie's work. Though this 'fairy play' and its prose variants were conceived earlier than either *Farewell* or *Mary Rose*, and would seem on the face of it unlikely Gothic exemplars, they distil those themes of fear, loss and bereavement even more sharply perhaps because they are mediated through the emblem of the lost child – 'the gothic child' (Georgiera 2013), 'the child that haunts us' (Hancock 2008). The key to the relationship between *Peter Pan* and the Gothic can be located in the iconic opening scene of the night nursery:

> [(]*As she [Mrs Darling] enters the room she is startled to see a strange, little face outside the window and a hand groping as if it wanted to come in*)
> MRS DARLING Who are you? (*The unknown disappears; she hurries to the window*) No one there. And yet I feel sure I saw a face. My children! (*She throws open the bathroom door and Michael's head appears gaily over the bath. He splashes; she throws kisses to him and closes the door. 'Wendy, John,' she cries and gets reassuring answers from the day nursery. She sits down, relieved, on Wendy's bed; and Wendy and John come in, looking their smallest size, as children tend to do to a mother suddenly in fear for them.*) (Barrie 1995: 89)

Before the nursery becomes the liberating threshold of Neverland, it is momentarily the home of a classic Gothic trope: the haunter at the window, seeking entrance, in a visual motif reminiscent of the popular spectral hands of the Victorian ghost story. 'Normality' is resumed but profound maternal anxiety has been articulated which is tenderly echoed in childhood's fear of the dark:

> MICHAEL Can anything harm us, mother, after the night-lights are lit?
> MRS DARLING Nothing, precious. They are the eyes a mother leaves behind her to guard her children. (Barrie 1995: 97)

From the outset, then, Peter is in part an embodiment of fear, the projection of unidentified but potent anxieties. As frequently observed, he is a hybrid and liminal creature, resisting fixed identity, termed 'a Betwixt-and-Between' in *Peter Pan in Kensington Gardens* (Barrie 2004: 172). Barrie's authorial instructions of the final 1928 play-text describe him 'dressed . . . in autumn leaves and cobwebs' (1995: 97) but associate him with emblems of birth and renewal; we know he still retains all his baby teeth (1995: 123); in *Peter and Wendy* (1911), they are 'gnashed' at Mrs Darling in a kind of vampiric miniaturism. He cannot be touched, like the spirits in medieval accounts of haunting who manifest 'resistance to physical contact with the living' (Schmitt 1998: 198). And yet, as Amy Billone strikingly puts it, his effect on other characters is of a 'heart-stoppingly gorgeous man who died as a child' (2004: 190).

Death and children are entwined throughout the *Peter Pan* narratives. This is where the absolute heart of Barrie's Gothicism can be located. The 'deathliness' of Peter himself, as it were, is ushered in from the start by the fact that he was the little boy who 'ran away to Kensington Gardens and lived a long time among the fairies' (1995: 99). The fairies' winged delicacy in Arthur Rackham's famous illustrations to *Peter Pan in Kensington Gardens* (1906), and Tinkerbell's beloved mischievous brilliance, has obscured the darker provenance of fairies in traditional Scottish folklore and belief which associated them with the world of the dead: 'folk customs, such as the offering of meal and milk to appease the fairies, were carried out to placate the dead' (Henderson and Cowan 2001: 19; cf. Briggs 1978, 1989; Kavey 2009). Later sixteenth-century first-hand accounts of fairy encounters, which often led to witchcraft persecution, were frequently initiated by the witness's visitation by the spirit of a dead person. The popular belief that fairies might represent, or incarnate, the souls of the deceased therefore renders them liminal creatures. As Diane Purkiss puts it, 'Fairies are the dead, and a category of the dead who are still active, still alive' (2007: 166). In that respect, Scottish fairies are already creatures of the Gothic. In *Peter Pan in Kensington Gardens*, the fairies are beautiful but lugubrious and vengeful as the little lost girl, Maimie, discovers almost to her peril. The gardens are where they and Peter live but they are also a graveyard, the potential burial ground for those lost children whom Peter has not successfully rescued. In the play, too, death and the realm of enchantment remain a thematic motif. When Peter airily tells Wendy that the fairies 'are nearly all dead now' (Barrie 1995: 99), it famously sets in motion the play's association between childhood belief and fairy survival but it also foregrounds the incomprehensibility of death as a word, a concept, to the children in the texts – 'To die will be an awfully big adventure', proclaims Peter (1995: 125); Curly says, 'I thought it was only flowers that die' (1995: 112), at Wendy's apparent death; whilst for Hook, the stopped clock 'is the fear that haunts me' (1995: 109). Far more poignantly, though, the Lost Boys are those children who have fallen out of their prams, stolen by fairies and (sometimes) rescued by Peter; but, in each instance, to their parents in the non-magical realm, they are dead.

In that sense, the *Peter Pan* texts, and *Mary Rose* too, are populated by Gothic children who are dead, or vanished, and therefore haunting their bereaved families. Barrie's 'ghost children', whilst seeming intrusively poignant within the genre of children's literature, evoke those dying children in Hans Christian Andersen's fairy tales – such as 'The Little Match Girl' (1845) – who find tragic but beautiful apotheoses; whilst in George MacDonald's fantasy writing children confront, as seen in his 1871 *At the Back of the North Wind* (2001) and are also transformed through, death. *Peter Pan* is also arguably shaped by the legacy of the late nineteenth-century ghost story in which children often play key roles. As Nina Auerbach observes, in Victorian literature 'children are always about to disappear . . . their admonitory, evaporating presences are most perfectly realised as ghosts' (1990: 24). In this respect, Margaret Oliphant (admired by both Henry James and Stevenson) is Barrie's significant predecessor in terms of Scottish exponents of the genre. In her ghost stories, children are often cast as sensitive and vulnerable percipients of the unseen ('The Open Door', 1882; 'Old Lady Mary', 1885). Moreover, as in *Mary Rose* and *Peter Pan*, her work is filled with hauntings that throw domestic and familial relationships into sharp relief ('The Open Door'). Like Barrie's, hers is arguably an intensely affective Gothic that focuses on bonds of love and trust between protagonists, and on the psychological relationships between past and present.

The 'ghostliness' of *Peter Pan* might therefore be constituted within a Scottish Gothic tradition of the ghost story, and within a tradition of the ghost story more broadly which is partly explicable in socio-cultural terms as a vehicle for confronting, and coming to terms with, the familiarity of death, and child mortality especially, an intimate experience in most Victorian families. Stories that evoked a spirit world were a way of retaining links with the dead (and therefore symbolically with the past), and of circumventing loss. In the 'old nursery' of the play's final scene, Mrs Darling sits waiting by the deliberately open window. An emblem of parental loss, her pain is what only Wendy can begin to imagine, and what the 'heartless' Peter refuses to believe can be experienced. Mrs Darling's fear in Act One comes true, but only temporarily for her children do return, like revenants, from Neverland. The Lost Boys too are 'found', or adopted – 'ghost children' who are restored to life – although they may grow up to be soldiers. As in *Mary Rose*, the war itself is a ghost, prefigured and retrospectively present, as Barrie developed the story pre- and post-conflict. It is perhaps understandable that in an age when cinema's 'lost object of desire, origin, and vanishing point', as Emma Wilson argues, has become 'the missing child' (2003: 15), *Peter Pan* should be a source of explicit and implicit allusion for one of the most notable recent examples of cinematic Gothic, Juan Antonio Bayona's *El Orfanato/The Orphanage* (2007).

Conclusion

Reasons for the prevalence of spirits, ghost mothers and vanished children in Barrie's work can be plucked from his own life. They include his brother's childhood death; his mother's; the surrogate family of the Llewellyn-Davies children whom he inherits through tragedy, and their own tragic afterlives. Ormond points to an essay by Charles Lamb, 'one of Barrie's favourite writers' (Ormond 1985: 124), as an aesthetic and psychological touchstone for his life and work: 'in ... "Dream-Children", the childless Lamb writes of an imaginary son and daughter who finally disappear. ... The essayist senses that they are calling to him: "We are nothing; less than nothing, and dreams"' (1985: 124). Even Peter Pan himself longs for his own dream-child: 'He is dreaming, and in his dreams he is always in pursuit of a boy who was never here nor anywhere' (1985: 135). There are, therefore, apparent biographical reasons why the 'dream-child' should figure so prominently in Barrie's writing but the relationship between Barrie's life and art can ultimately prove quite circular.

Barrie's Gothicism possesses qualities that have come to define the Scottish Gothic tradition, although the latter, as Baker cautions, remains a construct that always resists and questions its own unity (2014: 2). These texts inherit a Romantic fascination for traditional folkloric belief and culture, their ghost-children and spirit-protagonists bearing the imprint of the changeling, the fairy woman and the revenant. All three figures are prominent within the Scottish ballad tradition. In addition, *Farewell* explores the relationship between Scottish national and historical identity by means of what Ian Duncan describes as the characteristically 'uncanny recursion of an ancestral identity' (Duncan 2001: 70). However, the story is arguably less interested in the apparently troubling political and cultural implications of this 'ghost history' than in the more intimate psychological haunting of the central protagonist. This means that the trope of the resurrected past (so prominent in Scottish Gothic) is delicately and complexly inflected in Barrie's work, evoking not only dread and fear, but also – and especially when that past is emblematised by the figure of the missing or dead child – longing and nostalgia. This helps to explain why the influence of the nineteenth-century ghost story, and its associations both with spiritualism and with the figure of the ghost-child, is a helpful paradigm by which to understand these texts. In that respect, Barrie's writing also prefigures the way in which contemporary Scottish Gothic, according to Baker, deploys the mode as 'a space in which to appropriate loss' (2014: 163), and imaginatively to comprehend the processes of mourning. In its ambiguously celebratory desire to recover the dead and the vanished, then, *Peter Pan* can be seen as the ultimate Gothic fairy tale.

References

Auerbach, Nina (1990), *Private Theatricals: The Lives of the Victorians*, Cambridge, MA: Harvard University Press.

Baker, Timothy C. (2014), *Contemporary Scottish Gothic: Mourning, Authenticity, and Tradition*, Basingstoke: Palgrave Macmillan.

Bann, Jennifer (2009), 'Ghostly Hands and Ghostly Agency: The Changing Figure of the Nineteenth-Century Specter', *Victorian Studies*, 51: 4, 663–85.

Barrie, J. M. [1931] (1989), *Farewell Miss Julie Logan: A Wintry Tale*, ed. Alistair McCleery, Edinburgh: Scottish Academic Press.

— (1995), *J. M. Barrie: Peter Pan and Other Plays*, ed. Peter Hollindale, Oxford: Oxford University Press.

— (2004), *Peter Pan: Peter and Wendy* and *Peter Pan in Kensington Gardens*, ed. Jack Zipes, London: Penguin.

Bayona, Juan Antonio (dir.) (2007), *El Orfanato/The Orphanage*, film, Spain: Warner Bros.

Billone, Amy (2004), 'The Boy Who Lived: From Carroll's Alice and Barrie's Peter Pan to Rowling's Harry Potter', *Children's Literature*, 32, 178–202.

Bold, Valentina and Andrew Nash (eds) (2014), *Gateway to the Modern: Resituating J. M. Barrie*, Glasgow: ASLS.

Briggs, Julia (1997), *Night Visitors: The Rise and Fall of the English Ghost Story*, London: Faber.

Briggs, Katherine (1978), *The Vanishing People: Fairy Lore and Legends*, New York: Pantheon.

— (1989), *The Fairies in English Tradition and Literature*, London: Bellew Publishing.

Duncan, Ian (2001), 'Walter Scott, James Hogg and Scottish Gothic', in David Punter (ed.), *A Companion to the Gothic*, Oxford: Blackwell, pp. 70–80.

Freud, Sigmund (2003), *The Uncanny*, trans. David McLintock, intro. Hugh Haughton, London: Penguin.

Georgiera, Margarita (2013), *The Gothic Child*, Basingstoke: Palgrave.

Groom, Nick (2012), *The Gothic*, Oxford: Oxford University Press.

Hancock, Susan (2008), *The Child That Haunts Us: Symbols and Images in Fairytale and Miniature Literature*, London: Routledge.

Henderson, Lizanne and Edward Cowan (2001), *Scottish Fairy Belief*, East Linton: Tuckwell Press.

Jack, R. D. S. (2010), *Myths and the Mythmaker*, Amsterdam: Rodopi.

Kavey, Allison B. (2009), '"I do believe in fairies, I do, I do": The History and Epistemology of Peter Pan', in Allison B. Kavey and Lester D. Friedman (eds), *Second Star to the Right: Peter Pan in the Popular Imagination*, New Brunswick: Rutgers University Press, pp. 75–104.

McBride, Joseph (2001), 'Alfred Hitchcock's "Mary Rose": An Old Master's "Unheard Cri de Coeur"', *Cinéaste*, 26: 2, 24–8.

MacDonald, George [1871] (2001), *At the Back of the North Wind*, London: Everyman.

Macdonald, Kirsty (2009), 'Scottish Gothic: Towards a Definition', *The Bottle Imp*, 6 <http://www.arts.gla.ac.uk/ScotLit/ASLS/SWE/TBI/TBIIssue6/Scottish_Gothic.pdf> (last accessed 11 May 2015).

Nash, Andrew (2004), 'Ghostly Endings: The Evolution of J. M. Barrie's *Farewell Miss Julie Logan*', *Studies in Scottish Literature*, 33: 1, 124–37.

Ormond, Leonee (1983), 'J. M. Barrie's Mary Rose', *Yale University Library Gazette*, 58: 1(2), 59–63.

— (1985), *J. M. Barrie*, Edinburgh: Scottish Academic Press.

Pittock, Murray (2012), 'Is There a National Gothic?', in Mary-Ann Constantine and Dafydd Johnston (eds), *Footsteps of Liberty and Revolt: Essays on Wales and the French Revolution*, Cardiff: University of Wales Press, pp. 231–45.

Punter, David (2002), 'Scottish and Irish Gothic', in Jerrold E. Hogle (ed.), *The Cambridge Companion to Gothic Fiction*, Cambridge: Cambridge University Press, pp. 105–23.

Purkiss, Diane (2007), *Fairies and Fairy Stories: A History*, London: Tempus Publishing.

Riquelme, John Paul (ed.) (2008), *Gothic and Modernism: Essaying Dark Literary Modernity*, Baltimore: Johns Hopkins University Press.

Schmitt, Jean-Claude (1998), *Ghosts in the Middle Ages: The Living and the Dead in Medieval Society*, trans. Teresa Lavender Fagan, Chicago: University of Chicago Press.

Shaw, George Bernard (1993), 'Barrie: "The Man with Hell in his Soul"', *Shaw and Other Playwrights*, 13, 151–3.

Smith, Andrew (2010), *The Ghost Story, 1840–1920: A Cultural History*, Manchester: Manchester University Press.

Stevenson, Randall (2013), *Literature and the Great War 1914–1918*, Oxford: Oxford University Press.

Stewart, William Grant (1823), *Popular Superstitions and Festive Amusements of the Highlanders of Scotland*, Edinburgh: Archibald Constable.

Thurston, Luke (2012), *Literary Ghosts from the Victorians to Modernism: The Haunting Interval*, London: Routledge.

Wickman, Matthew (2007), *The Ruins of Experience: Scotland's 'Romantick' Highlands and the Birth of the Modern Witness*, Philadelphia: University of Pennsylvania Press.

Wilson, Emma (2003), *Cinema's Missing Children*, London: Wallflower Press.

Chapter 13

The *'nouveau frisson'*: Muriel Spark's Gothic Fiction
Gerard Carruthers

If Muriel Spark has strong elements of Gothic apparatus in her work, then this is generally of the kind that works through urban rather than 'wilder' or more 'sublime' settings. Gothic, supernatural, uncanny elements are used in Spark's fiction, most especially, to undermine and satirise the modern, material, town-based life of twentieth-century humanity and to signal an alternative immaterial, moral, spiritual reality in which, as a Christian, she believes. Alongside her crucial Catholicism, Spark's Scottishness provides a particular Gothic accent to her work through a set of texts on which she frequently riffs. These include the Scottish Border Ballads, James Hogg's *The Private Memoirs and Confessions of a Justified Sinner* (1824) and Robert Louis Stevenson's *Strange Case of Dr Jekyll and Mr Hyde* (1886). This set of texts does not make for any 'essential' Scottish Gothic canon, but rather relies on Hogg's steepage in the Ballads, Stevenson's knowledge of Hogg and Spark's interest in all of these things. These texts have tended to be given less emphasis in Spark criticism than her more explicit, critical engagement with English Gothic such as Mary Shelley or the Brontës, or even John Henry Newman whose religious writings belong, to some extent, within the context of the space mapped out by nineteenth-century Gothicism.

In her short stories, Spark develops a miniaturist sensationalism where human life is treated in shocking, seemingly gratuitous, ways. These also regularly feature an explicitly supernatural layer. 'The Portobello Road' (1958) is narrated by a ghost who acquires the nickname of 'Needle' after she finds one in a haystack. Our narrator has been murdered, her body being discovered in a haystack, and this concatenation between the two found needles mimics, in a way, the incremental repetition of the Ballads where lines/events are reiterated for intensity of effect. The violent death and the lingering revenant are also 'stock' ballad elements. The story ends in a way that hallmarks Spark's outlook on the world throughout her oeuvre, as Needle contemplates herself and some friends in a photograph, 'each reflecting fearlessly in the face of George's camera the glory of the world, as if it would never pass' (Spark 2011: 524). Humans are too complacent and secure in the mundane, quotidian world, and inattentive to the moral life, or indeed afterlife. Exemplary of a favourite Spark word that she associates with the ballads, there is 'economy' in her usage of 'the glory of the world', which is at once a feat of ironic compression (where the short life of Needle and her friends is treated reductively) and also a signal that the 'glory' really lies elsewhere in the less transient features of earthly existence. Sharply dissonant effect, where the cliché of 'needle in a haystack' and terrible murder are identically couched, displays what we might call the brittle Gothic texture of Spark's writing. We see this broad terrain also earlier in Spark's first published short story, 'The Seraph and the Zambesi' (1951) where a real angel, an exotically particular six-winged type, turns up at an African nativity play on a sweltering day and demands to take part. There is uncomfortable and clunking intrusion again in 'The Black Madonna' (1958) where a couple pray that their childless situation may be remedied via the intercession of Our Lady (and in particular apropos an icon of the Virgin made from Irish bog-oak). Seemingly, the white couple's prayers are answered and, in time, the woman gives birth to a baby. However, it is black and to avoid the gossip and the social stigma, they put it up for adoption. Amid possible explanations (the baby, in fact, is natural, a 'throwback') and public awkwardness, a point is being made about how earthly life is ungovernably, uncontrollably contingent, grotesque even, and that it is how we deal with such situations spiritually rather than socially that counts.

Spark's engagement with Gothic matter more than anything draws out and utilises its grotesque and sensationally shocking strand, both for darkly comic and also poignant effect (a duality we see also at the level of economical language in the simultaneously sardonic and lyrical ending of 'The Portobello Road'). In her novels, Spark's grotesque, quasi-Gothic characters are apparent from the start in *The Comforters* (1957) where the unpleasant, bullying and self-righteous Georgina Hogg sometimes simply disappears, a fictive rendering of her moral crassness. Both monstrously apparent and, at other times, a meta-fictional absence, the character shows what was to become a typically Sparkian ambivalence where her Gothic creations are somewhat casually taken 'off the peg' (in the case of Georgina Hogg, there is a play on James Hogg, with his central 'justified sinner' protagonist from his greatest novel) as well as subtly trick-laden within the formal fabric of the text. *Memento Mori* (1959) is similarly marked by Gothic intrusion, in this case an anonymous phone-caller apparently threatening people that they 'must die'. Rather than a petty, poisonous stalker, the reader might instead read a message from God, a *memento mori* that the elderly in receipt of this treatment ought, indeed, to remember: that the grave is near and that they should attend to their consciences, contemplating and being repentant of their moral flaws. We see here also that morally grey Sparkian terrain, where the agency of good and evil is not certain and represents a challenge of apprehension to Spark's characters (and, indeed, readers) as they negotiate, therefore, a rather Manichean or Gothicised world. Mary Shelley's *Frankenstein, or the Modern Prometheus* (1818) as well as Hogg's *Confessions* is a template here for a world which, in entangled oppositional fashion, is difficult to read. Moral ambiguity is unleashed in Dougal Douglas, the full-blown Gothic protagonist in *The Ballad of Peckham Rye* (1960), with its resonant supernatural title and its quotidian, suburban location. Dougal is both an exuberant modern-day agent of the devil – 'I'm only supposed to be one of the wicked spirits that wander through the world for the ruin of souls' (Spark 1999: 77), as he explicitly acknowledges – and another of Spark's fictive devices. He is constructed from the bricolage of Prometheus (as Dougal brings both light and heat to those he encounters in Peckham), and Satan in the ballad 'The Demon Lover'. With his hump, he also recalls William Shakespeare's Richard III and, in his role as a sinner bringing moral discernment (or as a 'justified sinner') Hogg's character, Robert Wringhim. As well as incorporating these materials, he relates to two great eighteenth-century writers, William Blake (who claimed to have encountered angels on Rye Common) as well as James Boswell (an archetypal 'Jock on the Make' in London, as Dougal might also be read).

The novel begins with an oral situation where the conversation mimics the incremental technique and predictable rhythms of the ballad:

> 'Get away from here, you dirty swine,' she said.
> 'There's a dirty swine in every man,' he said.
> 'Showing your face round here again,' she said.
> 'Now, Mavis, now, Mavis,' he said. (Spark 1999: 7)

At once we are plunged into mundane, clichéd, everyday speech though, at the same time, there is an undertow of something else: the *swinish*, which reverberates with the Satanic, after the Gospel passage of the Gadarene swine (Luke 8: 26–39). The folk supernatural terrain that is unobtrusively opened up develops through the plot. The 'dirty swine' is Humphrey Place who, under the influence of Dougal Douglas, has stood up at the altar with our first speaker's daughter, Dixie. It might be thought, however, that the real swine or devil is Douglas, whose demonic influence has transmitted itself into Humphrey (just as the demon is transported by Christ into the pigs in Gadara, as featured in all three Synoptic Gospels). Further enriching this demonic texture, Dixie is illegitimate, being conceived by her mother during the Second World War after a liaison with an American airman, and her behaviour further suggests that, in accordance with traditional, conservative folk-rules, she is a bad 'bastard' with a more than usual mark of the Devil upon her. However, Dixie's behaviour is far from being conventionally evil. She is seventeen and covets a comfortable marriage, for which she saves hard (employed in both a full-time and part-time job to this end), as well as the white goods that advertising teaches her to aspire to as a modern would-be housewife. This is a most curious kind of badness that resounds throughout *The Ballad of Peckham Rye* where ordinary, materialist behaviour stands for a moral laxness. Similarly, we find another situation of such small-mindedness, which Dougal works to encourage. He is a model tenant, eliciting his landlady's delight in a note praising his exemplary making of his bedclothes. This same woman is lacking any affection for her own brother when he appears as a tramp. Cleanliness and good housekeeping are things most certainly not next to godliness in this novel. In a third example of deep malaise of spirit signalled by quotidian conventionality, the married Mr Druce is having an affair with his secretary, Merle Coverdale. Before making love, he arranges his clothes neatly, signifying that even this illicit situation has become ground down into a bleak, joyless immorality. Dougal involves himself too with Merle so as to create a love triangle. Raising the pitch of the situation, he engenders jealousy in Druce who murders Merle by stabbing her in the neck with a corkscrew. Yet again, we see a typical Sparkian 'economy' or duplicity where the awful violence of the ballad world is replicated but in more threadbare, suburban fashion by means of the wine-opener, enabling device of the squalid evening couplings of the workplace lovers.

Dougal might be, as indeed he claims, an agent of the Devil sent to bring about the ruination of souls. As with the crucial model of Wringhim's doppelgänger, Gil-Martin in Hogg's *Confessions*, he obeys the 'folk-rules' where the Devil cannot simply bring about evil in people's lives, but instead encourages already pre-existing dispositions. In the case of Merle and Mr Druce, then, Dougal cranks up an already existing immoral situation. In Hogg's novel, Wringhim's pre-existing pride, arrogance and the fact that he is an extreme Calvinist believing that, in his vouchsafed salvation, he can do no wrong, make him prey to the suggestiveness of Gil-Martin. As a result, he carries on ever more impervious to morality, in a career that includes rape, murder and, ultimately, self-annihilation. Hogg's *Confessions* is also divided into two main parts, the Sinner's narrative and the Editor's account, with numerous places where each, implicitly, infects the other's perspective (see Hogg 2010). This makes for a duplicitous, double-tongued or demonic texture that *The Ballad of Peckham Rye* also replicates. We see this in the language throughout, as in the case of the opening already mentioned (with a discourse that is simultaneously inhabited with mundanity and the lyrical world of the ballads) and also in the oxymoronic title, where the poetic and the mundane, ballad and prose, collide. The duplicity occurs also in the character of Dougal who becomes his own doppelgänger or mirror image through the simple expedient of reversing his name to Douglas Dougal and finding employment in a second job. In this career situation, he also mimics the hardworking efforts of Dixie, though less honestly since he accounts the same time twice, cheating both his employers. The question arises, then, as to whether Dougal is truly a demon, or merely a petty conman (perhaps simply the devil 'deserved' by petty Peckham). In the nineteenth-century novel we have the options of either Wringhim's Satanic possession or non-supernatural psychological malaise. Something in Spark's writing becomes much more insistent in and after *The Ballad of Peckham Rye*, though it had clearly also been present in her earlier novels, and that is the reader's response. We are invited amid comically difficult, grimly humorous circumstances, to judge the status of reality, the supernatural and, indeed, the moral frame of reference to be employed. Here again a kind of Gothicism is at work as the reader is left at sea by a narrator who very ambiguously will not grant authority or finality of interpretation. The reader is also compelled to inhabit the bewildering, rather claustrophobic scenario with their own interpretative compass pointing in all directions at once.

Albeit with doubts about the notion of defining *Frankenstein* as a Gothic work, it is from Shelley's novel that Spark builds a Gothic apparatus in *The Prime of Miss Jean Brodie* (1961). Spark identifies the former as creating, at the start of the nineteenth century, a new intellectual energy to the mode, 'a wonderful and *nouveau frisson*. The limits of the horror-novel had been reached, and old props of haunted castles, hanged babes and moonlight dagger scenes were beginning to raise a shrug rather than a shudder' (Spark 1987: 154). One of Spark's more tender treatments of human life (the love is tangible towards a real-life model for the central protagonist who had taught the author), *Jean Brodie* contains horrific moments that mark it out as pervaded by a cruel, Gothic taste for suffering. The novel ends its first chapter with an episode concerning dull, bullied ten-year-old Mary Macgregor struggling to answer a question set by her teacher, Miss Brodie. We see Mary's discomfort and simultaneously we are shown the future:

> Mary Macgregor, lumpy, with merely two eyes, a nose and a mouth like a snowman, who was later famous for being stupid and always to blame and who, at the age of twenty-three, lost her life in a hotel fire . . . (Spark 1961: 13–14)

Here, in the brutal flash-forward ending of the life of a character we are witnessing presently as a somewhat vulnerable child, is a breathtakingly cruel narrator. This authorial-narratorial presence is chillingly insidious too, as we see Mary being not so much physically described as physically made, minimally moulded, 'like a snowman'. Chapter 2 ramps up the horrific pathos of Mary's situation as we are told that, aged twenty-three, a Wren during the Second World War, she has been dumped by her 'first and last boy-friend' and contemplates miserably:

> she thought back to see if she had ever really been happy in her life; it occurred to her then that the first years with Miss Brodie, sitting listening to all those stories and opinions which had nothing to do with the ordinary world, had been the happiest time of her life. She thought this briefly, and never again referred her mind to Miss Brodie, but had got over her misery and had relapsed into her habitual slow bewilderment, before she died while on leave in Cumberland in a fire in a hotel. (Spark 1961: 15)

For the reader here there is a double Gothic effect as the horrendous trapped demise of the young woman is supplemented by the prolepsis so that the form of the novel, in a sense, lends itself to a similarly claustrophobic entrapment. The unattractive, bullied Mary becomes here in adulthood the scapegoat that Miss Brodie had decreed her to be, a sacrificial offering almost in her horrifying death. The pathetic limits of Mary's life are tightly defined by an omniscient narrator who therefore seems complicit with Brodie in summing up the schoolgirl's value and worth. Of course we must assume a moral reckoning at work beyond this complicity of main character and narrator, and it is to be found, clearly, in the passage's cutting down of Miss Brodie herself. She is the petty dictator of standards and tidiness in the classroom worrying over, if not exactly 'spilled milk', then 'spilled ink'. Here we have an indicator of the trivial, clichéd Brodie who is very different from the person we seemingly find elsewhere in the novel. Brodie is as much an unpleasant bore as she is an imaginative plenitude, 'an Edinburgh Festival all on her own' (1961: 27). In one of Spark's most human novels, albeit with a typical formal trickery that goes against the grain of the typical 'humanist' novel, the reader should feel sympathy for the deeply disposable life-form that Mary seems to represent in both Brodie's contempt and in the heartless narration of schooldays and death.

Mary is not the only character in *The Prime of Miss Jean Brodie* whose life is appropriated for callous literary effect. Jean Brodie projects a lover, Hugh Carruthers who 'fell', she claims poetically, 'on Flanders' Field' during the First World War, 'the week before Armistice was declared' (1961: 12). Hugh's actual existence, however, is never verified. Like Frankenstein's monster, he is made from the body parts of others, living rather than dead, including Brodie's teaching colleagues Gordon Lowther (the music master) and Teddy Lloyd (the art master): 'He was very talented at both arts [singing and painting], but I think the painter was the real Hugh' (1961: 72), says Miss Brodie at one point discussing her two principal present-day suitors and revealing her preference. Brodie herself is described as part John Knox and part Mary, Queen of Scots, indicating her own ambiguous identity, part-Puritan, part-Romantic. She is also, generally, a 'Jekyll and Hyde' character in her frequent contradictions whose name has been appropriated from Deacon William Brodie, the real-life, respectable Edinburgh artisan who was also a burglar for the thrill of it, from whom Jean Brodie claims to be descended and who 'died . . . on a gibbet of his own devising' (1961: 88). From early on, her own body is appropriated by the girls she teaches, making use of the fanciful stories she tells them about herself. A high point of this characteristic Sparkian 'poetic justice' occurs as the prepubescent Sandy and Jenny invent a love epistle from Brodie to Lowther. A comical *tour de force* from the point of view of the adult reader, there is also something serious going on. It ends, 'Allow me, in conclusion, to congratulate you warmly upon your sexual intercourse, as well as your singing' (1961: 74). The point is that those who tell tall tales will have tall tales visited upon them, and with a kind of truth inevitably seeping out: here, the fact that the girls know their teacher to have been scandalously involved in premarital sexual intercourse with her lover.

Notoriously, Jean Brodie seeks to direct her girls' future lives, including her attempt to put one of her pupils in the bed of Teddy Lloyd as her 'proxy'. In the case of the letter, we see her girls in turn 'writing' the life of their teacher. Sandy Stranger herself exhibits an imagination in overdrive as she contemplates her teacher and, then, in more life-changing fashion, Lloyd's religion:

> The more she discovered him to be still in love with Jean Brodie, the more she was curious about the man that loved the woman. By the end of the year it happened that she had quite lost interest in the man himself, but was deeply absorbed in his mind, from which she extracted, among other things, his religion as a pith from a husk. Her mind was as full of his religion as a night

sky is full of things visible and invisible. She left the man and took his religion and became a nun in the course of time. (Spark 1961: 123)

Here Sandy has a veritable panoply of Gothic/supernatural functions. For a start, she is a wanton, unnatural (because fifteen-year-old) lover of a teacher at her school. She has also clearly decided to usurp Jean's role as Lloyd's lover. And she is too both demonic and, eventually will become, we are told, that other stock Gothic figure of papist immorality, a cloistered religious. The porcine metaphor ought to be noticed (as Sandy extracts Lloyd's religion 'as a pith from a husk', pigs, unlike other farmed animals, often being fed food with husks from which they are better equipped to derive nourishment). Sandy also has the porcine mark of the devil throughout the novel, where we find reference to her 'little pig-like eyes' (1961: 66).

We are confronted with the question: is Sandy Stranger a 'justified sinner' like Brodie herself, as she reports her teacher for involvement in 1930s politics so that the latter loses her job? Sandy is an outsider, part English, part Scottish, a 'stranger' in Calvinist Edinburgh, which she longs to have more fully in her background as 'something definite to reject'. Is this why she melodramatically projects Brodie as the God of Calvin, as a believer in predestination? Perhaps Brodie is not really any such thing, but merely a schoolteacher who attempts to exert a control that is ultimately imaginary and which only Sandy takes seriously. There is a Sparkian loop here that is very much like the self-parody so often found in classic Gothic fiction of an earlier age. As Sandy contemplates Calvin's views on the agency of God, she sums up that it is his 'pleasure to implant in certain people an erroneous sense of joy and salvation so that their surprise at the end might be the nastier' (1961: 109). This is what Sandy and/or Spark, or her author-narrator 'character', bring about for Brodie. Towards the end of the novel, Sandy is alternatively enlightened (good has come out of evil) or still haunted in a less pleasant way by her former teacher. We see her enclosed in her convent, seemingly desperate:

> And there was that day when the enquiring young man came to see Sandy because of her strange book of psychology, 'The Transfiguration of the Commonplace,' which had brought so many visitors that Sandy clutched the bars of her grille more desperately than ever. 'What were the main influences of your school days, Sister Helena? Were they literary or political or personal? Was it Calvinism?' Sandy said: 'There was a Miss Jean Brodie in her prime.' (Spark 1961: 127–8)

Is Sandy now feeling guilty over her betrayal of her schoolteacher, or are we seeing the uncomfortable 'unselfing' process, as described in the orthodox, Catholic depiction of the life of the religious? The claustrophobia that is one key element of the novel remains, but alongside it exists a kind of lyricism pertaining to the inspirational nature of Jean Brodie. Final judgement is sensationally suspended.

Spark's career continues with two novels that are equally historical, and indeed follow a trajectory from the largely 1930s setting of *The Prime of Miss Jean Brodie* with its sidelight on the rise of Fascism: *The Girls of Slender Means* (1963) is set for the most part during the Second World War, and *The Mandelbaum Gate* (1965) follows events in a post-war Middle East including the trial of Nazi Adolf Eichmann of 1961. *The Girls of Slender Means* reprises a horrific Mary Macgregor-like death as some characters are unable to escape their bombed hostel via a narrow toilet-window. It also features the crucifixion of an atheist dilettante turned Catholic missionary. Spark's God of grotesque horrors, then, remains very much in evidence in a novel that maintains the vivid and taught terror of classic Gothic fiction.

The Mandelbaum Gate is Spark's most obviously realistic novel. And yet it deals with the most contemporary of real-life horror stories, the Nazi death-camps. Barbara Vaughan attends the trial of Eichmann, key architect of the genocide:

> Barbara turned the switch of her earphones to other simultaneous translations – French, Italian, then back to English. What was he talking about? The effect was the same in any language, and the terrible paradox remained, and the actual discourse was a dead mechanical tick, while its subject, its massacre was living. She thought, it all feels like a familiar dream, and presently located the sensation as the one that the anti-novelists induce. (Spark 1967: 177)

Here, precisely, as Barbara switches across languages, there is no multivoicedness, no subtle ambiguity of message. There is no monster lurking, to be fearfully sensed; instead, there is merely Eichmann's dehumanisation, or self-vitiation. He is underwhelming (harking back to the fictive absence that is Georgina Hogg in *The Comforters*) and not even a 'justified sinner', but rather an unremarkable bureaucrat who seems not to signal evil in either an innate or dramatically obvious sense. *The Mandelbaum Gate* is a sort of crossroads in Spark's fiction where the trickery of fiction temporarily stops: indeed, it is associated in Barbara's apprehension of the *nouveau roman* with denuded humanity. Barbara's own complicated life and identity has taken her on pilgrimage in the first place, in search of some kind of moral truth. She is a Catholic convert from Judaism attempting to come to terms theologically with the relatively minor problem of a fiancé who is divorced. Instead of any easier, utterly logical certainty, however, she finds that the meeting place of the three great Abrahamic religions is a place of hyphenated, uncertain identity where the 'solution' is merely to live in a loving way.

Following *The Mandelbaum Gate*, Spark returns to her mode of exuberant fictionalising. In *The Public Image* (1968), a movie scriptwriter, Frederick Christopher, takes his own life, leaving behind 'evidence' that this has been precipitated by the orgiastic infidelities of his wife, Annabel, a glamorous actress. In fact, the husband has become jealous of his wife's greater success and because a particular director rather than himself is now moulding Annabel's image. Frederick's revenge is an attempt to ruin her new 'public image'. Out of this perfidy, as Annabel merely denies the allegations about her amidst press speculation, attempted blackmail and inquest, there emerges some hope. At the end of the novel we are left with the prospect that Annabel desires and might succeed in escaping from the falsity of public image altogether.

Mounting a particularly experimental platform following *The Public Image*, Spark writes her four most fictive works, which also see her at her most eschatological (where over-exuberant lives and deaths are essayed). *The Driver's Seat* (1970), *Not to Disturb* (1971), *The Hothouse by the East River* (1973) and *The Abbess of Crewe* (1974) are also starkly written in the present tense to give an ultimately false intensity to the impaired lives featured in all of these texts. All are also playfully uncomfortable for the reader, none more so than the poignant *The Driver's Seat*, which is relentlessly undemonstrative of emotion and, at the same time, heart-rending. Lise, from a city that might be London (only spare, inadequate references to locality are featured throughout), goes off to a southern European town ostensibly on holiday, and for romance but actually to bring about her own assisted suicide/murder. Early on, we are given the character's recent biography in a passage of claustrophobically managed detail that might be Spark's authorial-narrator at her cruellest or, alternatively, could be a focalisation of Lise's perspective:

> She walks along the broad street, scanning the windows for the dress she needs, the necessary dress. Her lips are slightly parted; she whose lips are usually pressed together with the daily disapprovals of the accountants' office where she has worked continually, except for the months of illness, since she was eighteen, that is to say for sixteen years and some months. Her lips, when she does not speak or eat, are normally pressed together like the ruled line of a balance sheet, marked straight with her old fashioned lipstick, a final and judging mouth, a precision instrument, a detail-warden of a mouth; she has five girls under her and two men. Over her are two women and five men. (Spark 1974: 9)

Lise is buried alive in her modern life, which makes for a kind of nightmarish alienation. The period of illness is the one hint we have of poor mental health in Lise. Is this brought on herself to some extent or visited upon her by an unjust world? Typically, Spark allows but does not necessarily encourage sociological interpretation (including Lise's employment situation which might be read as gender-unfair). Lise the individual is perhaps culpable with her 'final and judging mouth' of believing too much in her limited situation. She has given up on her own life, looking to bring it to an end or, in theological terms, she is guilty of the sin of despair. The flash-forwards telling the reader that soon Lise will be found violently killed make this the most mundanely horrific story. Details such as the 'necessary dress' that Lise is in search of make the narrative surface of the text appear like a *nouveau roman*, but the insouciant determinism of the narrator merely mirrors in ironic fashion the melodramatic plans of the central protagonist. Lise is going to find a psychopathic killer to give her the sensational notoriety, including press coverage, of which her life has been entirely devoid. This is the real mystery that the reader has to work out by the end. Very darkly humorous, the novel is a hyper-version of *Jean Brodie* where a single woman is driven by a warped sense of destiny. The extreme Lise though has become her own automaton, a zombie almost, so that autonomous action is never entirely allowed to her in plot description, including pro-lepsis and, ultimately, in a controversial ending about the detail of her demise at the hands of a sexual psychopath.

Spark's most obviously Gothic novel is *Not to Disturb*, which draws also on Jacobean drama, opening with a quotation from John Webster's *The Duchess of Malfi* (1613; published 1623) – '"Their life," says Lister, 'a general mist of error. Their death a hideous storm of terror' (Spark 1981a: 5) – and is divided (though in rather desultory fashion) into five chapters (or Acts). As Peter Kemp says, it is a novel full of 'flesh-creeper stereotypes (1975: 131). Baron Klopstock and his wife are locked in the library of their mansion near Lake Geneva and they have given orders to their servants that they are 'not to be disturbed'. They are never properly seen as their butler, Lister, stage-manages things around them, while their idiot, frothing heir rampages, as minor characters are killed by lightning, notoriously in a subordinate clause. Even more extremely than *The Driver's Seat*, a thoroughly threadbare, clichéd fiction is being played out as index of the debauched lives the Klopstocks have led. They are now devoid of any independent agency and are locked into a predetermined ending.

The Hothouse by the East River features a couple in their New York apartment who have actually died in London in 1944 slain by a V2 bomb, but whose continued, perfervid 'life' involves a staging of *Peter Pan* (directed by their 'son'), featuring a cast of geriatrics. This novel is a satire on 'the Big Apple' ('the city that never sleeps') with its bulging, variegated life that Spark depicts as a sea of heaving neuroses. Like *Not to Disturb*, *The Hothouse by the East River* is a riotously funny read, but unlike *The Driver's Seat* it is shorn of the poignancy that might allow the reader something beyond the experience of pure fictive farce, the Gothic-cum-*grand guignol*. In the case of *The Hothouse* especially, one feels that the critique of urban materialism has been mounted much more thoughtfully and wittily earlier in *The Ballad of Peckham Rye*.

The fourth of Spark's present-tense novels, *The Abbess of Crewe*, is all the more trenchant for being clearly a satire on the Watergate affair. Alexandra, the Abbess, is another iteration of Spark's Jean Brodie character, although different from Lise in *The Driver's Seat*, as she exhibits a sense of joyfulness with her frequent recourse to poetry. Alexandra places her nuns under surveillance, feeds them dog food and interferes with numerous affairs of the flesh as well as indulging in church politics. Here, we have diagnosed a system that has become self-contained within a withered version of its own power structures, running for its own sake, a kind of throw-away vision (by Catholic Spark) of the corrupt convent that classic anti-Catholic Gothic fiction had entertained in its earlier phases.

In her last thirty years as a novelist, we see the maintenance of the supernatural overtones of Spark's fiction, though with much more occasional and subdued grotesqueness. For instance, in *Loitering with Intent* (1981) Fleur Talbot becomes the secretary of the Autobiographical Association and witnesses, or perhaps (rather like an understated Dougal Douglas) cranks up, all kinds of nefarious fictions among its members. An avatar for Spark in some ways, Fleur ends the novel going 'on my way rejoicing' (Spark 1981b: 217). Is creativity a bad or a good thing, is the question that remains, pertaining to Spark's art itself? In later work such as *Symposium* (1990), the Border Ballads again, and a mad Scottish uncle inserted into the central event of a London dinner party, grant the narrative an air of the uncanny; in *Aiding and Abetting* (2000) the apparent Lord Lucan (we are never sure if it is really supposed to be him), makes an appearance as a patient to a fraudulent psychiatrist. For Spark, a well of Gothic elements is drawn upon throughout her oeuvre to inform her rich fictional recipe of horror and ordinariness, terrible lies and terrible truths.

References

Hogg, James [1824] (2010), *The Private Memoirs and Confessions of a Justified Sinner*, ed. Ian Duncan, Oxford: Oxford World's Classics.

Kemp, Peter (1975), *Muriel Spark*, New York: Barnes and Noble.

Spark, Muriel (1957), *The Comforters*, London: Macmillan.

— (1959), *Memento Mori*, London: Macmillan.

— (1961), *The Prime of Miss Jean Brodie*, London: Penguin.

— (1963), *The Girls of Slender Means*, London: Macmillan.

— [1965] (1967), *The Mandelbaum Gate*, London: Penguin.

— (1968), *The Public Image*, London: Macmillan.

— (1973), *The Hothouse by the East River*, London: Macmillan.

— (1974), *The Abbess of Crewe*, London: Macmillan.

— [1970] (1974), *The Driver's Seat*, London, Penguin.

— [1971] (1981a), *Not to Disturb*, London: Granada.

— (1981b), *Loitering with Intent*, New York: Coward, McCann & Geoghan.

— [1951] (1987), *Child of Light: Mary Shelley*, New York: Welcome Rain.

— (1990), *Symposium*, London: Constable.

— [1960] (1999), *The Ballad of Peckham Rye*, London: Penguin.

— (2000), *Aiding and Abetting*, London: Viking.

— (2011), *The Complete Short Stories*, intro. Janice Galloway, Edinburgh: Canongate.

Chapter 14

Scottish Gothic and the Moving Image: A Tale of Two Traditions

Duncan Petrie

Introduction

The Gothic has long been acknowledged as a significant cultural influence within Britain's cinematic heritage. In his seminal study of 'the English Gothic cinema', David Pirie asserts:

> It certainly seems to be arguable on commercial, historical and artistic grounds that the horror genre, as it has been developed in this country by Hammer and its rivals, remains the only staple cinematic myth which Britain can properly claim as its own, and which relates to it in the same way as the western relates to America. (Pirie 1973: 9)

Locating the roots of the British contribution to cinematic horror in the familiar literary terrain of classic Gothic fiction initiated in the late eighteenth century by Horace Walpole, Ann Radcliffe and M. G. Lewis, Pirie makes a persuasive case for the value of the genre and its centrality to the cultural specificity of a (then critically undervalued) 'national' cinema. But what is immediately striking from a contemporary, post-devolutionary vantage point is the Anglocentrism of the analysis as conveyed by the interchangeable use of the terms 'English' and 'British' throughout his book. Moreover, while acknowledging that 'the role of Ireland in Gothic literature is immense' (1973: 96), Pirie proceeds to co-opt C. R. Maturin's *Melmoth the Wanderer* (1820) – for him a foundational text alongside Lewis's *The Monk* (1796) – to a singularly English literary tradition. But just as Maturin's novel is now regarded as an exemplar of a distinctive tradition of Irish Gothic (Punter 2002: 105), so in this chapter I want to move beyond the limitations of Pirie's conceptual framework to consider the significance of the Gothic to Scottish cinema. This also necessarily transcends the confines of the horror genre to consider wider reverberations of a particular cultural sensibility or structure of feeling.

The cinematic representation of Scotland, its landscapes and inhabitants has benefited greatly from an increase in local production from the early 1980s onwards, stimulated by new sources of funding and creating the idea of a small national cinema connected to yet also distinct from a London-centric British film industry (Petrie 2000). This also brought about a shift of focus away from a vision of Scotland as a rural, remote and timeless place informed by romantic fantasy, towards a new engagement with the urban, the contemporary and the social, much of it rendered through the aesthetics of realism. An increase in indigenous production also generated a broader range of perspectives, stories and themes that dovetailed with the wider renaissance in Scottish cultural expression following the devolution debacle of 1979 (Petrie 2004).

The flourishing of a New Scottish Cinema has been accompanied by the emergence of a small but distinct field of film studies critically engaged with the aesthetic, industrial and cultural aspects of this emergent object of study. It has also prompted revisionist approaches to history, most notably a re-evaluation of indigenous cultural traditions that has challenged the overwhelmingly negative assessments associated with the 'Scotch Myths' perspective (McArthur 1982). As Cairns Craig (1996) has argued, this required a reconceptualisation of the notion of myth that replaced a Marxist understanding in which myths served to obscure the real conditions of economic and class oppression, with a Nietzschean perspective in which myths function to redeem humanity from the dissipating effects of history. Thus, rather than negating progressive cultural responses, the utilisation of myths facilitates creative human action. As Adrienne Scullion persuasively puts it:

> The role of mythology, legend and fable, the Gothic, the supernatural and the unconscious within the development of the Scottish imagination is not a symptom of psychosis but a sophisticated engagement with the fantastic that other cultures might celebrate as magic realism. (Scullion 1995: 201)

It is in this context that I will consider the significance of the Gothic within the history of Scotland and the moving image. This involves a distinction between two distinct trends and types of representation: the first rooted in the long-established association of Scotland with the Highlands and Western Isles in which the rural, the remote and the peripheral are key structuring factors; the second concerning a Lowland Gothic tradition in which the urban topography of Edinburgh and Glasgow feature in very significant, albeit differing and distinct, ways. While each trend at times dovetails with the traditional horror film as conceptualised by

David Pirie, the Gothic influence on Scottish cinema notably escapes any straightforward generic categorisation.

The Context of Scottish Gothic

While the concept of the Gothic is broad and complex, David Punter's identification of the heart (as opposed to the body) of the tradition as being concerned with the themes of paranoia, barbarism and the taboo, bound together by a preoccupation with fear (1996: 184), provides a useful starting point. Such expressions are often mapped onto particular socio-historical moments or processes, prompting Kelly Hurley to describe the Gothic as 'an instrumental genre, re-emerging cyclically, at periods of cultural stress, to negotiate the anxieties that accompany social and epistemological transformations and crises' (1996: 5). These can have a specifically national dimension, thus the development of a Scottish variant of the Gothic is frequently tied to the trauma and identity crisis that followed Scotland's Union with England in 1707 and its subsequent status as a 'stateless nation'. Ian Duncan identifies the disjunction between the Lowland Protestant modern present and the Highland Catholic primitive past as a recurring feature in Scottish Gothic. While the modernity of the Scottish Enlightenment affirmed the ascendancy of Anglo-British culture, it also generated a ghostly 'Other', an 'uncanny recursion of an ancestral identity alienated from modern life' (2000: 70). In this schema, the past comes to assume a particular significance in its power to haunt the present in Scottish cultural expression. This perspective also invokes the (seemingly inescapable) figure of duality that has dominated Scottish cultural analysis from G. Gregory Smith's 'Caledonian Antisyzygy' (Smith 2010) onwards, reinforcing the key role played by myth, distortion and fabrication in constructions of Scottish national identity (including the much-derided Scotch myths of Tartanry and Kailyard).

While neglecting to use the term 'Gothic', Craig's (1996) elaboration of the counter-historical in Scottish cultural expression, traced from the nineteenth-century literary tradition of Walter Scott, James Hogg and Robert Louis Stevenson through the interwar renaissance to the more recent flourishing of the Scottish novel, provides very similar insights. Craig's analysis of how Scotland's Calvinist heritage has fundamentally shaped the national cultural imagination is also crucial to an understanding of the significance of the Gothic. Central to this is a dialectic of fear, turning on the ambiguity of the term 'fearful': on one hand 'the fear-stricken submission to a greater power', the community cowed by a vengeful Calvinist God; on the other, the 'fear-inspiring . . . denial of the ordinary limits of human suffering' embodied by the terrifying individual who, in rejecting the values and morality of the community, fearlessly defies the wrath of God (Craig 1999: 37). The most potent and influential expression of Craig's dialectic of fear is provided by Hogg's 1824 novel, *The Private Memoirs and Confessions of a Justified Sinner*, and its tale of Robert Wringhim, the Calvinist fanatic whose downfall is engineered by a sinister shape-shifter called Gil-Martin who may either be the Devil or a hellish projection of Wringhim's irreparably damaged psyche. In this way Hogg offers a foundational manifestation of duality – echoed in the divided form of the novel itself – which proved influential to Stevenson's 1886 novella *Strange Case of Dr Jekyll and Mr Hyde*. Stevenson's doppelgänger, in turn, became one of the most adapted literary works by film-makers (Butt 2007: 52), leading to the rise of a cinematic horror archetype ranking alongside Frankenstein's monster, Count Dracula and the Werewolf (another version of the divided self). The dialectic of fear is arguably the key recurring Gothic trope in Scottish cinema, one that links not only works clearly informed by the fantasy and horror genres but also films that on the surface may appear to engage with contemporary social realities.

Where No One Can Hear You Scream

Until the 1980s, the cinematic representation of Scotland was of a predominantly remote, rural and backward environment located far from the modern, metropolitan world and culture of the film-makers responsible for the construction of these images. Representations of the nation were, therefore, informed largely by fantasy, romance and myth rather than any appeal to or connection with contemporary reality. Scotland's cinematic image was synonymous with the Highlands and Western Isles, with the recurrent trope of the island serving to intensify the theme of isolation. While in part the product of a discourse of heritage and tourism dating back to the Georgian era (Womack 1989), the other-worldliness underpinning this dominant image chimes with Craig's 'out of history' thesis and the related Gothic themes of distortion, fragmentation and unease. Key structural tensions between present and past, rationality and superstition, modernity and tradition are underscored by the persistent narrative and thematic concerns of films centred on the arrival of an outsider into a strange – sometimes enchanting, sometimes threatening, always unsettling – rural Scottish environment, initiating an encounter that invariably proves to be profoundly transformative for the visitor. This is a manifestation of 'the journey North', identified by Kirsty Macdonald as a recurring trope in the Scottish Gothic that is essentially a trajectory 'back in time, to a more primitive location where the conventional rules do not apply' (2009: 2). Macdonald traces the tradition back to Radcliffe's 1789 novel, *The Castles of Athlin and Dunbayne: A Highland Story*, subsequently resurfacing in the works of Scott, Hogg, Stevenson and even J. M. Barrie's 1932 novella *Farewell Miss Julie Logan*.

In some films the encounter between outsider and environment proves to be life-affirming, with key examples including *I Know Where I'm Going* (Michael Powell and Emeric Pressburger, 1945), *Brigadoon* (Vincente Minnelli, 1954) and *Local Hero* (Bill Forsyth, 1983), in which the forces of tradition, myth and enchantment provide a welcome escape from the stresses, strains and empty materialism of modern life. But this strand ultimately constitutes more of a romantic than a truly Gothic vision of Scotland. However, in other films the experience is much darker, unsettling and ultimately destructive, as in the Gainsborough melodrama *The Brothers* (David MacDonald, 1947) and the post-Hammer horror film *The Wicker Man* (Robin Hardy, 1973). In both, the incomer's encounter with an insular island community culminates in their death; a fate indelibly marked by a deadly combination of fear, superstition, folklore and repressed sexuality.

Set on Skye at the turn of the twentieth century, *The Brothers* charts the arrival on the island of Mary Lawson, a teenage orphan raised in a Glasgow convent, sent to work as a domestic servant for a widower and his two sons. But the presence of a young woman in the all-male, God-fearing household immediately creates a hotbed of barely contained, sado-masochistic sexual tension, the inevitable resolution of which is the destruction of all concerned. The backward community is riven with superstition and inter-family rivalry, and the pervading atmosphere of Gothic melodrama is heightened by the expressionistic black-and-white cinematography and the locations, which present Skye as a striking but harsh landscape dominated by the brooding Cuillin mountain range and dark lochs. *The Wicker Man* is set in the present and concerns a policeman investigating a report of a missing child on the fictional Summer Isle. Sergeant Howie discovers that the islanders' lives are governed by pagan worship and fertility rites that he considers blasphemous. Howie suspects that the missing girl has been sacrificed to appease the gods, but ultimately the wily islanders turn the tables on him and he is lured into a trap that culminates in his being burned alive in a huge wicker man on the cliff top. Howie is revealed to be not only a devout Christian but a virgin, and it is his fear and sexual repression that seals his fate. While on one level an innocent, Howie is also guilty of blind arrogance that leads him to underestimate the islanders, which paves the way for his ultimate destruction.

While the arrival of the New Scottish Cinema tended to displace this narrative of the outsider's fateful encounter with rural Scotland, the early 2000s saw the release of two new manifestations of 'the journey North'. The first of these, *Blinded* (2004), written and directed by Eleanor Yule, features a young Danish traveller, Mike, who, in shades of *The Brothers*, comes to reside with a family in their dilapidated remote farmhouse situated next to a black swamp. Inspired by Émile Zola's *Thérèse Raquin* and the muted, melancholy images of the Danish painter Vilhelm Hammershøi, the film is suffused with the Gothic theme of a dark, oppressive past clinging to and dictating the present. This is signified by the bleak house and its occupants, suitably named 'Black' and comprising the blind, bitter, domineering – but symbolically castrated – Francis, his frail and doting mother, Bella, and his abused young wife, Rachel, an orphan, seemingly 'out of time' in her shabby, old-fashioned clothes. There are hints that Francis is a victim of circumstance, trapped by his responsibility to his mother who was born in the house. The farm does not seem to produce anything, Mike's job being limited to consigning rusting and dead machinery to the swamp, and as such is a place of destruction rather than cultivation. An intense attraction develops between Mike and Rachel, which is sensed by the pathologically jealous Francis, prompting a fight between the two men that culminates in Francis falling into the swamp. Mike subsequently remains at the farm with Rachel, but a combination of guilt, Bella's suspicions and the revelation that Mike had been charged with murder in Denmark for smothering his terminally ill mother, propels the film towards its suitably Gothic climax. Rachel's misunderstanding that Mike has murdered Bella in the same way he had killed his own mother causes her to panic and throw boiling water in his face, an act that, in blinding him, replays the fate that befell Francis and underscores Mike's inability to escape his own past.

The Last Great Wilderness (2002) provides a different take on the theme. It begins in familiar fashion with two travellers, Charlie and Vince, finding refuge among the psychologically damaged residents of a remote Highland hotel, generating much unease and trepidation. Director David Mackenzie knowingly builds a sense of dread (including a direct reference to *The Wicker Man*), before revealing that the community's nocturnal participation in pagan rites is benign and celebratory rather than deadly. Moreover, the source of barbarity in the film comes from outside – Vince ends up horribly crucified, blinded and castrated by London hitmen who have followed him to Scotland, but is subsequently freed from his torment in a mercy killing by the local gamekeeper. Ultimately for Charlie, who has come to Scotland seeking vengeance against his estranged wife and her lover, the encounter functions as a kind of healing process (Martin-Jones 2005). In her analysis of the film as a key example of 'the journey North', Kirsty Macdonald cites a moment when the psychotherapist leader of the community explains to Charlie that the last great wilderness is not out there but in here – pointing to his own head, suggesting that '(t)he real hauntings, magic and liminality come from the mind' (2007: 335): the scene directly acknowledges the central role played by psychic metaphors in discourses of Scottish culture.

The most recent contribution to the tradition, *Under the Skin* (Jonathan Glazer, 2014), provides yet another twist in that the visitor is a predatory alien, who has come to Scotland to lure young men to their deaths – transfixed by their desire, their naked bodies slowly sink into a black void as if into a swamp or quicksand. This new version of the fatal woman, played with suitably emotional blankness by Hollywood star Scarlett Johansson in a black wig, becomes curious about the human world, developing an empathy that motivates her escape from inner-city Glasgow to the solitude of the Highlands. While the alien is the initial locus of fear and destruction, this is challenged by Glazer's rendition of what Kirsty Macdonald calls 'this desolate and appalling landscape' (2011), the most terrifying sequence in the film being when the sea claims the lives of an innocent man and woman attempting to rescue their dog, leaving their distraught toddler alone on the shore. The landscape is also the site of the alien's death at the hands of a rapist whose violence reveals the alien's real uncanny form, 'under the skin', its shiny blackness recalling the substance into which she had lured her prey. In a striking image, the alien contemplates the now detached 'human' face that she holds in her hands – an imaginative take on the theme of dualism – before her assailant returns with a can of petrol and sets her alight. As the alien is consumed by the fire, the camera follows the thick black smoke as it rises into the air, mingling and merging the film's two sources of Gothic 'otherness': the alien outsider (whose monstrosity has been displaced by the barbarity she has encountered at the hands of a human), and the brooding Highland landscape.

The Urban: Dark Closes and the Devil

The most significant Scottish contribution to the horror film remains Stevenson's *Strange Case of Dr Jekyll and Mr Hyde* (1886). While the story is set in London, various commentators from Roderick Watson (1995) to Ian Rankin (2007) have persuasively argued that its tale of duality is clearly inspired by the city of Edinburgh divided between the Enlightenment rationality of James Craig's New Town and the vertiginous buildings and meandering streets of the medieval Old Town. The latter location also features strongly in Hogg's *Confessions* and in several of Stevenson's short stories, notably 'The Body Snatcher' (1884), inspired by the exploits of the notorious resurrectionists who provided specimens for the city's medical school. This story was adapted in 1945 by director Robert Wise and producer Val Lewton for the Hollywood studio RKO, a feature which is also notable as the final pairing of horror stars Boris Karloff and Béla Lugosi. This was also the first of a small group of films, most of which feature the notorious figures that collectively established an enduring Gothic cinematic topography of old Edinburgh – albeit a facsimile created in the studio – comprising the imposing castle on its volcanic rock, looming tenements, sinister closes and labyrinthine wynds. One of the most interesting of these films, *The Flesh and the Fiends* (John Gilling, 1960), also explored the city's topographical duality through the contrasting representation of the dark and macabre world of fear and superstition in which Burke and Hare commit their crimes, and the bright and affluent New Town respectability and scientific rationality of the anatomist Doctor Knox. Significantly, the point of contact and of mutual dependence between the two environments is the illicit trade in cadavers.

Gothic Edinburgh was itself resurrected, albeit obliquely, in 1994 by Danny Boyle's stylish thriller *Shallow Grave*, one of the films that heralded the arrival of a New Scottish Cinema. The story concerns the exploits of a trio of self-centred yuppies whose lives are turned upside down when they find their mysterious new flatmate dead in his room with a suitcase of cash. They decide to keep the money and dispose of the corpse, but the trauma of dismembering and burying the body leads the ostensibly most sober and sensible of the three, accountant David, to suffer a nervous breakdown. He subsequently takes to the attic with the money, from where he spies, unseen, on the activities of his flatmates, Alex and Juliette, below. While the increasing sense of paranoia, suspense and sudden eruptions of violence provide a familiar thematic landscape, the Gothic sensibility of *Shallow Grave* is most interestingly conveyed in the memorable opening sequence that anticipates the narrative trajectory and neatly encapsulates the sense of duality discussed above. This pivots on the contrasting images of, on one hand, the distinctive New Town Georgian buildings, appropriately illuminated in bright sunshine and filmed in exhilaratingly fast motion;

on the other, an unidentified, sinister and artificially illuminated forest – subsequently revealed as the site of the 'shallow grave' – through which the camera appears to prowl, evoking the 'Other' realm of fear, irrationality and the supernatural into which the protagonists are inevitably drawn.

The physical topography of the city's Old Town is more central to *16 Years of Alcohol* (2004), ostensibly a very familiar story about a young working-class man whose formative experiences have left him emotionally retarded and addicted to violence and alcohol. The narrative charts Frankie Mac's attempts to live a normal existence, most hopefully through his relationship with a fellow troubled soul, Mary. But the past misdemeanours are impossible to shake off and ultimately prove Frankie's undoing, beaten to death in a dark Old Town close by the skinhead gang he had previously led. The film's director Richard Jobson utilises the Gothic inventively to heighten this tale and relate it to a very different tradition, that of urban social realism. The narrative point of view is intensely subjective, beginning and ending with Frankie's subterranean encounter with the three assailants. As such, it is framed as a series of autobiographical memories conjured at the point of death. Throughout the story, Frankie is inexorably drawn downwards into the darker recesses of the Old Town, also the site of his symbolic fall, when he discovers that his idolised father is a philandering drunk. In this way, the Gothic topography functions symbolically as the backdrop to Frankie's (predestined?) fate. Significantly, one of the brightest and most optimistic moments in the film occurs at the foot of the Scottish National Monument on Calton Hill (a symbol of Enlightenment rationality) during Frankie's brief relationship with Helen, a young art student who provides the opportunity for him to leave the gang.

The theme of the supernatural is also subtly explored via Frankie's conflict with Miller, one of his fellow gang members and ultimate nemesis. In one scene, Miller pulls a knife on Frankie during some horseplay, an altercation that culminates with the latter being stabbed in the side. Writhing about in agony on the ground, Frankie's voice-over invokes familiar themes:

> There is a time when you never think of things like survival. Fearless people know that this is something that cannot last for long. The brave ones know the truth. They know about fear. Sometimes it's not possible to tell people you are afraid. It just wouldn't help the situation. It's not a good feeling. Fear . . . Fear. (Jobson 2004)

The direct invocation of fear immediately moves beyond the surface drama of male violence to a deeper realm of Gothic unease and irrationality.

This is confirmed when Jobson then cuts to a scene featuring an apparently unscathed Frankie with Helen, disrupting the logical continuity of the filmic world. This rupture occurs again when an inebriated Frankie has his next violent encounter with Miller in which he gains the advantage, taking a bite out of his assailant's cheek before bringing a hammer down on his head (out of frame) with a dull and apparently fatal crunch. Yet on this occasion it is Miller who is resurrected, reappearing later to menace Mary in a bar at the very moment when Frankie seems to have finally mustered the strength to move on. In disrupting narrative logic, Miller functions as either a diabolical force or a projection of Frankie's damaged self, an ambiguity that directly invokes Robert Wringhim's relationship with Gil-Martin in Hogg's *Confessions*. In his discussion of the counter-historical trends in the nineteenth-century fiction of Scott, Hogg and Stevenson, Craig argues that

> what these narratives foretell is that history is no benign progress, gradually exiling from the present all that is destructive and barbaric in humanity: the blindness of the historian is the very condition for the resurrection of the 'evil' – whether of barbaric conduct or the dominance of the imagination over fact – which he cannot believe to be real because it is inexplicable within his conception of the world. The more insistently he exiles the evil, the more insistently he buries it, the more insistently will it return to take its revenge upon him. (Craig 1996: 81)

This final sentence could equally apply to Frankie Mac's struggle with Miller, a struggle that culminates in his violent demise in the subterranean depths of old Edinburgh. The revelation of the narrative as Frankie's memories of his life at the moment of his death reinforces the compelling force of the Scottish Gothic sensibility that infuses the film at almost every level.

In contrast, the representation of Glasgow and the Clyde estuary in film and television has been much more dependent on the codes of realism and representations of tough and gritty working-class life enshrined in the overtly masculine discourse of Clydesidism. Even this environment has proven amenable to the Gothic, as anticipated in the 1951 feature film *Flesh and Blood*, directed by Anthony Kimmins, an adaptation of James Bridie's play *The Sleeping Clergyman* (1933), which concerns three generations of a Glasgow family and combines a melancholic obsession with heredity and such familiar themes as madness, murder and suicide. More significant is the 1987 Channel 4 mini-series *Brond* (1987), adapted by Frederic Lindsay from his novel and directed by Michael Caton-Jones. An enigmatic political thriller in which a young student becomes inadvertently embroiled in a murky world of sectarianism, political assassination and the hunt for an IRA terrorist, the drama alludes to a complex imperial history that includes the (then still active) war in Ulster, a nascent armed struggle for independence in Scotland and the ruthlessness of the British state. But just as *Brond* appears to put Scotland back into history, it invokes the dark forces of the Gothic in the sinister and seemingly all-powerful eponymous villain whose ultimate identity and purpose remains enigmatic.

In the opening sequence, Robert, a student at Glasgow University (whose distinctive Gothic architecture features in one of the opening images) witnesses a stranger casually pushing an innocent child off a city-centre bridge in broad daylight. The shock is intensified when the man acknowledges Robert with a complicit wink and smile. Their next encounter is at a party given by a university lecturer, where a still shocked Robert overhears the man – now identified as Brond – holding forth on the invincibility of the Devil. Robert subsequently becomes caught up in a web of manipulation orchestrated by Brond and aided by Primo, an emblematic 'Scottish Soldier' who is resentful yet bound by duty to serve his imperial master. Brond's motivations and allegiances remain unclear and his uncanny presence is underscored by the use of extreme close-ups, distorted camera angles and low-key lighting (often featuring a red glow) that disrupt the otherwise naturalistic surface of the drama. In this way the fear-inspiring mystery man may be yet another Gothic manifestation of 'auld Nick', whose numerous appearances in Scottish literature have been linked to 'the overdriven Calvinist perception of the fallen world' (Carruthers 2008: 1). *Brond* ends with the death of Primo, who is in pursuit of his master following the discovery that it was his son whom Brond had killed in the opening scene. This revelation involves a hint of complicity on the part of Robert, which is underscored when he looks out of a window expecting to see Brond but is confronted instead by his own doubled image playfully winking back at him, a replay of their first encounter that deftly invokes Hogg's shape-shifter.

A similar influence can be discerned in Peter Mullan's debut feature, *Orphans* (1998), which depicts the bizarre escapades of four Glasgow siblings in the twenty-four hours preceding the funeral of their beloved mother. A key work in the New Scottish Cinema, *Orphans* is distinguished by Mullan's rejection of the constraints of realism, inspired use of Biblical metaphor, and the Catholic theme of redemption that leaves open an alternative outcome for his apparently damned protagonists. The links with the Gothic are perhaps most productive in relation to the character of John, the youngest of the 'orphans', who has sworn to find and kill the man who had earlier stabbed his brother Michael in a bar brawl. John's desire for vengeance is fed by the malevolent figure of

Tanga, a classic portrayal of the insecure hard man who demonstrates his own warped view of the world when he attempts to rape a woman whose husband insulted him. Under Tanga's baleful influence – he also provides a gun and ammunition – John is transformed from a mild-mannered young man poised for a bright future into a fear-inspiring presence driven by hate, cackling like a demon from the window of Tanga's minivan as the storm brews and he goes in search of blood. Mullan even underscores John's descent into hell with a shot of the white van disappearing into a sinister red tunnel. When John finally catches up with and confronts his intended victim, the latter reveals a baby strapped to his chest, a shocking image that breaks the spell. In this way and in contrast to the enigmatic dénouement of *Brond*, John achieves his own redemption. His sanity and humanity restored, he leaves Tanga damned by fate, seriously injured by his own malfunctioning shotgun.

Conclusion

The Gothic has reasserted itself in recent Scottish film-making, informing a range of films that, while apparently part of the wider cinematic engagement with different facets of contemporary Scotland, also harks back to an older tradition of representation rooted in a counter-historical valorisation of fantasy and myth. In common with contemporaneous developments in the Scottish novel, the Gothic has encouraged film-makers to challenge and transcend the limiting constraints of realism, redeeming aspects of a deeper cultural tradition that provides new interpretations of contemporary social experience and existential crises, and sometimes even offer new creative aesthetic solutions to old problems and predicaments. As I have attempted to demonstrate, this influence can be explored via two distinct – if ultimately linked – traditions: on one hand, the projection of Scotland as a Romantic or sublime rural wilderness, a 'land beyond the stars'; on the other, a contemporary urban environment reflecting the forces of economic, political and social change. Despite their ostensible differences, both traditions share a self-conscious playfulness in their recognition and utilisation of Gothic themes and motifs. While rural-set films like *The Last Great Wilderness* and *Under the Skin* rework the long-established anti-realist tradition that itself oscillated between the Romanticism of *Brigadoon* and the terror of the *Wicker Man*, the urban Gothic of *16 Years of Alcohol* and *Orphans* arguably owes more to the enduring influence of Hogg and Stevenson than the late twentieth-century social realism of Peter MacDougall or Ken Loach. In their shared dependence on the uncanny, the supernatural, the irrational and, above all, the dialectic of fear, both traditions ultimately intermingle, a testament to the creative vitality and cultural relevance of a deep-rooted Gothic tradition and sensibility that continues to inspire cinematic creativity in Scotland.

References

Boyle, Danny (dir.) (1994), *Shallow Grave*, film, UK: Polygram Filmed Entertainment.

Butt, Richard (2007), 'Literature and the Screen Media Since 1908', in Ian Brown (gen. ed.), *The Edinburgh History of Scottish Literature*, 3 vols, Edinburgh: Edinburgh University Press, vol. 3, pp. 53–63.

Carruthers, Gerard (2008), 'The Devil in Scotland', *The Bottle Imp*, 3, 1–7.

Caton-Jones, Michael (dir.) (1987), *Brond*, television mini-series, UK: Channel 4.

Craig, Cairns (1996), *Out of History: Narrative Paradigms in Scottish and British Culture*, Edinburgh: Polygon.

— (1999), *The Modern Scottish Novel: Narrative and the National Imagination*, Edinburgh: Edinburgh University Press.

Duncan, Ian (2000), 'Walter Scott, James Hogg and Scottish Gothic', in David Punter (ed.), *A Companion to the Gothic*, Oxford: Blackwell, pp. 70–80.

Forsyth, Bill (dir.) (1983), *Local Hero*, film, UK: 20th Century Fox.

Gilling, John (dir.) (1960), *The Flesh and the Fiends*, film, UK: Regal Film Distributors.

Glazer, Jonathan (dir.) (2014), *Under the Skin*, film, UK: Studio Canal.

Hardy, Robin (dir.) (1973), *The Wicker Man*, film, UK: British Lion Films.

Hurley, Kelly (1996), *The Gothic Body: Sexuality, Materialism, and Degeneration at the* Fin de Siècle, Cambridge: Cambridge University Press.

Jobson, Richard (dir.) (2004), *16 Years of Alcohol*, film, UK: Metro Tartan.

Kimmins, Anthony (dir.) (1951), *Flesh and Blood*, film, UK: British Lion Film Corporation.

McArthur, Colin (ed.) (1982), *Scotch Reels: Scotland in Cinema and Television*, London: BFI.

MacDonald, David (dir.) (1947), *The Brothers*, film, UK: General Film Distributors.

Macdonald, Kirsty (2007), 'Against Realism: Contemporary Scottish Literature and the Supernatural', in Berthold Schoene (ed.), *The Edinburgh Companion to Contemporary Scottish Literature*, Edinburgh: Edinburgh University Press, pp. 328–35.

— (2009), 'Scottish Gothic: Towards a Definition', *The Bottle Imp*, 6, 1–2.

— (2011), '"This Desolate and Appalling Landscape": The Journey North in Contemporary Scottish Gothic', *Gothic Studies*, 13: 2, 37–47.

Mackenzie, David (dir.) (2002), *The Last Great Wilderness*, film, UK: Feature Film Company.

Martin-Jones, David (2005), 'Sexual Healing: Representations of the English in Post-Devolutionary Scotland', *Screen*, 46: 2, 227–33.

Minnelli, Vincente (dir.) (1954), *Brigadoon*, film, USA: MGM.

Mullan, Peter (dir.) (1998), *Orphans*, film, UK: Downtown Pictures.

Petrie, Duncan (2000), *Screening Scotland*, London: BFI.

— (2004), *Contemporary Scottish Fictions: Film, Television and the Novel*, Edinburgh: Edinburgh University Press.

Pirie, David (1973), *A Heritage of Horror: The English Gothic Cinema 1946–1972*, London: Gordon Fraser.

Powell, Michael and Emeric Pressburger (dirs) (1945), *I Know Where I'm Going*, film, UK: General Film Distributors.

Punter, David (1996), *The Literature of Terror, Volume 2: The Modern Gothic*, rev. edn, London: Longman.

— (2002), 'Scottish and Irish Gothic', in Jerrold E. Hogle (ed.), *The Cambridge Companion to Gothic Fiction*, Cambridge: Cambridge University Press, pp. 105–23.

Rankin, Ian (dir.) (2007), *Ian Rankin Investigates: Dr Jekyll and Mr Hyde*, television documentary, first broadcast 16 June 2007, UK: BBC Four.

Scullion, Adrienne (1995), 'Feminine Pleasures and Masculine Indignities: Gender and Community in Scottish Drama', in C. Whyte (ed.), *Gendering the Nation: Studies in Modern Scottish Literature*, Edinburgh: Edinburgh University Press, pp. 169–204.

Smith, G. Gregory [1919] (2010), *Scottish Literature: Character and Influence*, London: Kessinger Publishing.

Watson, Roderick (1995), 'Introduction', in Robert Louis Stevenson, *Shorter Scottish Fiction*, Edinburgh: Canongate, pp. vii–xxii.

Wise, Robert (dir.) (1945), *The Body Snatcher*, film, USA: RKO.

Womack, Peter (1989), *Improvement and Romance: Constructing the Myth of the Highlands*, London: Macmillan.

Yule, Eleanor (dir.) (2004), *Blinded*, film, UK: Guerilla Films.

Chapter 15

New Frankensteins; or, the Body Politic

Timothy C. Baker

In the introduction to his 2001 anthology of 'New Scottish Gothic Fiction', Alan Bissett argues that Gothic 'has always acted as a way of re-examining the past, and the past is the place where Scotland, a country obsessed with re-examining itself, can view itself whole, vibrant, mythic' (2001: 6). While virtually every contemporary Scottish author has made use of Gothic elements or tropes in some part of their work, many of the most important recent texts to be labelled 'Scottish Gothic' are centrally concerned with such a re-examination of the past. For many authors, however, the past is not to be found in historical events or cultural contexts, but specifically in the interrelation between established Scottish and Gothic literary traditions. Beginning with Emma Tennant's *The Bad Sister* (1978), one of numerous twentieth-century reworkings of James Hogg's *The Private Memoirs and Confessions of a Justified Sinner* (1824), many contemporary Gothic novels have explicitly relied on earlier texts; adapting the work of Hogg, Stevenson or even Shelley becomes a way of challenging preconceived notions of stable national and individual identities. While critics including David Punter have argued that any contemporary conception of 'Scottish Gothic' must 'remain under a certain erasure' lest the criticism develop an essentialist paradigm in contrast to both a modern global marketplace and the emergent recognition of Gothic as an international form (Punter 1999: 103), many of the novels themselves replace such categorical anxieties with a focus on the interpretative possibilities suggested by a return to tradition. More precisely, revisiting literary tradition allows for a focus on the text as a body, and the body as a text: in the novels discussed below, human bodies are both formed by, and read as, texts, suggesting that national and literary traditions are best approached not as abstractions, but in individual instances of embodiment. Whether looking to the past or the future, and whether writing in an explicitly

Gothic mode or incorporating Gothic tropes within other genres, each of these novels problematises the relation between the embodied self and larger discourses of identity.

The relation between text, body and nation is foregrounded in three pivotal novels from the period between the unsuccessful Scottish Devolution Referendum of 1979 and the successful referendum of 1997: Iain Banks's *The Wasp Factory* (1984), Alasdair Gray's *Poor Things* (1992) and Elspeth Barker's *O Caledonia* (1991). Each of these texts situates the development of individual and collective identity in relation to literary tradition, as is made clear both by intertextual allusions and the protagonists' own reading habits. While for many critics Gothic writing can be seen as an index of contemporary social concerns, each of these novels demonstrates the way social concerns are shaped by Gothic texts.

The Wasp Factory is the cornerstone of many accounts of contemporary Scottish Gothic. The novel is in part an adaptation of Mary Shelley's *Frankenstein* (1818), and is especially notable in presenting an isolated world known only through naming. While Victor Frankenstein and his creation journey across Western Europe and the Arctic, the Cauldhame family is confined to a geographically and intellectually secluded existence. Angus Cauldhame fixes precise but arbitrary labels on every object in his house, while his son, Frank, orients his life around a series of named and capitalised 'Signs', all of which show that 'From the smaller to the greater, the patterns always hold true' (Banks 1990: 37). Frank's construction of the titular Wasp Factory, a method for predicting death, as well as his naming of 'Sacrifice Poles', the 'Rabbit Grounds' and the 'Snake Park', can be seen as an attempt to impose order on a chaotic existence. The novel's final revelation, that Frank is not 'Francis Leslie Cauldhame' but 'Frances Lesley Cauldhame' (1990: 181), similarly points to the way naming creates identity: Frank's identification as male and his subsequent hatred of women are manifested through language. Frank's life is designed as a series of misreadings and misinformation. His education is filled with 'utter rubbish', such as Angus's claim that 'Pathos was one of the Three Musketeers' (1990: 14), while the two books Angus gives Frank, Gore Vidal's *Myra Breckinridge* (1968) and Günter Grass's *The Tin Drum* (1959), remain unread despite their parallels with Frank's story and potential explanatory power. Nevertheless, Frank's life is shaped by literary history: just as Angus's experiments echo those of Victor Frankenstein, so too can Frank's Factory be seen as a version of the chambers in Edgar Allan Poe's 'The Masque of the Red Death' (1842), an allusion reinforced by Frank's drinking 'a couple of cans of the old Red Death' (1990: 135). As in many Romantic-era

Gothic novels, there is 'a secret in the study' (1990: 16) while, in a nod to older traditions, the Factory is described as 'a little Grail legend of its own' (1990: 121). One of the novel's central tensions lies between Angus's and Frank's desire to name everything around them and their failure to recognise that their story has, in many senses, already been written. Both characters express agency through acts of writing and naming, but ultimately find themselves slaves to a pre-existing set of tropes and narratives.

As much as Frank's identity is textually determined, however, he also positions himself in more universal terms:

> Often I've thought of myself as a state; a country or, at the very least, a city. It used to seem to me that the different ways I sometimes felt about ideas, courses of action and so on were like the differing political moods that countries go through. (Banks 1990: 62)

While a purely allegorical interpretation of Frank as Scotland might appear overdetermined, Frank's jingoistic sensibility, confused identity and isolationist despair echo political sentiments found in many of Banks's other novels. Numerous critics have located a similar allegorical impulse in Alasdair Gray's *Poor Things*, not least in the protagonist Victoria Blessington/Bella Baxter's portrayal as 'Bella Caledonia'. Although this appellation might imply that Bella can be taken as a figure for Scotland more generally, it is only one of the many identities Bella is given over the course of the novel. Like Frank, Bella receives many names throughout the novel, each of which fixes a particular referential identity: each name notably corresponds with how she is seen by particular males. Like Frank, Bella is, in one version of her story, the product of a Frankenstein-like experiment, involving the replacement of her brain with that of her unborn child. Even more than Banks, however, Gray presents the novel's narrative ambiguities and contradictions as a product of intertextuality. If some of the plot and characterisation of the novel is derived from Shelley, the structure is explicitly modelled on Hogg, as well as Scott and Boswell. The introduction and notes by 'Alasdair Gray' include references to real and imagined texts, while the main body of the novel is divided into a fantastical narrative by Archie McCandless and a more traditionally realist narrative by Bella, now known as Victoria McCandless. In her commentary on Archie's manuscript, Bella notes echoes of Stevenson, Stoker, Haggard, Doyle, Carroll and many other Victorian fantasists. In the novel's first half, meanwhile, she explicitly models herself after Cathy in *Wuthering Heights* (1847), while reflecting that, despite not having read Ruskin and Hugo, she has 'been told enough about these mighty epics of our race to know most folk think God and me a very gothic couple' (Gray 1992: 51). If Bella's identity cannot be tethered to a unified national tradition, it is almost entirely constituted in reference to a canonical Gothic tradition; her relationship to her creator Godwin Baxter, for instance, can only be understood in connection to Gothic texts.

While the explicit textual allusions in *Poor Things* are largely centred on nineteenth-century Gothic and fantastic fiction, however, Gray also incorporates more recent texts, most notably V. S. Naipaul's *In a Free State* (1971), an episode from which is adapted in the account of Bella's Grand Tour. Gray's explicitly intertextual strategy, which also includes the creation of imagined passages from 'real' books, highlights the extent to which each of the characters in the novel must be seen in relation to textual antecedents, but simultaneously cannot be confined by any single national or generic category. Although the relation between the editor's introduction and the two contradictory texts that make up the bulk of the novel is modelled on Hogg's *Confessions*, the layering of textual evidence is far more complex. The most 'authentic' or reliable text in the novel, in part reproduced in handwritten pages marred by tears, is found in Bella's letters detailing her travels. Yet this manuscript is translated by Baxter, reported by Bella's eventual husband Archie McCandless, placed in a text discovered by Michael Donnelly, and both analysed and placed by the figure of Gray as editor. As Gavin Miller argues, this interweaving of texts is not simply 'mere playfulness' on Gray's part, nor even an example of the postmodern metafiction found in the famous 'Index of Plagiarisms' included in Alasdair Gray's *Lanark* (1981). Instead, the layering of texts is 'a species of the truly fantastic' in the sense developed by Tzvetan Todorov (Miller 2005: 83): Gray's novel highlights the boundary between the real and the marvellous to the extent that resolution is not just difficult but contrary to the text. The central question of the novel is not whether McCandless's supernatural explanation of Bella's life or her own natural explanation is more reliable or likely. Instead, the novel highlights the extent to which all lives, and all narratives, are predicated on the existence of other texts. While many readers dismiss McCandless's fantastic narrative in favour of Bella's/Victoria's more historically familiar one, Gray maintains parity between them. In the novel's closing lines, for instance, the reader is informed of Victoria McCandless's death:

> Reckoning from the birth of her brain in the Humane Society mortuary on Glasgow Green, 18th February 1880, she was exactly sixty-five years, forty weeks and four days old. Reckoning from the birth of her body in a Manchester slum in 1854, she was ninety-one. (Gray 1992: 317)

The fantastic story is given scientific and historical credence that directly contradicts Victoria's own account of her life. Even her body is ultimately subject to textual interpretation.

In both Gray's and Banks's novels, then, the self – whether seen in terms of psychological development or physical embodiment – is ultimately revealed as a series of intertextual references with no resolution. Yet unlike their characters, Banks and Gray display little anxiety over this essential ambiguity. As one character reflects in Banks's Gothic-inflected family saga *The Crow Road* (1993), '"because the real stories just happen, they don't always tell you very much. Sometimes they do, but usually they're too ... messy"' (1993: 236). 'Pretend' stories are valued over 'real' ones because the former offer explanations unavailable elsewhere in the world. Similarly, the castle that is the central image in Banks's apocalyptic fantasy *A Song of Stone* (1998), hovers between being 'a civilised thing', or a remnant of a rational world, and 'a figment of the cloud, something dreamed from mist-invested air' (1998: 123, 255). This divide is especially clear in Banks's *The Bridge* (1986) and Gray's *Lanark*, both of which juxtapose a 'realistic' and a 'fantastic' world without ultimately favouring either one. Both novels combine explicitly Gothic and science-fiction passages with more conventional realism: the space between traditional Scottish settings and fantastic realms is easily crossed, while the threat of barbarism, in the figure of the Scots-speaking Barbarian of Banks's novel or the dragon-hide-covered residents of Gray's Unthank, is always present. Both texts destabilise categorical determinations at the level of both genre and body: no judgement of the nature of reality is ever certain. As such, both authors' novels exemplify Jacques Rancière's argument that fiction should be seen as a way of 'building new relationships between reality and appearance, the individual and the collective' (2010: 141). Rather than forcing the reader to choose between pre-existing categories of the real and the fantastic, Banks and Gray highlight the new sensibility formed from their combination. In their more explicitly Gothic texts, however, they go further to show that the reader's expectations of both realistic and fantastic worlds are textually mediated, as are the characters' understandings of themselves: the text is the ground of the body.

Few contemporary Scottish Gothic texts have made this relationship as clear as Elspeth Barker's *O Caledonia*. The text is book-ended with the brutal murder of its protagonist Janet. In both passages she is explicitly Othered as death places her in relation to the animal realm: she is killed with a rabbit-skinning knife, and mourned only by her pet jackdaw. The body of the text, however, concerns Janet's coming-of-age. Like Bella and Frank, Janet is deprived of most human contact, and subjected to the arbitrary cruelties of a patriarchal world. Like those characters, too, Janet defines herself through language and reading. Her world is shaped by allusions to Shakespeare, Scott and the Border Ballads. Exploring the Aberdeenshire countryside, for instance, she believes 'that if only she had the courage to go on she, like True Thomas, might reach a fairyland, another element, the place of ballads, of "La Belle Dame Sans Merci"' (Barker 1992: 52). As in Andrew Greig's *When They Lay Bare* (1999), the external world and the actions of people within it are simultaneously clarified in relation to, and constrained by, the ballad tradition.

All three protagonists find that their world has already been interpreted; their only agency lies in identifying the story of which they are already part. Each of these novels looks to literary tradition in order to clarify the relation between fantasy and reality, as well as to position characters within familiar narratives. Yet counter to Bissett's claim, contemporary Gothic's focus on historical tradition does not provide a whole or vibrant sense of either individual or national identity. Instead, in all three novels, identity is fractured. Each of the protagonists can only come to an understanding of themselves in reference to textual antecedents, but such understanding is necessarily partial. If the texts are examined as political allegory, as each has been, this suggests a view of Scotland as inherently multiple: rather than presenting a unified nation, the nation must be seen as composed of often contradictory components from a variety of traditions. To a similar extent, the novels challenge the idea of a unified Scottish Gothic, foregrounding instead their broad national and chronological intertextual range. Banks, Gray and Barker thus highlight the tension between adherence to literary and national traditions and the way such traditions can be revisited to create new grounds for identity.

Following Gray and Tennant, more recent Scottish Gothic novels have revisited tradition by focusing on specific antecedents, particularly as a way of interrogating the notion of the 'divided self' as developed by Hogg and Stevenson. Kevin MacNeil's *A Method Actor's Guide to Jekyll and Hyde* (2010) begins with a struck-out epigraph from Stevenson, while the first line is 'I'm in two minds' (2010: 3). Robert Lewis, the protagonist, is not only an actor appearing in a stage production of *Jekyll and Hyde*, but someone whose entire life is shaped by a Scottish literary tradition. He looks to Hugh MacDiarmid for advice on method acting, visits the Burke and Hare strip club and the Jekyll and Hyde pub in Edinburgh and, after a bicycle accident, is tended by a Nurse Stevenson. Lewis's account of the world is filled with allusions and textual echoes. As he argues late in the book, Stevenson did not create Jekyll and Hyde, but 'revealed them' in order to 'shed the right amount of shadowy light upon that which is within us all' (2010: 158); the novella demonstrates that the 'solid core of self is not a fixed entity, it is an illusion' (2010: 200). Textual allusions do not reinforce a particular view of self, but rather demonstrate the multiplicity of selves. This is true not only of the individual, but of the nation: 'There is no Scotland. No Edinburgh. They exist in the plural' (2010: 158). Stable notions of individual and collective identity are not only constituted by fiction, but are themselves a fiction. Gothic texts haunt the self as much as they haunt other Gothic texts. As Peter Schwenger articulates this tension, 'Passing through the woods of narrative, self is continually intersected by words – words that function now as foreground, now as background to the equally unstable figurations of fictional identity. And ours' (1999: 72). More explicitly than in the novels previously discussed, MacNeil presents a world in which perception is always shaped by fiction. Stevenson not only describes the multiple selves of modern Scotland, but also shapes them such that Scotland can only be seen through the palimpsest of Stevenson's text.

The frustration engendered by such a potentially monolithic view of Scottish culture and literary tradition is voiced by Andrew Carlin, the protagonist of James Robertson's *The Fanatic* (2000). Carlin's appearance as the Covenanter Major Weir on Edinburgh ghost tours leads him to further research, which in turn leads him to madness. Reflecting on Jekyll and Hyde, he states:

> Fuckin Scottish history and Scottish fuckin literature, that's all there fuckin is, split fuckin personalities. We don't need mair doubles, oor haill fuckin culture's littered wi them. . . . I mean how long is this gaun tae go on, for God's sake? Are we never gaun tae fuckin sort oorsels oot? (Robertson 2001: 25)

Robertson's text articulates an anxiety not only of influence but of tradition and genre more generally. If Hogg's and Stevenson's novels are repeatedly held as paradigms of Scottish life and art, it becomes difficult to imagine how any text, or any self, could exceed them. History may be no more than 'hearsay and handed down stories and a lot of paper', but at the same time, 'the past was never over' (2001: 197, 306). The hold of the literary past over both Carlin and Lewis is so extreme that both, to a certain extent, lose their conception of a unified self: there is neither an authentic past nor an authentic self, and any individual can only be seen as a combination of echoes. Critics of contemporary Scottish Gothic are often similarly frustrated: so great is the influence of Hogg and Stevenson that the genre can seem remarkably restricted. Novels as diverse as Christopher Whyte's *The Warlock of Strathearn* (1997), Robertson's *The Testament of Gideon Mack* (2006), Denise

Mina's *Sanctum* (2002), Alice Thompson's *Burnt Island* (2013), Ian Rankin's *Hide and Seek* (1991) and Iain Banks's *Complicity* (1993), as well as lesser-known pastiches of Hogg such as Angus McAllister's *The Canongate Strangler* (1990) and J. P. McCondach's *The Channering Worm* (1983), all replay these familiar themes of doubling and literary inheritance. From this perspective, Scottish Gothic can appear a closed circle, where each new text reinforces the authority of a previous one.

One potential solution to this pervasive anxiety is to disrupt the idea of textual inheritance altogether. Alice Thompson's *The Falconer* (2008) is filled with literary allusions, beginning with the characters' names: Iris Tennant evokes both Iris Murdoch and Emma Tennant, while her sister Daphne echoes du Maurier. Unlike the protagonists of the novels previously discussed, however, Iris does not read: in the novel's opening page the train she takes to the remote estate of Glen Almain judders 'so much that the words of her book began to dance about on the page', and she never returns to the printed text (Thompson 2008: 1). Glen Almain is depicted as an 'Eden before the fall' (2008: 11), but is also filled with violence: even the rose garden is filled with threat, while animals, and even people, are sacrificed to a legendary beast. The beast of Glen Almain is said to be 'half-human, half-beast', but the novel is also full of 'beasts in human form' (2008: 54, 72). The unstable relation between humans and animals is figured in part as allegory; Iris has been hired to annotate Hitler's speeches for Lord Melfort, who is in favour of appeasement. While Lady Melfort dismisses National Socialism as 'profoundly *unnatural*', based in a 'romantic neopaganism' and 'worship of forests and nature and strange beasts' (2008: 50; original emphasis), the world of Glen Almain operates along identical principles. The world of political machinations and the world of the fairy tale are closer than they might appear. Rather than embracing these more mythic aspects, Thompson presents a world in which identity is known only through embodiment and metamorphosis: Iris realises over the course of the novel that she will never be more than flesh and bone, and that is what will remain of her when she dies. Her encounters with animals, like Janet's in *O Caledonia*, lead her to understand her life primarily in relation to her physical presence in the world and eventual death. Yet such a focus on embodiment implicitly gives rise to moral or ideological ambiguity: without texts or, indeed, other people around to provide an intellectual foundation, the insular world of Glen Almain succumbs to madness.

The Falconer works along much broader mythic and fairy-tale lines than the novels previously discussed: although the reader finds echoes of many twentieth-century English novels (not only du Maurier, but also L. P. Hartley and D. H. Lawrence), the only texts presented in the novel are political speeches. If a view of the world predicated on literary history leads to endless circularity, as in MacNeil's and Robertson's novels, a world that denies literary history can be overly insular. This paradox is exemplified in John Burnside's first novel, *The Dumb House* (1997). The protagonist, like Iris Tennant, sees physical death as a sign of reality; in childhood he hunts for animal corpses with his mother, finding that 'animals I had only ever encountered in books became real as corpses, life-size, as it were' (Burnside 1997: 15–16). The protagonist, named late in the novel as Luke, moves from collecting animal skulls to live dissection and, eventually, murder. He frames his actions, however, as a quest to understand the importance of language, and the degree to which it separates humans from other animals. In a term that would fit equally well in *The Wasp Factory*, he categorises animals as 'wet machines' (1997: 82) that he can take apart and examine. Unlike Frank Cauldhame, however, Luke sees animals neither as auguries to tell his own future nor as personal enemies, but rather as tools with which he can investigate the nature of the soul. Like Angus, Luke's experiments culminate in the manipulation of his own children: he first keeps them imprisoned in a cellar so that they are not exposed to language; when they begin singing to each other he removes their larynxes, and he finally kills them for his own protection. Luke is ultimately a much more disturbing figure than is found in either *The Wasp Factory* or *Poor Things*: far less introspective, he excuses his actions in a gracefully written set of philosophical preoccupations located on an entirely different plane than his actions. Like both the Cauldhames and Melforts, isolation leads to a form of monstrosity; Luke is rendered further distinct by his inability to perceive the abnormality of his actions. Near the close of the novel, Luke acknowledges that his isolation has made the world into 'nothing more than a jumble of meaningless and disquieting sensations' (1997: 175), but reintegration is impossible. Unlike the Cauldhames and Melforts, however, Luke learns nothing from his exploration of the world.

In these novels, Gothic tropes and themes are used to explore the dangers of literary and cultural inheritance; viewed together they demonstrate that neither fidelity to literary tradition nor withdrawal provides an adequate solution to the problems of political and personal life. Moreover, each can be viewed as an example of Marshall Brown's definition of Gothic novels 'as thought experiments that test the limits not just of human endurance but more specifically of human reason' (2003: 12). Like Victor Frankenstein and Robert Wringhim before them, virtually all of the protagonists view their actions through the lens of justification and reason: the experiments performed by Luke, Godwin Baxter and both Cauldhames reinforce the authority of reason, while characters such as Iris Tennant, Janet, Robert Lewis and Andrew Carlin find themselves subject to an external authority, whether textual, political or historical, that they are unable to resist. In each of these works, reason and authority are coded as patriarchal, yet neither upholding these norms nor rejecting them provides any stability. Instead, each of these novels turns to the individual body as the source of knowledge. The central mystery in each text is not the traditional secret in the study, but the nature of individual embodiment. By moving from general to specific concerns, each novel calls into question the stability not only of ideas of nation and text, but of every foundational discourse: no explanation of identity is ever sufficient. Contemporary Scottish Gothic fiction foregrounds both the impossibility of forgetting the past and the dangers of nostalgia: conforming to tradition and acting in isolation both lead to madness and despair. Instead, questions of politics and history are always seen in relation to individual identity.

The relationship between politics and ideas of embodiment is made clear in a number of novels that integrate Gothic tropes with elements of other genres. For Judith Halberstam, Gothic 'is the breakdown of genre and the crisis occasioned by the inability to "tell," meaning both the inability to narrate and the inability to categorize' (1995: 23). Both of these aspects are visible in recent crime novels by Ian Rankin and Val McDermid that incorporate Gothic tropes into detective fiction. McDermid's *The Skeleton Road* (2014) begins with a skeleton found in an abandoned, explicitly Gothic school building; attempts to 'read' the body lead to a broader exploration of both Scottish nationalism and the legacy of the Balkan conflict. As one character explains, '"the very act of describing a geopolitical relationship can bring it into being"' (McDermid 2014: 17). The same is true of the corpse: assigning it an identity, and building a story for it, creates its place in the world. The corpse is both unspeakable and unspeaking; McDermid's novel demonstrates the dangers in narrating and categorising the body. Rankin's *Saints of the Shadow Bible* (2013), like McDermid's novel set in the lead-up to the 2014 independence referendum, explores the relationship between contemporary politics and the legacy of the past. The 'Saints' of the title are an organisation defined by silence and loyalty: '*Whatever happens among the Saints, we never talk, we never grass*' (Rankin 2013: 234; original emphasis). The mystery turns on John Rebus's attempts to uncover things that could not be said, at the same time that he refuses to speak of contemporary politics. Like other recent novels in the series, Rebus's reticence to discuss his own past is central to the narrative. Although less explicitly tied to the Gothic tradition than earlier Rebus novels such as *The Black Book* (1993), *Saints*, like *Skeleton Road*, uses Gothic tropes to reflect on the constitution of both individual and national identity, and the way bodies do and do not speak. The secrets of the past cannot be thought, but are revealed in the physical body.

Ken MacLeod's *The Night Sessions* (2008), on the other hand, moves a discussion of the past into a narrative of the future, combining the religious themes of Hogg with humanoid robots and science-fiction tropes. Juxtaposing a detective inspector named Adam Ferguson and a group of Covenanters inspired by Major Weir with mention of witchcraft and werewolves, the novel explores the legacies of religion and superstitious belief in a near-future Edinburgh, where the streets and pubs have their present-day names but society is shaped by the end of the 'Faith Wars' and widespread secularism. The history of religious struggle haunts this society: while the various artificial and transhuman characters have no concept of 'original sin', the narrative is nevertheless shaped by 'fanatical suicidal religious robots' (MacLeod 2009: 218, 246). Although the various characters in the novel continually question the idea of the human, they are united in their debt to the past. As in Robertson's and MacNeil's novels, the past is inescapable; despite the science-fiction setting, the characters can only replay conflicts from Scotland's history. In each of these novels the past is neither vibrant nor whole, as in Bissett's formulation, but nevertheless must constantly be re-enacted.

The most surprising Gothic trope to re-emerge in the past decade is a focus on Hell, which returns us to the themes of Gray's *Lanark*, where physical punishment and transformation is the necessary consequence of embodiment. Rankin and Mina have both written graphic novels featuring the DC character John Constantine, or Hellblazer, while Christopher Brookmyre's *Pandaemonium* (2009) locates a portal to Hell in Western Scotland. While Hell is also depicted in high fantasy novels such as Alan Campbell's *Scar Night* (2006), its most interesting, and most Gothic, appearance is in Banks's *Surface Detail* (2010), from his series of science-fiction novels about The Culture. The novel broadly concerns a war between multiple cultures over the existence of simulated Hells to which religious believers are banished after death. Although some action takes place in 'the Real', the world of traditional embodiment, much more is located in various simulated worlds: characters are kept alive after death by 'neural laces', or computer-backed-up memory that creates an 'absolutely identical' version of a person (Banks 2010: 78), while the personalities of enormous interstellar vessels are presented as humanoid avatars, or other creatures. Like MacLeod, Banks combines science-fiction and Gothic tropes to explore the nature of suffering and its necessity in a 'civilised' world. The academic Chayleze

Hifornsdaughter becomes trapped in Hell and is turned into a destroying angel. At the same time, however, she doubts her own experience:

> She had denied the existence of the Real while she was here, surrendering all too easily to the grinding actuality of the horror all around her; why would she not likewise deny the unbelievable gruesomeness of Hell once she was safely back in the Real? (Banks 2010: 99)

Banks presents an absolutely liminal world where every question of environment, embodiment, history, politics, art and language is subsumed into a question of the nature of reality: neither the novel nor the worlds within it can be categorised. For both Banks and MacLeod, the combination of Gothic tropes with science-fiction settings permits a wider investigation into the religious and historical nature of society, and of the 'Real' itself.

Contemporary Scottish Gothic novels cannot be said to have identical aims or relations to a canon of Gothic literature. In these texts Gothic is seen both in terms of literary tradition and as a tool for exploring the relation between the body and the world: Gothic becomes a textual body. As much as many of these texts display an anxiety of influence, tying their narratives to nineteenth-century antecedents, they also demonstrate the extent to which contesting earlier texts allows for the expression of new ideas. Most significantly, conventional political and historical narratives are destabilised in order to foreground the relation between the individual body and death: these novels reveal the extent to which the embodied self, like the very idea of nation, is potentially more unstable than has been previously recognised. Contemporary Scottish Gothic presents a world in which identity is forever multiple, highlighting the contradictory way the self can only be known in relation to pre-existing narratives, but must also break free of them. 'Scottish' and 'Gothic' are not stable categories but the grounds for individual self-creation. This focus on individual identity suggests that rather than simply repeating earlier tropes, contemporary Gothic novels productively use them to question the relation between self and others, as well as past and present, in relation to literary inheritance.

References

Banks, Iain (1986), *The Bridge*, London: Macmillan.
— (1990), *The Wasp Factory*, London: Abacus.
— (1993), *The Crow Road*, London: Abacus.
— (1998), *A Song of Stone*, London: Abacus.
Banks, Iain M. (2010), *Surface Detail*, London: Orbit.

Barker, Elspeth (1992), *O Caledonia*, London: Penguin.

Bissett, Alan (2001), '"The Dead Can Sing": An Introduction', in Alan Bissett (ed.), *Damage Land: New Scottish Gothic Fiction*, Edinburgh: Polygon, pp. 1–8.

Brown, Marshall (2003), *The Gothic Text*, Stanford: Stanford University Press.

Burnside, John (1997), *The Dumb House*, London: Jonathan Cape.

Gray, Alasdair (1981), *Lanark*, Edinburgh: Canongate.

— (1992), *Poor Things*, London: Bloomsbury.

Halberstam, Judith (1995), *Skin Shows: Gothic Horror and the Technology of Monsters*, Durham, NC and London: Duke University Press.

McDermid, Val (2014), *The Skeleton Road*, London: Little, Brown.

MacLeod, Ken (2009), *The Night Sessions*, London: Orbit.

MacNeil, Kevin (2010), *A Method Actor's Guide to Jekyll and Hyde*, Edinburgh: Polygon.

Miller, Gavin (2005), *Alasdair Gray: The Fiction of Communion*, Amsterdam: Rodopi.

Punter, David (1999), 'Heart Lands: Contemporary Scottish Gothic', *Gothic Studies* 1: 1, 101–18.

Rancière, Jacques (2010), *Dissensus: On Politics and Aesthetics*, ed. and trans. Steven Corcoran, London: Continuum.

Rankin, Ian (2013), *Saints of the Shadow Bible*, London: Orion.

Robertson, James (2001), *The Fanatic*, London: HarperCollins.

Schwenger, Peter (1999), *Fantasm and Fiction: On Textual Envisioning*, Stanford: Stanford University Press.

Thompson, Alice (2008), *The Falconer*, Ullapool: Two Ravens.

Chapter 16

Queer Scottish Gothic
Kate Turner

This chapter's analysis of queer Scottish Gothic originates from a simple observation: there is a large and coherent scholarship on queer Gothic and Scottish Gothic respectively; however, there is notably little analysis of the way Scottish and queer Gothic may interact. With the exception of one recent article by Fiona McCulloch, queer Scottish Gothic has not yet been given full critical attention. This chapter explores revisions in the treatment of Gothic monsters, traditionally viewed as 'all that is dangerous and horrible in the human imagination' (Gilmore 2003: 1), in Louise Welsh's *The Cutting Room* (2002), Luke Sutherland's *Venus as a Boy* (2004) and Zoë Strachan's *Ever Fallen in Love* (2011). More specifically, this analysis considers the dissociation of the monstrous figure from fear and terror in these texts, and suggests that they are repositioned as elusive figures through which the peripheral identities of Scottish and of queer may be simultaneously explored.

Torn between a dual British and Scottish identity, positioned as a marginal borderland to a civilised England, and haunted paradoxically by simultaneous ideas of its erased national identity and imperial sins, the Gothic resonates for Scotland in that it provides a site for the exploration of haunting and fracturing incoherencies inherent in the Scottish position as 'other' (Wright 2007: 73; Germanà 2011: 1–5; Morace 2011: 26). Meanwhile, critics of the queer Gothic draw attention to the genre's focus on transgression, perversion and the haunting disquiet of the conservative norm in their interlinked analyses of Gothic and queer (Haggerty 2004–5: 1; O'Rourke and Collings 2004–5: 15; Hughes and Smith 2009: 1). Clearly, then, Scottish and queer have both turned to the Gothic to explore that which is other, marginal and potentially disturbing to the (hetero)normative centre. Significantly, in exploring the origins of the word 'uncanny', Nicholas Royle deduces that 'the "uncanny" comes from Scotland, from that "auld country" that has so often been represented as "beyond the borders", liminal, an English foreign body' (2003: 12). Elsewhere in *The Uncanny*, Royle writes that 'the uncanny *is* queer. And the queer is uncanny' (2003: 43; original emphasis). In making this association, Royle refers to Eve Kosofsky Sedgwick's famous definition of queer as 'the open mesh of possibilities, gaps, overlaps, dissonances and resonances, lapses and excesses of meaning when the constituent elements of anyone's gender, of anyone's sexuality aren't made (or *can't be* made) to signify monolithically' (1994: 8; original emphasis). Queer is the taboo breaker that cannot find a 'place' in understanding or language; like Scotland, queer is 'beyond the borders' and 'liminal', while, like queer, Scotland represents 'lapses and excesses of meaning'. Punter has described the way in which the Gothic resonates for Scotland in that 'issues of suppression in a stateless national culture can find a mode of expression which has much to do with the Gothic' (1999: 101). Yet, simultaneously, the Scottish Gothic encompasses Scotland's haunting imperial sins. James Robertson's *Joseph Knight* (2003), which explores Scotland's participation in the slave trade, exemplifies the Scottish Gothic exploration of 'the burden of unsolved issues and uncomfortable knowledge' (Germanà 2011: 4). In these terms then, Scotland, both outward and inward, both foreign and familiar, shares in Sedgwick's understanding of queer as that which does not 'signify monolithically'. As a site of the uncanny disturbance of borders then, the Gothic emerges as a space of potential common ground for both queer and Scottish.

Despite their commonalities, little attention has been paid to the possibilities of a queer Scottish Gothic. This may be, in part, due to Scotland's traditional masculine heterosexism, which remained a central point of contention in Scottish literary criticism at the turn of the century and was the subject of Christopher Whyte's famous contestation that 'to be gay and to be Scottish ... are still mutually exclusive conditions' (1995: xv; see also Gifford and McMillan 1997; Stirling 2008; Jones 2009; Germanà 2010). On the other hand, queer criticism of canonical Scottish Gothic texts also reveals little attention to their Scottish context. Sedgwick introduces *Between Men* (1985), which includes her queer reading of James Hogg's *The Private Memoirs and Confessions of a Justified Sinner* ([1824] 2002), stating that 'the subject of this book is a relatively short, recent, and accessible passage of English culture, chiefly as embodied in the mid-eighteenth to mid-nineteenth century novel' (1985: 1). Although now dated and contentious, Whyte once asserted that 'Scottishness is visible, anomalous, problematic in a way Englishness has not yet, and may never become' (1995: xvi). This 'invisible' Englishness is the one implemented in these readings; it does not indicate intention to analyse a specific 'Englishness' but refers to a generalised view of the literature produced in the British Isles within the specified period. This is not to argue that these critics exclude the central or most significant aspect of these texts; of course texts can hold pertinence beyond their national context. Rather, these queer readings raise questions about what it would mean to 'place' the queer Gothic in Scotland and to bring Scottishness in line with its previously excluded queerness.

Whereas Sedgwick's open conception of queer as that which 'can't be made to signify monolithically' might align with Gothic exploration of the transgressive space 'beyond', in her analysis of lesbian Gothic, Paulina Palmer recognises that the genre 'also reveals . . . misogynistic/homophobic attitudes' (1999: 13), as it casts 'others' as threatening abject monstrosities. In exemplifying this point, Palmer refers to Diana Fuss's location of 'a fascination with the specter of abjection, a certain preoccupation with the figure of the homosexual as specter and phantom, as spirit and revenant, as abject and undead' (1991: 3). Thus, Palmer concludes, 'writers of lesbian Gothic, in paradoxically reworking the homophobic and misogynistic images associated with the genre, similarly engage in an attempt to resignify the boundaries of the abject' (1999: 16). The Gothic, then, may provide fertile ground for an exploration of that which is queer but this must also involve a renegotiation of the coding of transgressive sexualities and bodies as abject, repulsive and monstrous. This chapter's suggestion, then, is that in recasting the terms of the abject away from fear and terror, the texts of Welsh, Sutherland and Strachan present monstrous figures and peripheral locations as elusive, excessive and uncontainable sites through which the shared 'off-centre' positions of queer and Scottish may interact.

The Cutting Room

Louise Welsh's *The Cutting Room* is narrated by Rilke, a gay auctioneer who discovers a selection of violent and disturbing photographs while clearing out the house of the deceased Mr McKindless. Rilke becomes obsessed with the authenticity of the images, moving through the dark underworld of Glasgow in his quest. Welsh draws a boundary between a civilised world of 'normal people' (2002: 201) and Rilke, who is playfully coded as monstrous throughout the text. He narrates, 'they call me Rilke to my face, behind my back the Cadaver, Corpse, Walking Dead' (2002: 2) and, in comic reference to Gothic homophobia, suggests 'all queers are unstable – who knows when I might turn?' (2002: 121). These knowing references to the casting of queer as monstrous are intertwined with Rilke's abject descriptions of his queer fantasies, 'I was in a tunnel way beneath the city ... the smell of ordure in my lungs ... the scuttle of rats around me ... fucking a stranger against the rough brick of a wall' (2002: 153). Welsh's divide between the civilised surface and the immoral, abjected underbelly calls to mind the typical dispelling of the 'other' beyond the healthy body politic.

However, Rilke's first-person narrative permits the reader access to his queer underworld and, as such, the civilised and normative are recast as marginal and spectral. His reference to 'normal people', for instance, evokes a strange and detached world impossible for Rilke to comprehend: 'I tried to imagine myself working in an office, travelling home to a warm hearth, children, a salary at the end of the month, pension for old age. It was too difficult; the image refused to appear' (2002: 201). This notion of the 'image' that 'refuses to appear' grants an unreal and spectral quality to the bourgeois heteronormative world of home, family and stability. In contrast, the marginal, subversive experience of anal sex is detailed and clinical:

> In anal sex it is of great importance that your partner is relaxed. Too much resistance can lead to tearing of the anal sphincter, resulting in infection, or a loss of muscle tensions, leading to leakage of the back passage – unpleasant. Other possible side effects include a split condom – which may result in the contraction of HIV or several other harmful infections – piles, and a punch in the face for inflicting too much pain. All this aside, I like my sexual partners to have as good a time as I can give them. I find it stimulating. (Welsh 2002: 152)

This clinical and informative description departs from panicked Gothic evocations of queer sexuality; it is overt, casual and factual, as Rilke focuses instead on pleasure: 'I find it stimulating.' Images of abjection and contagion appear through reference to 'infection', 'leakage of the back passage' and 'contraction of HIV', but are subverted by Rilke's offhand, unthreatened response to these as he shifts from discussing HIV to humorously listing 'several other harmful infections', such as 'piles, and a punch in the face'. *The Cutting Room* thus recasts the positioning of the healthy body politic and its spectral threat as Rilke's narrative shifts the queer abjected underbelly to the centre of the text, permitting the reader unthreatened access to this world. Catherine Spooner has suggested a turn in the contemporary Gothic, which constitutes a 'Gothic Carnivalesque' where 'one of the most prominent features ... is sympathy for the monster' (2006: 69). While *The Cutting Room* may not constitute sympathy for the monster, it undoubtedly dissociates abjection from fear and terror, as it revels in Rilke's queer underworld of excess, spectacle and chaos. The spectral and 'threatening', then, shifts to the forefront of the narrative in a carnivalesque celebration of 'otherness'.

Moreover, Rilke's queer world is irrevocably 'placed' in the text as Welsh maps her divided spaces of civilisation and abjection onto competing versions of Glasgow. Rilke refers to the way in which the 'industrial age had given way to a white-collar revolution and the sons and daughters of shipyard toilers now tapped keyboards and answered telephones in wipe-clean sweatshops' (Welsh 2002: 65). The world of normality is cast into the faceless conglomerate of the globalised world here as the 'white-collar revolution' is reduced to 'wipe-clean sweatshops'. Meanwhile, the nostalgic reference to 'the sons and daughters of shipyard toilers' suggests an inward turn to Glasgow's past as an alternative to what McCulloch has referred to as 'capitalist globalization and its alienating entropic affects on our ever shrinking planet' (2012b: 2). Rilke continues, 'dark suits trampled along Bath Street, past the storm-blasted spire of Renfield St Stephen's, home to prepare for another day like the last and another after that' (Welsh 2002: 65). The uniform monotony of apparent 'normality' is juxtaposed here, not with an explicit example of Rilke's queerness, but with the sublime Gothicism of 'the storm-blasted spire of Renfield St Stephen's'. Thus, Welsh looks to the Gothicism of Glasgow's Victorian setting and the chaos of its industrial age as a locus of texture, variation and excess that provides fertile exploration for a queer alternative to the faceless, sterile monotony inherent in the apparent 'normality' of the globalised city.

Significantly, the Gothicism inherent in the image of 'the storm-blasted spire of Renfield St Stephen's' is inscribed into queer scenes throughout the novel. Glasgow's notorious cruising grounds, Kelvin Way, are cast as a particularly abject queer space: 'everywhere I could sense decay. The pigeons were roosting on a skeletal willow poised above the water ... winged rats' (2002: 28). Rather than signify an abhorrence that must be dispelled, Rilke's narration positions this image at the centre of the text and allows the abject to function aesthetically to cast queer cruising as excessive and subversive. In other scenes where Rilke enters a stranger's house for sex, his description of the Glasgow tenement clearly harks back to Victorian Gothicism:

> paper peeled from the walls in jagged tongues, exposing the dark treacle of Victorian varnish on the plaster beneath ... the light came from two tall picture windows which let in the glow of the street lamps ... he turned towards me ... 'you like fucking young boys?' (Welsh 2002: 149–50)

The Gothicism of 'jagged tongues' resonates with the Gothic imagery of Kelvin Way while the 'dark treacle of Victorian varnish' and 'tall picture windows' intertwines the Gothicism of Glasgow's architecture with queer dissonance and excess in this scene. This inward turn to the Gothic architecture and industrialism of Glasgow's Victorian age evokes a textured place of queer excess that forms the underbelly to sterile, uniform globalisation. In this way, Glasgow's past evokes an aesthetics that may be aligned with Sedgwick's reference to queer gender and sexuality; it presents excess and subversion that is not 'made (or *can't be* made) to signify monolithically' (1994: 8; original emphasis).

Venus as a Boy

In a contemporary take on the Gothic-framed narrative, Luke Sutherland's *Venus as a Boy* opens with a narrator (L. S.) who describes how he came to possess and then transcribe a package of minidisks onto which Désirée, the text's supernatural protagonist, had recounted his life story. Désirée narrates his discovery of his 'gift' for sex and his subsequent debauched life, which begins on Orkney and ends in Soho. Désirée's supernatural 'gift' for sex that '[makes] folk melt' (Sutherland 2004: 50) casts him explicitly as the irresistible queer abject monster who threatens heteronormality. He references the 'conflict in [men's] eyes . . . taking for granted they were a hundred per cent heterosexual in any case, and yet wanting to hump the arse off me' (2004: 67). Vampiric images are explicit in Désirée's descriptions of how he gets 'kind of drunk on spunk and cunt juice. All these bodily fluids are like delicious liqueurs to me . . . some nights I finish, I feel like I've been at a feast' (2004: 50). Thus, where *The Cutting Room* playfully references the conservative coding of queer monsters, *Venus as a Boy* presents a supernatural, vampiric protagonist who is unequivocally monstrous.

The transcription of Désirée's audio-recorded life story poses a contemporary twist on the Gothic trope of the found manuscript. Threatening monstrous figures do not typically gain authorial control in Gothic narratives. Bram Stoker's Dracula, for instance, is described by those around him; the journals of Jonathan and Mina Harker, Dr Seward's diary and letters between characters cast the monster as the elusive 'other' and align the reader with the normative perspective it threatens. Similarly, Hyde has no voice in Stevenson's text; he is constructed entirely through other characters' terrified descriptions of him (Stevenson 2006). The Gothic monster's narrative position thus tends to be spectral in that they are produced from the anxieties of the characters they threaten. Similarly, the narrative device of the text as transcript grants the queer monster a voice, therefore bypassing the traditional construction of the monstrous through the terrified 'normative' response, and presenting instead a monster dissociated from 'fear and terror'. Following Gilmore's recognition that monsters tend to represent 'all that is dangerous and horrible in the human imagination' (2003: 1), Sutherland's repositioning of Désirée outside of a framework of fear opens possibilities for alternative explorations of the symbolism of monstrous figures. Mary Shelley's *Frankenstein* (1818) is perhaps the most famous Gothic text granting its monster a voice. In the chapters where Frankenstein's monster takes over the narrative, he is conveyed as sensitive, humane and vulnerable to the mercy of Victor Frankenstein, his 'creator', and, as such, this narrative device inverts the monster–victim relation. Sutherland's text, however, poses no clear-cut lines between monster and victim. Indeed, the text constitutes multifaceted contradictions that refuse comfortable delineation at all turns. This might be termed 'queer disorientation' in the text and it is explored as much through the landscape of Orkney as it is through Désirée, the elusive monster. In many ways, for instance, Sutherland looks to Orkney as the peripheral space that provides an apt setting for his elusive queer monster. Désirée recalls:

> in winter I'd sit in the attic. Watch storms start to form over the Atlantic. Up there, the sky would break open, give you a quick flash of bloody sunlight then spew its guts. The thrill was in the roof shaking and you still feeling safe, at the same time knowing, if anything really did go wrong, what with Orkney being so remote, you'd be fucked. (Sutherland 2004: 15)

This description of landscape clearly evokes Edmund Burke's sublime in which 'the passion caused by the great and sublime in nature' excites 'ideas of pain and danger' leading to 'Terror'; 'the strongest emotion which the mind is capable of feeling' (2008: 39). Here the sublime landscape appears as a complementary setting for this supernatural, elusive, queer monstrosity as the excessive imagery in which the sky would 'give you a quick flash of bloody sunlight then spew its guts' mirrors the vampiric images of gluttony and excess that evoke Désirée's insatiable queer desire. As such, Gothic evocations of excess and marginality intertwine the queer body and the peripheral landscape throughout Sutherland's text. This is evidenced further as Désirée reflects, 'I see how [Orkney is] almost everything I am' (Sutherland 2004: 9) and, later, 'a map of Orkney's a map of my emotions, pretty much. A map of me' (2004: 52). In their intertwining, then, the text inscribes Orkney as a queer supernatural entity and simultaneously evokes the queerness inherent in Orkney's position as 'beyond', peripheral and 'other'.

Yet, at the same time, the narrative challenges essentialist definitions of the (queer) other. Elsewhere, the island is presented as an insular community where local thugs are 'the cream of South Ronaldsay' (2004: 39), and all forms of otherness are persecuted; Désirée describes 'boys at school who wanted to kill me and the Jehovah's Witnesses and the English' (2004: 17). In these presentations of Orkney, Désirée and his friend Finola, daughter of a 'Czechoslovakian countess', are cast as others. Following the story of Finola's mother's magical flight from an unwanted marriage in a wedding dress which 'made a kite out of her', Désirée describes a scene on 'Christmas day, Finola in Eva's wedding dress and me in a mock eighteenth-century ballgown Eva got in some West End musical, skydiving off Hoxa Head' (2004: 20), inscribing this episode with queer escapism. Orkney, then, is juxtaposed as, on the one hand, an insular community that violently excludes otherness and, on the other, the peripheral setting that accommodates fantastic and escapist imagery. This contradictory presentation of Orkney nuances traditional evocations of the magic inherent in this peripheral location, famously depicted in George Mackay Brown's poetry. In this nuance, Orkney's landscape appears 'queered' as it is no longer permitted to realise the simplistic fulfilment of an escapist fantasy for those 'who'd done a runner from the rat race and come to Orkney in the hope of finding an island Utopia' (2004: 11), and instead appears as a violent and contradictory space that intertwines with Désirée's queer monstrosity.

Just as Orkney functions as a conflicting space in the text, queer images are similarly evasive of simple delineation. Upon failing to help Finola when she is horrifically gang-raped by boys on the island, Désirée breaks into her house and becomes fixated on wearing her clothes and makeup. He recalls:

> I got a trick going alone in my bedroom, with lipstick and eyeshadow . . . I'd sit a bit away from the mirror and cross my eyes, defocus and focus until I saw Finola. We had the same kind of build, same colour hair, and what with her undies on and this trick with my eyes, I turned into her . . . I touched myself . . . hmm . . . it was like she was playing with me. Possession, I guess. (Sutherland 2004: 27)

Queer functions here neither as an image of drag nor as easily delineable queer desire. Dualism resonates across the Gothic genre, of which Stevenson's Jekyll and Hyde and Hogg's Robert and Gil-Martin are two of its most famous examples. The doubling of Désirée and Finola, however, also presents an image of union, which calls to mind doublings such as Cathy and Heathcliff in Emily Brontë's *Wuthering Heights* (1847) and, as this chapter later considers, Strachan's Luke and Richard. Sutherland's image of queer Gothic doubling thus alludes to traumatic fragmentation yet simultaneously evokes a space for exploration of shared peripheral experience. In her analysis of the unnameable monster in literature and film, Maria Beville refers to 'a general problem in teratology, which is the avoidance of the ultimate excess and unrepresentability of the monster due to obsessive concentration on processes of labelling, cataloguing, and rationalisation' (2014: xi–xii). Sutherland's exploration of monstrosity presents an image akin to Beville's focus on the unnameable monster. By encountering the voice of this monster we gain some recognition that if Dracula, or Hyde, or Gil-Martin were given a voice then similarly linearity and simple categorisation would break down as the 'other' is permitted control of the narrative. Désirée states, defiantly, 'as for my sexual orientation, I hadn't any . . . some days I'd be all yin, others all yang, sometimes both. So what?' (Sutherland 2004: 90). Thus, in giving his monster a voice, Sutherland departs from the monster–victim relation and monster–healthy body politic relation, allowing the monstrous figure to emerge as the elusive body through which multifaceted ideas of otherness are explored. Meanwhile, Orkney surfaces as a landscape of distortion that accommodates Désirée's monstrous queerness in the text; both function as the confronting spaces of 'ultimate excess' that refuse 'labelling, cataloguing, and rationalisation'.

Ever Fallen in Love

Zoë Strachan's *Ever Fallen in Love* comprises two narratives: one details Richard's present-day life living in the remote Highlands of Scotland, and the other constitutes his memories of his university days and his queer friendship with promiscuous Luke, who is coded throughout the text as excessive, abject and vampiric, yet ultimately desirable. Richard recalls, 'you could see inside his mouth more than seemed usual; his tongue, his teeth. His lips were dry' (Strachan 2011: 20) and 'a shadow passed above me . . . Suddenly I felt fingers in my mouth . . . Luke of course. His papery hand, prone to eczema, and a surge of unwilling arousal at his rough fingers against my tongue' (2011: 99). Richard's memories haunt his present and slowly reveal the crux of his trauma, which involves his complicity in the sexual exploitation/rape of fellow student Lucy, which precedes her accidental drowning/suicide.

McCulloch acknowledges that Strachan provides 'her own contemporary view of Scotland's alterity' (2012a) in passages where Richard and Luke are estranged by 'floppy fringed public school boys' (Strachan 2011: 15) at St Andrews, who 'called me Jock and went through a whole routine of see you Jimmy jokes' (2011: 19). McCulloch also introduces Fred Botting's notion that 'Romance, as it frames Gothic, seems to clean up its darker counterpart . . . the Gothic genre's usual trajectory is reversed: a flight from figures of horror and revulsion is turned into a romantic flight towards them' (Botting 2008: 1). Botting's concept provides fruitful terms through which to consider 'the pattern followed by Richard who pines for the monstrous manipulator Luke' (McCulloch 2012a). McCulloch, then, has identified the terms through which Strachan's text explores the peripheral identities of Scottish and queer and revises the traditional terms of the monstrous via the romantic flight towards Luke.

Additionally, the text's intertextual relationship with Hogg's *Confessions* allows queer Gothicism to resonate across the Scottish Gothic tradition. Richard's reflection that 'it must have been fate that brought us together, chance was never so precise' (Strachan 2011: 7) intertwines the men. Meanwhile, the narrative split between the authorial tone of the third-person narrative and Richard's account of past events, in which he casts Luke as the otherworldly manipulator, aligns Luke with Hogg's Gil-Martin. In her queer reading of *Confessions*, Sedgwick proposes triangulation as the mediation of desire in bonds between men via the appropriation of women. In this respect, she offsets Robert's failed triangulation with George's successful homosociality suggesting that, 'unlike Robert . . . George relates to his male acquaintance as a man, because he has the knack of triangulating his homosocial desire through women' (1985: 102). Luke and Richard's friendship undoubtedly echoes Sedgwick's reading of *Confessions*; indeed, the pinnacle sex scene involving Lucy presents an unmistakeable scene of triangulation:

> while I stayed still but still hard in position, he eased himself in from the front. He began, slowly to move, and I thought I would explode then expire for the pleasure of feeling him so close to me . . . he smiled, as if he would have kissed me. As if he would have pressed his dry lips to mine. If she hadn't been between us. He reached over and stroked my hair back from my face, and his touch, his touch, the feel of him against me, his fingers brushing my throat, my lips, made me shudder and slow, and as I relaxed I saw his beautiful face contort, as if it was the sight, the sound, the feel of my ecstasy that had brought his own . . . (Strachan 2011: 194)

Lucy fulfils the role of the woman in triangulation as her presence creates a literal distance between the men that prevents the encounter becoming explicitly homosexual. As if to leave no question about the presence of queer desire, however, the scene takes triangulation one step further as Lucy, for all the significance of her presence, is made absent in the moment of contact – 'his touch, his touch' – that prompts both men's orgasm. This scene, then, enacts a confirmation of Sedgwick's exploration of the possibility of desire in homosocial relationships in *Confessions* and presents a queer Scottish Gothicism that invites renewed queer analysis of this cornerstone text of the Scottish Gothic.

Further intertextual references map a specifically queer Scottish landscape across the text. Readers of *Brideshead Revisited* (1945) will note similarities between the university friendship replete with queer subtext and Sebastian and Charles's relationship in Evelyn Waugh's novel. Indeed, Richard reflects on a passage from Waugh's novel in which Charles recalls '"that faint, unrecognized apprehension that here, at last, I should find that low door in the wall, which others, I knew, had found before me, which opened on an enclosed and enchanted garden"' (Strachan 2011: 131). Richard ponders 'How those words had resonated in his mind, once upon a time, when he'd searched for just such a low door in the wall of his university town, ready to stoop and enter, willing himself to be enchanted' (2011: 131). This passage maps the imagery of 'that low door in the wall' onto his desire for Luke and casts St Andrews as the surreal space of queer exploration. Moreover, Richard introduces the narrative with an explicitly queer reference to St Andrews: 'It was quite an old-fashioned place. Luke was quite old-fashioned too. Cast himself as a latter day Dorian or Valmont, sinned the old sins' (2011: 1). The references to the Gothic 'old sins' clearly inscribe homosexuality onto Luke; as McCulloch recognises, 'there is something "elsewhere" about Luke's old worldly otherworldliness of depravity, drawn from other literary texts' (2012a). Furthermore, the alignment of that 'old-fashioned university town by the sea' clearly positions St Andrews as the literal 'elsewhere' for this queer 'otherworldliness'.

Landscape is layered throughout Strachan's novel; St Andrews appears as a surreal queer space that interjects Richard's present-day existence and simultaneously, in a move that alludes to the monstrous, these memories of St Andrews detail Luke and Richard seeking solace in the Gothic hiding-place of a derelict mansion: 'anyway, he said. Want to go to the castle? Get away from the Yahs for an hour or two?' (Strachan 2011: 179). Their justification of squatting due to the fact that there is 'no law of trespass in Scotland' (2011: 51) inscribes the castle as a specifically Scottish uncanny space in which the boys find belonging in unbelonging. On their first visit Richard reflects: 'I had a sense, almost, of time blurring' (2011: 51). As such, the castle emerges as both a space of escapism for these Scottish Gothic others and simultaneously a space of distortion replete with queer potential. The homosocial/homosexual intertwines, for instance, in their fight:

I forgot, I think, who it was I was struggling against and why, got lost in the physical sensation of the fight . . . I realised that he was looking at me and that our bodies were touching. This was the moment, my chance, to reach out and push the hair back from his face, to lean in and kiss him. (Strachan 2011: 249)

The distortion of the space is inherent in the disoriented physicality of the scene in which Richard 'got lost in the physical sensation of the fight', which leads to the queer moment in which he contemplates kissing Luke. Thus, the castle, alongside St Andrews, functions as a specifically queer Scottish Gothic space through which the schizoid figuring of Luke/Richard's queerness and Scottishness simultaneously intertwine in an exploration of fragmenting and distorting otherness. Moreover, the intertextual relationship between Strachan's homosocial/sexual Scottish double and Hogg's Wringhim/Gil-Martin presents queerness that resonates across the Scottish Gothic tradition.

Conclusion

In her study of the unnameable monster, Beville claims that 'consistent attempts to manage the monster have overshadowed considerations of the phenomenology and aesthetics of the monster and monstrous' (2014: 179). Meanwhile, as Palmer notes, the lesbian Gothic involves '[resignifying] the boundaries of the abject' (1999: 16). In the contemporary Queer Scottish Gothic, then, Welsh, Sutherland and Strachan look to the abject and monstrous as that which disorientates boundaries and limits and thus provides opportunity for the exploration of multifaceted otherness that simultaneously encompasses the positions of Scottish and queer. As such, from Welsh's excessively subversive Victorian Glasgow, Sutherland's abrasively queer Orkney, to Strachan's disorienting queer Gothic spaces, Scotland emerges as a multifaceted topography across the contemporary Gothic that provides a fitting space for these reconfigured queer monsters. Following Beville's analysis of the unnameable monster and Spooner's consideration of sympathy for the monster, the queer Scottish Gothic's reappropriation of monstrosity provides further terms through which monstrous figures are increasingly available for the exploration – and at times celebration – of various manifestations of 'otherness' outside of a framework of expulsion and fear.

References

Beville, Maria (2014), *The Unnameable Monster in Literature and Film*, New York: Routledge.

Botting, Fred (2008), *Gothic Romanced: Consumption, Gender and Technology in Contemporary Fictions*, Abingdon and New York: Routledge.

Burke, Edmund [1757] (2008), *A Philosophical Enquiry into the Sublime and Beautiful*, London and New York: Routledge.

Fuss, Diana (1991), 'Introduction', in Diana Fuss (ed.), *Inside/Out: Lesbian Theories, Gay Theories*, New York: Routledge, pp. 1–10.

Germanà, Monica (2010), *Scottish Women's Gothic and Fantastic Writing: Fiction Since 1978*, Edinburgh: Edinburgh University Press.

— (2011), 'Introduction: The Sick Body and the Fractured Self: (Contemporary) Scottish Gothic', *Gothic Studies*, 13: 2, 1–8.

Gifford, Douglas and Dorothy McMillan (1997), *A History of Scottish Women's Writing*, Edinburgh: Edinburgh University Press.

Gilmore, David D. (2003), *Monsters: Evil Beings, Mythical Beasts, and All Manner of Imaginary Terrors*, Philadelphia: University of Pennsylvania Press.

Haggerty, George (2004–5), 'The Horrors of Catholicism: Religion and Sexuality in Gothic Fiction', *Romanticism on the Net*, 36–7 (November 2004, February 2005), <http://erudit.org/revue/ron/2005/v/n36-37/011133ar.html?lang=en> (last accessed 24 October 2014).

Hogg, James [1824] (2002), *The Private Memoirs and Confessions of a Justified Sinner*, ed. Peter Garside, Edinburgh: Edinburgh University Press.

Hughes, William and Andrew Smith (2009), 'Introduction: Queering the Gothic', in William Hughes and Andrew Smith (eds), *Queering the Gothic*, New York and Manchester: Manchester University Press, pp. 1–10.

Jones, Carole (2009), *Disappearing Men: Gender Disorientation in Scottish Fiction 1979–1999*, Amsterdam and New York: Rodopi.

McCulloch, Fiona (2012a), '"Looking Back": Scottish Queer Gothic Returns in Zoë Strachan's *Ever Fallen in Love*', *The Irish Journal of Gothic and Horror Studies* (June), <http://irishGothichorrorjournal.homestead.com/EverFalleninLove.html> (last accessed 6 October 2014).

— (2012b), *Cosmopolitanism in Contemporary British Fiction: Imagined Identities*, New York and Basingstoke: Palgrave Macmillan.

Morace, R. (2011), 'James Robertson and Contemporary Scottish Gothic', *Gothic Studies*, 13: 2, 22–36.

O'Rourke, Michael and David Collings (2004–5), 'Introduction: Queer Romanticisms: Past, Present and Future', *Romanticism on the Net*, 36–7 (November 2004, February 2005), <http://www.erudit.org/revue/ron/2005/v/n36-37/011132ar.html?vue=biblio> (last accessed 24 October 2014).

Palmer, Paulina (1999), *Lesbian Gothic: Transgressive Fictions*, London and New York: Cassell.

Punter, David (1999), 'Heart Lands: Contemporary Scottish Gothic', *Gothic Studies*, 1: 1, 101–18.

Royle, Nicholas (2003), *The Uncanny*, Manchester: Manchester University Press.

Sedgwick, Eve Kosofsky (1985), *Between Men: English Literature and Male Homosocial Desire*, New York: Columbia University Press.

— (1994), *Tendencies*, London: Routledge.

Spooner, Catherine (2006), *Contemporary Gothic*, London: Reaktion Books.

Stevenson, Robert Louis [1886] (2006), *Strange Case of Dr Jekyll and Mr Hyde*, London: Penguin Books.

Stirling, Kirsten (2008), *Bella Caledonia: Woman, Nation, Text*, Amsterdam and New York: Rodopi.

Strachan, Zoë (2011), *Ever Fallen in Love*, Dingwall: Sandstone Press.

Sutherland, Luke (2004), *Venus as a Boy*, London: Bloomsbury.

Welsh, Louise (2002), *The Cutting Room*, Edinburgh: Canongate.

Whyte, Christopher (1995), *Gendering the Nation: Studies in Modern Scottish Literature*, Edinburgh: Edinburgh University Press.

Wright, Angela (2007), 'Scottish Gothic', in Catherine Spooner and Emma McEvoy (eds), *The Routledge Companion to Gothic*, London: Routledge, pp. 73–82.

Chapter 17

Authorship, 'Ghost-filled' Islands and the Haunting Feminine: Contemporary Scottish Female Gothic
Monica Germanà

Introduction

While scholars are certainly indebted to Ellen Moers's pioneering work on women's writing, it would be difficult to agree, with almost four decades of Gothic criticism behind us, that 'Female Gothic is easily defined' (1977: 90). The topic has been the subject of contested definitions and critical revisions informed by both the contentious boundaries of the critical category in question, and the changing perspectives in feminist and gender studies (Fitzgerald 2009). While the link between Female Gothic and the biological sex of its authors has been frequently challenged, in one of the most recent works, we are also reminded that 'Gothic and feminist categories now demand a self-criticism with respect to their totalising gestures and assumptions' (Brabon and Genz 2007: 7).

Adding the national element to a discussion of Female Gothic amplifies the sense of categorical marginalisation of this critical analysis, for, as Douglas Gifford and Dorothy McMillan have argued, 'Scottish women's writing arguably suffers from the double bind of being Scottish and being by women' (1997: ix–x). The inclusion of English author Amy Sackville in this chapter aims to challenge the boundaries of Scottish literature and, in this specific context, Scottish Gothic. The view purported here is that, as a category identifying a specific kind of literary production, 'Scottish' ought not to be reductively used in relation to the birthplace or residence of the writers who produce it, but to indicate, instead, a text's relationship with a nation's diverse cultural production. Paradoxically, it is a distinctive anxiety about boundaries and authenticity – both authorial and historical – rather than an endorsement of national values that characterises Scottish Gothic, as it emerges in non-linear genealogies and textualities from James Hogg's and Robert

Louis Stevenson's canonical works to more recent works such as Iain Banks's *The Wasp Factory* (1984), Alan Warner's *These Demented Lands* (1997) and Michel Faber's *Under the Skin* (2013).

Bearing this complex framework in mind, this chapter seeks to explore the question of authorship exposed by contemporary Scottish Female Gothic. Uncertain textual origins, and, consequently, authorship, have distinctly pervaded Scottish Gothic since the publication of James MacPherson's Ossian's 'fake' *Fragments of Ancient Poetry* in 1760, and have continued to preoccupy Scottish writers to the present day. Following Angela Wright's claim that Scottish Gothic exposes textuality as a site of contestation (2007: 76), this chapter suggests that the self-reflective employment of intertextuality and metafictional references to problematic authorship are a pervasive feature of contemporary Scottish Female Gothic. As this chapter demonstrates, such concerns emerge strongly in connection with the haunting feminine, which challenges authorial control to destabilise the centre/margins dichotomy and, ultimately, point to the story of the Other.

Authorial control – and patriarchal authority behind it – are threatened by the disruptive function of the haunting feminine, a theme pervasively present throughout Scottish Gothic, from the ballad tradition and the Ettrick Shepherd's folk tales, to the more recent fictional apparitions in George Mackay Brown's 'Andrina' (1983), Elspeth Barker's *O Caledonia* (1991), and Ali Smith's *Hotel World* (2001) (see Germanà 2010). Commenting on Mary R. Beard's notion of the 'haunting idea', which refers to the omnipresent spectral woman of Western literature, Diana Wallace argues that Beard's claim points 'to the way in which woman has been consistently depicted as "ghostly", haunting in the sense that she is disembodied/disempowered through being subjected to "*male* man"' (2009: 26; original emphasis). Whilst tracing the recurrence of the motif in both literature and theory from Mary Wollstonecraft to Virginia Woolf, Wallace also notes that in the twentieth century, 'metaphors of burial, imprisonment and spectrality . . . are no longer used to theorise women's "subject" position specifically within marriage but to analyse the repression of women's "subjectivity" in a wider sense' (2009: 34). Looking, more specifically, at Scottish Female Gothic, this chapter claims that the haunting feminine performs an even more subversive function. Without wanting to generalise, and bearing in mind the diversity of contexts in which it emerges, the haunting feminine disrupts the coherence of authorial narrative, insinuating doubts about the authenticity of the main story and, simultaneously, exposing the possibility of (an)Other story. In the three representative novels analysed in this chapter – Louise Welsh's *Naming the Bones* (2010), Amy

Sackville's *Orkney* (2013) and Alice Thompson's *Burnt Island* (2013) – the haunting feminine establishes important links between the treatment of femininity and authorial control. In dealing with the decentred authority of the male author-figures, the haunting feminine casts a shadow on the limits of their authority in these stories and, consequently, the authenticity of their texts.

Such interrogations are significantly rooted in the spectrality of the novels' insular settings that distinctly inscribe these questions in the uncanny landscape of Scotland and its haunted history, pointing to the nation's contested autonomy. The island setting, a frequent locus in contemporary Scottish Gothic, as seen in A. L. Kennedy's *Everything You Need* (1999), Alice Thompson's *Pharos* (2002) and Sarah Moss's *Night Waking* (2011), does not merely function as a suitably haunted background to these narratives, but most importantly serves as a reminder of Scotland's peripheral liminality (see Baker 2014: 92). Indeed, Scotland's hybrid political condition of being a devolved nation within the United Kingdom arguably places its literature in the complex in-between position of the colonial Other. Gothic's obsession with otherness has prompted postcolonial critics such as Tabish Khair to claim that 'An uneasy negotiation with the "foreign" runs through the Gothic tradition' (2009: 7). Channelling a dual kind of Otherness – nation and gender – Scottish Female Gothic deploys the haunting feminine to question the authority of the centre, and write back from the margins.

Naming the Bones

Naming the Bones is the story of Murray Watson, a University of Glasgow academic working on the biography of poet Archie Lunan, drowned, under mysterious circumstances, off the coast of the island of Lismore in Argyll. His research puts him in touch with a number of people who met Archie when he was alive, including his head of department, Professor Fergus Baine; a retired academic, Professor James; and, crucially, Christie Graves, a writer and Archie's girlfriend at the time of his death. The research project gradually turns into investigative work, as Murray, who is also haunted by the memory of his father's recent death in a mental institution, visits the island to unearth the secrets surrounding Archie's death.

With other contemporary Scottish novels, including Alasdair Gray's *Poor Things* (1992), Luke Sutherland's *Venus as a Boy* (2004) and James Robertson's *The Testament of Gideon Mack* (2006), *Naming the Bones* shares a self-reflective engagement with authorship channelled through a web of textual references that permeate the main story. The narrative of *Naming the Bones* is haunted by the elusive story of the missing poet, which Murray puts together from an array of textual and oral sources: accounts given by Fergus, Professor James and book-finder George Meikle all provide complementary information, whilst also opening up gaps in Archie's life. From the start, the narrative is a patchwork of texts: beside Archie's collection of poetry, an unpublished science-fiction novel and notebooks, Murray is exposed to the notes of another scholar, the late Alan Garrett (who, incidentally, also dies in an unexplained accident on Lismore), Christie's own books and a juvenile poetry collection by Fergus. In combination with the influence of these fictional texts, possessing Murray's narrative is a plethora of literary references – including James Hogg, Oscar Wilde and Seamus Heaney – the most significant of which is to Stevenson's *Strange Case of Dr Jekyll and Mr Hyde* (1886), whose duality also pervades Archie's character: 'you could say that Archie had two sides to him, the Glaswegian who wasn't going to take any shit and the mystical islander' (Welsh 2010: 33).

In line with Angela Wright's observation that 'Scottish Gothic is intimately concerned with distilling the right narrative from any story' (2007: 76), the novel's deployment of intertextuality poses questions about authorial control and authenticity. While Murray's research into the late Archie Lunan assumes a progressively more personal dimension, the boundaries between author and subject matter become increasingly blurred. When talking to Christie about his project, she astutely remarks that 'Archie's in every word, even when you're writing of something else, just as he's in your thoughts, even when he's absent' (Welsh 2010: 369). When Murray – perhaps as a result of his identification with the subject of his writing, perhaps out of guilt for letting his father die in an institution – attempts to hang himself, the image of the dead poet returns to haunt him: 'Murray stepped from the table, seeing Archie's face at the window as he fell' (2010: 375). Finally, as the novel draws to an apparently more positive outcome, Murray's brother, Jack, simply tells him: 'You resurrected Archie Lunan' (2010: 388). Despite drawing attention to the problematic questions of authorship and authorial control, simultaneously *Naming the Bones* demonstrates distrust in the concept of the 'Death of the Author'. In fact, by the end of the story Murray plans to reissue a collection of poetry previously published under the name of none other than Fergus Baine. It was Fergus, significantly, who had discouraged Murray from looking further into Archie's life: 'The poetry was the thing, the life an unfortunate distraction from the art. They should delete authors' names from all books and let the works stand or fall on their own merit' (2010: 277). The story, however, would appear to resurrect – rather than kill – legitimate authorship, whilst still questioning the text's so-called authenticity.

Such questions about authenticity are strongly reflected in the novel's evocative engagement with the geology and archaeology of Lismore. Talking of the 'monument' and the 'ruin' as recurrent tropes in Scottish and Irish Gothic, David Punter argues that 'both of these notions . . . point us toward the "uncanny", in that they speak always of history, but of a history that is constantly under the threat of erasure' (2002: 105). Almost as a response to Punter's reading of Scottish history, Murray's landlady in Lismore, Mrs Dunn, speaks of the island's archaeology as a way of holding on to the island's elusive past: 'The only chance we have of preserving the past now is by recording it' (Welsh 2010: 297), she claims, fuelling Murray's own obsessive hunt for the truth about Archie's death. But the threat of erasure deeply permeates Lismore's ambiguous heritage. Beside the fact that the island has claimed the lives of both Archie and the only other researcher interested in his work, Lismore is, from the start, allusively captured as a land haunted by 'the souls of dead sailors welcoming the travellers home' (2010: 234). As John Berger has suggested, 'The address of western Ireland or Scotland is tidal, recurring, ghost-filled' (1992: 69), and it is this uncanny scenery that accommodates the elusive spectrality of Lismore and, as will be illustrated, the haunting feminine. Berger reads geography as narrative, an untold story written on landscape. In the sense that it alludes to meaning (albeit unknowable), scenery becomes text. In *Naming the Bones*, while the landscape might lend itself to claims of authenticity, it also resists singular interpretations, being simultaneously adjacent and juxtaposed to the urban environs of Glasgow and Edinburgh. The island's history is one of exploitation; as Christie reminds Murray, 'A lot of those fine townhouses and tenements in Edinburgh and Glasgow wouldn't be standing if it weren't for lime made on this little island' (Welsh 2010: 281). Moreover, although the landscape retains its unspoilt character, the island's historical and recent pasts share similar, or worse, kinds of sin with those of the mainland's largest cities. While on the ground level, Lismore's topography remains, at best, elusive – 'not all of [the limekilns] have been mapped', warns Christie (2010: 281) – the underground layers of its archaeological past disclose the island's ambiguous past. The notion that 'They were big into sacrifice, our ancestors' (2010: 323) foreshadows the exhumation of Christie's own daughter from the limekilns, whilst endorsing a link between earlier and more recent sacrifices performed on the island.

Notably, the question of authorial control is linked to the haunting feminine, which serves the function of destabilising the foundations of patriarchal discourse, whilst challenging the notions of authorship and textual authenticity. Significantly, Christie is initially presented as a peripheral figure – 'She was Archie's shadow or maybe he was hers, who knows?' – whose influence on Archie's work remains ambiguous, and whose Gothic beauty – 'big eyes, pale skin and . . . red hair' (2010: 90–1) – conceals the dangerous sensuality of a femme fatale. Moreover, while Christie's surname overtly points to the figurative 'buried woman' of Gothic fiction, the horrific death of her baby and exhumation of her corpse thirty years later further cements her haunting role within Murray's story. In line with the Female Gothic's thematic recurrence of difficult (after-)births and absent mothers noted by Moers, here the conflation of the mother with the haunting feminine speaks of the sub-version of gender normativity, noted in many examples of problematic/ absent motherhood in contemporary Scottish Gothic, including Iain Banks's *The Wasp Factory* (1984) and Emma Tennant's *Two Women of London* (1989). Such disruption is apparently assuaged, at the end, in Christie's embracing the corpse of her baby before committing suicide in what prefigures a gesture of self-burial.

The influence of the haunting feminine does not end, but, arguably, comes to the foreground with Christie's death. When DNA testing reveals that the baby is in fact Fergus's and not Archie's, as Christie 'like[d] to think' (2010: 338), the revelation points to the novel's underscoring of the gaps in the narrative of Archie's life that Murray has attempted to reconstruct. While all manuscripts relative to Archie's biography are destroyed in Christie's house fire at the end of the novel, the only clues left about Archie's life are in Christie's autobiography, *Sacrifice*. Linked with the anti-normative maternal space she occupies, and the unclear paternity of her child, Christie's role as the haunting feminine is cemented by the survival of her memoir, which ultimately defies the centrality of both Archie and Murray as author figures.

Orkney

Orkney tells the story of Richard, an academic like Murray, albeit of an older generation, and his honeymoon trip to a remote island of the Orkney archipelago. Richard's first-person narrative is an intensely evocative account of his new marriage to an elusive young woman, his former student, who remains significantly unnamed throughout the story. The plot shifts between the present tense, in which Richard's attachment to his new wife slowly develops into the kind of supernatural bewitchment investigated by his academic research, and flashbacks to the recent past, which reveal inconsistent memories of their courtship. At the end, the wife's mysterious disappearance coincides with his psychological meltdown, which is preceded by writing block.

Opening the novel, in a passage that prefigures the uncanny association between Orkney's tidal scenery and the haunting feminine, is a description of Richard's wife standing on the 'barren beach, all wrapped up in her long green coat' (Sackville 2013: 1). From the outset, Richard is positioned as the narrator-observer – and, by extension, the author-figure – juxtaposed to his wife, who is constructed as the object of her husband's authorial narrative and controlling gaze. Laura Mulvey has argued that the principal function performed by female characters in classic cinematography is that of supporting – and pleasing – the male gaze, and, consequently, reinforcing masculinity and patriarchal authority (Mulvey 1975). Following Mulvey, John Berger has also commented on the gender asymmetry of the gaze politics in Western visual art, arguing that 'men act and women appear. Men look at women. Women watch themselves being looked at' (1972: 41). The narrative repeatedly exposes Richard's obsession with keeping the girl, literally, in his frame: 'I close my eyes to fix her there' (Sackville 2013: 124), he says, even when his gaze is not directly focused on her.

Simultaneously, however, the narrative points to the wife's awareness of the gaze, and her elusiveness; 'I'm sorry I moved beyond your frame' (2013: 165), she says, towards the end of the novel, when she disappears, temporarily, from his sight. Moreover, in spite of Richard's constant watch, his wife remains uncannily inscrutable throughout the narrative, and his failure to capture her in the still frame of a photograph discloses her persistent resistance to his gaze (2013: 96). This implies the subversion of her apparent compliance with the politics of the male gaze in a performative strategy that, as Diane Long Hoeveler has identified, is central to the feminist ideology of earlier Female Gothic novels: 'the female gothic novelist constructs female characters who masquerade as professional girl-women caught up in an elaborate game of play-acting for the benefit of an obsessive and controlling male *gaze*' (1998: 4; original emphasis). 'Gothic feminism', Hoeveler further explains, draws attention to the performance of the heroine's 'staged weakness' – a form of 'victim feminism' to resist patriarchal control (1998: 7). In *Orkney*, the character's subversive elusiveness is further endorsed by the wife's insubstantial physicality – an ambiguous manifestation of her 'staged weakness' – with her thin body described in spectral terms – 'so slight and young, so strange and pale' (Sackville 2013: 10) – while her 'silver eyes . . . wide, wet, [and] *inscrutable*' (2013: 211; my emphasis) reinforce the notion of her resistance to the male gaze. As Diana Wallace reminds us, 'With its roots in the Latin "specere" (to look), the metaphor of the spectre has obvious appeal as a way of exploring representations of femininity within a symbolic based on visual difference' (2009: 37). To Richard's gaze, the wife represents the feminine Other, whose physical ethereality is endorsed by her unknown past (Sackville 2013: 27).

Significantly, once on Orkney, the remote place of her nebulous origin and her choice for their honeymoon, the wife's body exists in seamless continuity with the island's scenery. Moreover, the narrative points to a supernatural link between the woman and the sea: 'there is a trace of webbing' (2013: 11) between her fingers, so that she cannot wear her wedding ring; her skin has a 'salty tang' (2013: 14); she cooks with too much salt, pulls a lobster apart with her own hands, and has 'dreadful' table manners (2013: 56–7). The symbiotic bond between the woman and the sea is strongly evocative of Scotland's selkie-lore, an allusion supported by the reference to the tales of selkies and finfolk she tells Richard (2013: 185) the night before she disappears (see Thompson 2000). Like the selkie-women of many Scottish folk tales, Richard's wife retains an ambiguous relationship with the sea: she claims to be afraid of it, but keeps playing close to the water. Elsewhere, he refers to her as 'The storm-witch on the shore' (Sackville 2013: 180), thus drawing a comparison with the *Cailleachs*, the 'divine hags' of Celtic lore (2013: 159; see also Ross 1973).

What all these references to the supernatural world of Scottish marine superstitions reveal is the unsettling continuity between Richard's research project – a compendium of nineteenth-century enchantment narratives – and the fantasy he constructs around his elusive wife: 'Beautiful terrible women. Vulnerable lonely cursed women. Strange and powerful women. It's an old obsession' (2013: 21). The problem with his project is that it attempts to contain and categorise that which cannot, in fact, be easily contained – the haunting feminine – a conundrum mirrored in the relationship with his wife whom he also wants to own but, significantly, cannot name. Yet, as the narrative progresses, the object of Richard's fixation shifts away from the fictional creatures of his texts to focus on his wife: 'I am supposed to be working', he admits, 'My concentration wanes with every passing day, every troubled night. These *paper-thin creatures on the page fail to fascinate as she does, although she is hardly more substantial*' (2013: 158; my emphasis). As in *Naming the Bones*, where Murray's identification with the subject of his biography destabilises authorial control, there is an increasing sense of confusion, as the narrative of *Orkney* unfolds, between the subject of Richard's research and his relationship with his new wife. Towards the beginning of the narrative, he disturbingly frames his feelings within a mythological incestuous fantasy: 'She is my maligned, molested daughter, not my spouse; and I am a monster to flaunt it in their faces . . . she *could be lifted out of my library*' (2013: 11–12; my emphasis). Such references are suggestive not only of the permeable boundaries between the world of Richard's books and the 'real' world, but also of the more disquieting effect of the textual enchantments on the 'real' events of his life, and the darker corners of his desire. As with the enigmatic Gil-Martin in Hogg's *The Private Memoirs and Confessions of A Justified Sinner* (1824), the effect, at the end of *Orkney*, is of interpretive hesitation between a supernatural and a rational explanation about the wife's existence (see Williams 2013).

Significantly, as well as drawing ostensibly from Scottish superstition and folklore, the source of the uncanny narrative, as the title announces, is firmly grounded in Orkney's scenery, history and literature, as suggested in the reference to George Mackay Brown in one of the novel's epigraphs. Orcadian landscape is, like Lismore in *Naming the Bones*, constructed as a spectral text. 'A place of fluid borders and edges' (Sackville 2014), the tidal landscape of Scotland accommodates the quintessential setting for Gothic spectrality, pointing, in turn, to a reading of insular Scotland as eminently 'Other' both outwardly, in relation to England, but also inwardly, in relation to mainland Scotland. Orkney's sublime scenery, with its dark sea and 'bloated purple, tumorous' sky (Sackville 2013: 54), and the unknown ancient history of its people – and their 'burial mounds; old worship, old defences, long-forgotten tombs' (2013: 145) – complicate interpretation. As inscrutable and elusive as his unnamed wife, Orkney represents the uncanniness of a place with shifting scenery and an obscure past.

Instead of complying with Richard's authorial intentions, neither the scenery nor the woman sits easily within the frame of his gaze; the result of the wife's haunting collusion with the land exposes, in turn, Richard's damaged psyche. In the end, reader and narrator are left only with the cryptic clues in the isolated lines from a book she has been reading that invoke a supernatural reading of the novel whilst underscoring the subversive drive of the haunting feminine – 'A stranger came in / So beautiful / She seemed to be a woman from the sea' (2013: 248).

Burnt Island

Burnt Island tells the story of Max Long, an unsuccessful writer who travels to Burnt Island to be on a residency organised by the best-selling author James Fairfax, in the hope of revitalising his waning career. His stay on the island, however, is disturbed by a series of strange events, the authenticity of which remains questionable throughout the story, and his interaction with the island's women. Following his progressive breakdown, the end of the story marks Max's death by drowning and, simultaneously, the publication of James's new novel.

From the start, Burnt Island is shrouded in Gothic darkness. As the ferry approaches the harbour, 'the sea was darkening, as if a malevolent spirit had entered its depths and taken on the form of the shifting, rising black water' (Thompson 2013: 4); 'The sky was eternally dramatic; the sun appeared apocalyptic behind a coastline of jagged black rocks' (2013: 16). As fog enshrouds 'the island in enticing shapes' (2013: 41), the island scenery speaks of the liminality of a space that challenges characters' and readers' perceptions of the 'real'. Moreover, as in *Naming the Bones*, it is not just the geology, but also the archaeology of the island that resists definition: when a stone circle mysteriously shifts its millennial alignment, there is a strong suggestion that the island's ground might be untrustworthy, or, at least, deceptive to the gaze. Significantly, similar monuments elicit recurrent questions about authenticity throughout the Scottish canon, including Lewis Grassic Gibbon's *Sunset Song* (1932), Iain Crichton Smith's *Consider the Lilies* (1968) and especially James Robertson's *The Testament of Gideon Mack* (2006), a Gothic rewriting of Hogg's *Confessions*. That the stone circle on Burnt Island encapsulates a critique of narrative and textual reliability is further emphasised by the fact that 'Engraved on the stones, in indecipherable script, was faded lettering' (2013: 51).

The island's past – and its written texts – thus remains unreadable, echoing the notion of history 'under the threat of erasure' (Punter 2002: 105), which underpins Scotland's condition as colonial Other. Just as monuments no longer support a coherent narrative of national history, equally, in *Burnt Island*, the stone circle's shifting alignment foreshadows Max's increasingly complex relationship with the 'real'. Such metaphorical reading of the island is also endorsed by the novel's intertextual body, and, as discussed later, its relationship with the haunting feminine. While the setting of *Burnt Island* owes much to the sublime aesthetics of the Scottish landscape, and Thompson's personal experience of Shetland and the West Coast (Foley 2013), the island gestures toward the fictional islands of other Gothic novels, including Stephen King's *The Shining* (1977), which Rose, James's daughter, is reading. As she admits, 'Burnt Island is a place where your imagination can come alive' (Thompson 2013: 80); it is the spectral 'address' of the fictional island, in conjunction with the haunting feminine, that accommodates the metafictional interrogation of authorship, which has preoccupied Thompson since her debut novella, *Killing Time* (1990).

The novel's concern with authorial control is reinforced by the coexistence of multiple author figures, whose texts, metaphorically at least, bleed into each other: besides Max, Rose and James are also authoring their own stories. Significantly, Max's discovery of another manuscript, Daniel Levy's *The Song of the Imagination*, penned by the previous resident writer, leads to the novel's major twist – namely, Max's realisation that *Lifeblood*, James's masterpiece, is in fact a plagiarism of Daniel's work. Simultaneously, Max's anxieties about the originality of his own work also emerge as a form of metaleptic inversion, whereby Max no longer identifies with the author figure, but fears he might be a character in Rose's book (2013: 168). This mirrors his suspicion at the beginning of the story, that his therapist 'already had a book written of his life' (2013: 3).

The spectrality of 'real' and textual worlds is complicated by the disruptive presence of the haunting feminine in *Burnt Island*. As James warns Max, 'All the women on the island are demons' (2013: 120), and there is more than a trace of the Gothic demon in Dr Macdonald who, like a vampire, fears the light: her black-polished fingernails contrast with her 'pearly-white' teeth (2013: 22), while 'Her languid, dark, eyes' (2013: 23) reveal 'a certain loucheness' (2013: 36), and her neck is bruised with love-bites. To the authority of the male author, Dr Macdonald functions as a predatorial ideal reader: although she has read all of Max's books, her 'appetite' for his fiction, however, is not received without anxiety by Max, who observes her carry a 'pile of [his] seven books like the charred bones of a ritual sacrifice' (2013: 23). His concern about the reader's 'dissecting' – and emasculating – powers is mirrored in an episode towards the end of the novel when Max believes he sees 'a naked young man . . . lying [in her surgery]', 'her hands . . . bruised and the nails engrained with blood' (2013: 156).

Like Dr Macdonald, all the female characters in the novel remain ambiguously elusive. Dot, Max's ex-wife, is only heard on the phone, and even then, Max is dubious about the authenticity of her voice. Natalie, James's wife, is missing, and there are no pictures of her, while Esther, his youngest daughter, is mute, possibly as a result of her witnessing of his incestuous relationship with Rose. As previously seen in *Orkney*, the notion of an incestuous relationship – bearing in mind this might be Max's own paranoid fantasy – is strongly suggestive of the threat posed to female autonomy by patriarchal authority, pointing, simultaneously, to the emasculating effect this Oedipal tension might have on Max's own authority.

While the lack of female presence – and voice – is problematic in Max's world, it is Rose who, as the most enigmatic female character in the novel, encapsulates the novel's important questions about authorial/ patriarchal control. Like the unnamed wife in Sackville's *Orkney*, Rose's elusiveness bears strong associations with the island world, and particularly the sea; Max notes, for instance, that she moves 'as if her body was liquid' (2013: 34), while Rose claims to 'hear a Siren song coming from the sea. An irresistible sound, the song of my imagination' (2013: 79). Such ambiguous references may seem to point to the woman as *tabula rasa*, the passive recipient of the author's imagination, but when Max has a vision of 'Her lower body . . . in the twisting convoluted shape of a serpent, writhing and twisting in the water as if with its own *independent* life' (2013: 160; my emphasis), Rose's identification with a sea-monster points to a different reading. Counteracting the notion of female oppression conjured up by the drowned woman – including the allusion to Scottish witches, as well as Natalie (2013: 79) – the haunting feminine's association with the sea would appear instead to signal female emancipation. As a marine monster, Rose can free herself of the patriarchal/authorial shackles with which Max and her father bind her. Behind the appearance of pliability, then, the haunting feminine functions instead to destabilise authorial control and challenge the male gaze by embodying the threat of the uncontrollable sea-monster.

Following the long tradition of haunting femininity that pervades oral ballads and the works of authors as diverse as James Hogg, Ellen Galford and Ali Smith, *Burnt Island* deploys the haunting feminine to challenge the control and authority of the masculine gaze/author. Not only does Rose represent a character that refuses to be written, but also, in writing about Max, she threatens to subvert the hierarchical structure of authorship. Framed by the uncanny island scenery, as in *Naming the Bones* and *Orkney*, the novel's use of the haunting feminine, decentring the authority of the central author figure, points to the proliferation of Other stories.

Conclusion

Self-consciously informed by the Scottish/Female Gothic tradition behind it, contemporary Scottish Female Gothic appears to be distinctly preoccupied with authorial control. Such concerns arise from a deeply rooted interrogation of textual authenticity at the heart of Scottish Gothic, and particularly its self-reflective use of textuality. Within this context the haunting feminine can be read as an elusive construct that destabilises authorial control while, simultaneously, laying bare and subverting the politics of the male gaze. While dismantling the foundations of authorship, what these texts also question is the authenticity of writing, challenged both by the intertextual traces of other texts as well as by the conflation of 'real' and 'imagined' worlds. Significantly, such interrogations are set against the backdrop – both haunting and haunted – of Scottish islands: far from echoing the conventional representations of Scotland as a land perennially stuck in its primitive past, Scotland's ghostly scenery in fact aids in the deconstruction of categorical certainties within the three stories. As the fluid lines of the Scottish landscape form an illegible text, and the spectral woman escapes the frame of the male gaze, these novels reveal the dual critical intention of Scottish Female Gothic, which, while decentring authorial control, pushes the story of the Other – female, Scottish – from the narrative margins to the centre.

References

Baker, Timothy C. (2014), *Contemporary Scottish Gothic: Mourning, Authenticity, and Tradition*, Basingstoke: Palgrave Macmillan.

Berger, John (1972), *Ways of Seeing*, London: Penguin.

— (1992), *Keeping a Rendezvous*, London: Granta Books.

Brabon, Benjamin A. and Stéphanie Genz (eds) (2007), *Postfeminist Gothic: Critical Interventions in Contemporary Culture*, Basingstoke: Palgrave.

Fitzgerald, Lauren (2009), 'Female Gothic and the Institutionalisation of Gothic Studies', in Diana Wallace and Andrew Smith (eds), *The Female Gothic*, London: Palgrave, pp. 13–25.

Foley, Matt (2013), 'In Conversation with Alice Thompson', *The Gothic Imagination*, 13 June, <http://www.gothic.stir.ac.uk/blog/in-conversation-with-alice-thompson> (last accessed 5 December 2014).

Germanà, Monica (2010), *Scottish Women's Gothic and Fantastic Writing: Fiction Since 1978*, Edinburgh: Edinburgh University Press.

Gifford, Douglas and Dorothy McMillan (eds) (1997), *A History of Scottish Women's Writing*, Edinburgh: Edinburgh University Press.

Hoeveler, Diane Long (1998), *Gothic Feminism: The Professionalization of Gender from Charlotte Smith to the Brontës*, University Park: University of Pennsylvania Press.

Khair, Tabish (2009), *The Gothic, Postcolonialism and Otherness: Ghosts from Elsewhere*, London: Palgrave.

Moers, Ellen (1977), *Literary Women*, London: W. H. Allen.

Mulvey, Laura (1975), 'Visual Pleasure and Narrative Cinema', *Screen*, 16: 3, 6–18.

Punter, David (2002), 'Scottish and Irish Gothic', in Jerrold Hogle (ed.), *The Cambridge Companion to Gothic Fiction*, Cambridge: Cambridge University Press, pp. 105–23.

Ross, Anne (1973), 'The Divine Hags of the Pagan Celts', in Venetia Newall (ed.), *The Witch Figure*, London: Routledge and Kegan Paul, pp. 139–64.

Sackville, Amy (2013), *Orkney*, London: Granta.
— (2014), 'Amy Sackville: Reliable Narrator', *Booktrust*, <http://www.book trust.org.uk/books/adults/interviews/210> (last accessed 1 September 2014).
Thompson, Alice (2013), *Burnt Island*, Cromer: Salt Press.
Thompson, David (2000), *The People of the Sea: Celtic Tales of the Seal-Folk*, Edinburgh: Canongate.
Wallace, Diana (2009), '"The Haunting Idea": Female Gothic Metaphors and Feminist Theory', in Diana Wallace and Andrew Smith (eds), *The Female Gothic*, London: Palgrave, pp. 26–41.
Welsh, Louise (2010), *Naming the Bones*, Edinburgh: Canongate.
Williams, Holly (2013), 'Review: Orkney, by Amy Sackville', *The Independent*, 17 February, <http://www.independent.co.uk/arts-entertainment/books/revi ews/review-orkney-by-amy-sackville-8498004.html> (last accessed 1 September 2014).
Wright, Angela (2007), 'Scottish Gothic', in Catherine Spooner and Emma McEvoy (eds), *The Routledge Companion to Gothic*, London: Routledge, pp. 73–82.

Notes on Contributors

Timothy C. Baker is Senior Lecturer in Scottish and Contemporary Literature at the University of Aberdeen. He is the author of *George Mackay Brown and the Philosophy of Community* (Edinburgh University Press, 2009) and *Contemporary Scottish Gothic: Mourning, Authenticity, and Tradition* (Palgrave Macmillan, 2014).

Barbara A. E. Bell has researched and published on the nineteenth-century Scottish Theatre, Victorian Medievalism, Fannish Making and Contemporary Scottish Playwriting, alongside pedagogical studies around E-learning and the Performing Arts student.

Scott Brewster is Reader in Gothic Studies at the University of Stirling. He has published widely on the Gothic, Irish writing and psychoanalysis, and is currently working on a study of Gothic, tourism and travel.

Gerard Carruthers is Francis Hutcheson Professor of Scottish Literature at the University of Glasgow. Recent books include *The Cambridge Companion to Scottish Literature*, co-edited with Liam McIlvanney (Cambridge University Press, 2012) and *Scottish Literature* (Edinburgh University Press, 2009). He is the author of half a dozen essays on Muriel Spark.

Carol Margaret Davison is Professor and Head of the Department of English Language, Literature and Creative Writing at the University of Windsor. She is the author of *History of the Gothic: Gothic Literature 1764–1824* (University of Wales Press, 2009) and *Anti-Semitism and British Gothic Literature* (Palgrave Macmillan, 2004), and has published on a wide variety of Gothic-related authors and topics. She is currently at work on a casebook of criticism of the British Gothic,

1764–1824, and has just completed an edited collection of critical essays on the Gothic and death (Manchester University Press, 2017).

Sarah Dunnigan is a Senior Lecturer in Edinburgh University's English Literature Department. She has published on a wide variety of Scottish literature, including medieval Scottish literature; ballads; fairy tales and myth; and Scottish women writers.

Monica Germanà is Senior Lecturer in English Literature and Creative Writing at the University of Westminster. Her research concentrates on contemporary British literature, with a specific emphasis on the Gothic and gender. Her publications include *Scottish Women's Gothic and Fantastic Writing* (Edinburgh University Press, 2010) and *Ali Smith: New Critical Perspectives* (Bloomsbury, 2013) co-edited with Emily Horton. She is currently working on a new monograph called *Bond Girls: Body, Dress, Gender* (Bloomsbury).

Nick Groom is Professor in English at the University of Exeter. He is the author of several books, including *The Gothic: A Very Short Introduction* (Oxford University Press, 2012). His anniversary edition of *The Castle of Otranto* was published by Oxford University Press in 2014, and his editions of *The Monk* and *The Italian* followed in 2016 and 2017, respectively.

Hamish Mathison lectures at the University of Sheffield. His most recent work has been on the connections between print culture and patriotic sentiment in the eighteenth-century Scottish newspaper press, part of a larger interest he has in developing the literary history of early Scottish newspapers. His publications include 'On Robert Burns: Enlightenment, Mythology and the Folkloric', in *The Voice of the People*, ed. Matthew Campbell and Michael Perraudin (Anthem Press, 2012); 'Robert Burns and National Song', in *Scotland, Ireland, and the Romantic Aesthetic*, ed. David Duff and Catherine Jones (Bucknell University Press, 2007); and *Instruments of Enlightenment*, ed. and intro. Hamish Mathison and Angela Wright, a special issue of *History of European Ideas*.

Alison Milbank is Associate Professor of Literature and Theology at the University of Nottingham and author of *Daughters of the House: Modes of the Gothic in Victorian Fiction* (St. Martin's Press, 1992) as well as a number of articles on the Gothic and religion. She has also edited two novels by Ann Radcliffe in the World's Classics series.

Robert Morrison is Queen's National Scholar at Queen's University, Kingston, Ontario. He is the author of *The English Opium-Eater: A Biography of Thomas De Quincey* (Weidenfeld and Nicolson, 2009), which was a finalist for the James Tait Black Memorial Prize for Biography. He is the editor of Thomas De Quincey's *Confessions of an English Opium-Eater* (Oxford University Press, 2013) and Jane Austen's *Persuasion* (Harvard University Press, 2011). With Chris Baldick, he co-edited *The Vampyre and Other Tales of the Macabre* (Oxford University Press, 1997) and *Tales of Terror from Blackwood's Magazine* (Oxford University Press, 1995).

Duncan Petrie is Professor of Film and Television at the University of York. His long-standing engagement with Scottish film and television has generated two monographs: *Screening Scotland* (BFI, 2000) and *Contemporary Scottish Fictions* (Edinburgh University Press, 2004), one co-edited book: *Bill Douglas: A Lanternist's Account* (BFI, 1993), and numerous book chapters and journal articles. He was a member of the Scottish Screen lottery panel, which provided production funding for Scottish feature films, documentaries and shorts, between 2001 and 2003.

Alan Riach is the Professor of Scottish Literature at Glasgow University and the author of *Hugh MacDiarmid's Epic Poetry* (Edinburgh University Press, 1991), *The Poetry of Hugh MacDiarmid* (Association for Scottish Literary Studies, 1999), *Representing Scotland in Literature, Popular Culture and Iconography* (Palgrave Macmillan, 2005) and, with Alexander Moffat, *Arts of Resistance: Poets, Portraits and Landscapes of Modern Scotland* (Luath, 2008), which the *Times Literary Supplement* described as 'a landmark book'. He is the author of five books of poems, most recently *Homecoming* (Luath, 2009). He is General Editor of the *Collected Works of Hugh MacDiarmid* and co-editor of *Lion's Milk: Turkish Poems by Scottish Poets* (Kennedy & Boyd, 2012), *The Edinburgh Companion to Twentieth-Century Scottish Literature* (Edinburgh University Press, 2009), *The Radical Imagination: Lectures and Talks by Wilson Harris* (Liège Language and Literature, 1993) and *Scotlands: Poets and the Nation* (Scottish Poetry Library, 2004).

Fiona Robertson is Professor of Eighteenth- and Nineteenth-Century Literature at the University of Durham and an Honorary Fellow of the Association for Scottish Literary Studies. Her publications include editions of Walter Scott, Stephen Crane and women's writing for Oxford University Press; *Legitimate Histories: Scott, Gothic, and the Authorities* *of Fiction* (Clarendon Press, 1994); *The Edinburgh Companion to Sir Walter Scott* (Edinburgh University Press, 2012); and the forthcoming monograph *The United States in British Romanticism* (Oxford University Press).

Kate Turner is a doctoral candidate at the University of Westminster under the supervision of Dr Monica Germanà. Her project 'The Queer Moment: Post-devolution Scottish Literature' explores the intersections of queer theory and Scottish national identity from 1999 to the present.

Roderick Watson is Professor Emeritus at the University of Stirling. He has lectured and published widely on Scottish literature, the poetry of Hugh MacDiarmid, modern Scottish culture, language and identity. He currently co-edits the *Journal of Stevenson Studies*.

Index